BIBLICAL EXEGESIS IN THE APOSTOLIC PERIOD

Richard N. Longenecker

William B. Eerdmans Publishing Company

Printed in the United States of America

Library of Congress Cataloging in Publication Data

Longenecker, Richard N.
Biblical exegesis in the apostolic period.

Bibliography: p. 221
1. Bible—Criticism, interpretation, etc.—History—
Early church. 2. Bible. N.T.—Relation to O. T.
I. Title.
BS500.L66 220.6′6 74-13757
ISBN 0-8028-1569-3

CONTENTS

ACKNOWLEDGMENTS

I wish to thank the Institute for Advanced Christian Studies for a grant enabling me to complete the present manuscript. Also, my thanks are due Mr. Alan Millard, editor, for permission to incorporate in revised form material from my article, "Can We Reproduce the Exegesis of the New Testament?", *Tyndale Bulletin,* XXI (1970), pp. 3-38. My debt to many others who have written in the areas of biblical exegesis and hermeneutics is all too feebly indicated in the footnotes.

ABBREVIATIONS

General

ET	English Translation
I.F.	Introductory Formula
MSS	Manuscripts
LXX	Septuagint (A=Alexandrinus; B=Vaticanus)
MT	Masoretic Text
Str.-Bil.	*Kommentar zum Neuen Testament aus Talmud und Midrasch*, 5 vols., H. L. Strack and P. Billerbeck, 1922-56
TDNT	*Theological Dictionary of the New Testament*, 9 vols., ed. G. Kittel and G. Friedrich, 1932ff., trans. G. W. Bromiley, 1964-74

Journals

ALUOS	*The Annual of Leeds University Oriental Society*
BA	*The Biblical Archaeologist*
BASOR	*Bulletin of the American Schools of Oriental Research*
Bib	*Biblica*
BJRL	*Bulletin of the John Rylands Library*
CBQ	*Catholic Biblical Quarterly*
CJT	*Canadian Journal of Theology*
CTJ	*Calvin Theological Journal*
ExpT	*The Expository Times*
HTR	*Harvard Theological Review*
HUCA	*Hebrew Union College Annual*
IEJ	*Israel Exploration Journal*
IJT	*The Indian Journal of Theology*
Interp	*Interpretation*
JBL	*Journal of Biblical Literature*
JQR	*Jewish Quarterly Review*

JTS	*Journal of Theological Studies*
NRT	*Nouvelle Revue Theologique*
NTS	*New Testament Studies*
PAAJR	*Proceedings of the American Academy of Jewish Research*
PIJSL	*Papers of the Institute of Jewish Studies, London*
RQ	*Revue de Qumran*
RSR	*Recherches de Science Religieuse*
TS	*Theological Studies*
VT	*Vetus Testamentum*
ZNW	*Zeitschrift für die neutestamentliche Wissenschaft*
ZTK	*Zeitschrift für Theologie und Kirche*

Philo

De Abr.	De Abrahamo
De Cherub.	De Cherubim
De Decal.	De Decalogo
De Exsecrat.	De Exsecrationibus
De Fuga	De Fuga et Inventione
Leg. All.	Legum Allegoria
De Migrat. Abr.	De Migratione Abrahami
De Mutat. Nom.	De Mutatione Nominum
De Plant.	De Plantatione
De Post. Cain.	De Posteritate Caini
De Prof.	De Profugis
Quaes. et Sol. Gen.	Quaestiones et Solutiones in Genesin
Quaes. et Sol. Exod.	Quaestiones et Solutiones in Exodus
Quis Rer. Div. Heres	Quis Rerum Divinarum Heres sit
Quod Det. Pot. Insid.	Quod Deterius Potiori insidiari soleat
Quod Deus Immut.	Quod Deus sit Immutabilis
Quod Omnis Prob. Liber	Quod omnis Probus liber
De Sacrif. Ab. et Cain.	De Sacrificiis Abelis et Caini
De Somn.	De Somniis
De Spec. Leg.	De Specialibus Legibus
De Vita Mos.	De Vita Mosis

Dead Sea Scrolls

1QS	Manual of Discipline (*serek hayoḥad*)
1QH	Psalms of Thanksgiving (*hodayot*)

1QM	War Scroll (*milḥamah*)
1QpHab	Commentary on Habakkuk 1 and 2
1QIs^a	Isaiah Scroll, exemplar a (complete)
3Q2	Portion containing Ps. 2:6f.
4QTest	Testimonia Fragment
4QFlor	Florilegium: Comments on Selected Portions
4QPatr	Patriarchal Blessings
4QDt	Deuteronomy Scroll
CDC	Cairo Damascus Covenant (6QD and 4QD^b of Qumran)
11QMelch	Melchizedek Scroll

Talmudic materials are abbreviated as in H. Danby, *The Mishnah*, and the Soncino editions of the Gemaras and Midrashim. The letters j and b signal the Palestinian Talmud (*Talmud jerusalmi*) and the Babylonian Talmud (*Talmud babli*) respectively; R signifies Rabbah in the Midrashim, and Tos. indicates the Tosephta.

All other abbreviations are customary or self-explanatory.

INTRODUCTION

The New Testament's use of the Old Testament is a subject of perennial interest and vast dimensions. It involves a number of important theological issues as to the relation of the two testaments, the development of biblical religion, the nature of prophecy, and the meaning of fulfilment. And it encompasses a number of significant critical questions as to the provenance of the various writings, their purposes and theological perspectives, the nature of their literary structures, the identification of quotations and allusions within them, the specification of particular text-forms used by them, their procedures of interpretation, their development of biblical themes, and their employment of biblical phraseology. It is further complicated by a paucity of primary materials in certain areas of importance to the discussion and frustrated by uncertainties as to the exact nature of the biblical text in its various traditions during the first Christian century. Nevertheless, the subject is a vitally important one. Historically, differences between Judaism and Christianity can in large measure be traced back to and understood in light of differing exegetical presuppositions and practices. And personally, it is of greatest importance to appreciate something of how the Old Testament was interpreted during the apostolic period of the Church and to ask regarding the significance of this upon one's own convictions, exegesis and life today.

With such an all-encompassing and involved subject, some controls must be exercised if the work of investigation and presentation is to be kept within reasonable and workable bounds. And it is well here to indicate the limitations we have imposed in what follows. To speak of "Biblical Exegesis in the Apostolic Period" is to suggest, of course, something of our concerns and limitations. But more particularly it must be said that, in the first place, our interest is primarily with *exegetical procedures*—that is, with specific exegetical practices, the presuppositions that underlie these practices, and the manner itself in which biblical exegesis was carried on in the apostolic period—and only secondarily and as derived from such an inquiry will we concern ourselves with the broader issues of the relation between the testaments and the development of biblical religion. Secondly, the focus of our attention will be on the *biblical quotations* employed by the various writers of the New Testament, and less directly upon their development of biblical themes, the structure of their compositions, their allusive use of biblical materials, or their employment of biblical language. And thirdly, our desire is to trace out distinguishable *patterns of usage and development* that appear in the various strata of the biblical citations within the New Testament, particularly as seen when compared with Jewish exegetical practices and patterns of roughly contemporaneous times. All the theological and critical considerations to which we have alluded above will, of course, need to be dealt with to some extent at various places in the presentation that follows, for they are inseparably related to the data of our interest. But our discussion will be structured along the lines of these three primary concerns, believing that a proper understanding of these matters will illumine a path through the maze of many more important and tangled issues.

As for our manner of treatment, it need hardly be argued at any length here that for an understanding of the New Testament one must seek to determine as far as possible the circumstances, influences, modes of conceptualization, and ways of expression of the people among whom it came to birth. That, by now, is surely an axiom of scholarship.[1] But in carrying out such an historico-grammatical endeavor with

[1] J. W. Doeve has formulated the axiom as follows: "The possibilities of coming to a proper understanding of an antique document accrue according to the degree in which one knows the milieu whence it came" (*Jewish Hermeneutics in the Synoptic Gospels and Acts* [1954], p. 1).

regard to the biblical citations of the New Testament, a number of methods could be followed—and each has its own contribution to make to the discussion. Analysis could be done, for example, (1) of the exegetical presuppositions and practices of any one group within either Judaism or Christianity, (2) of any particular exegetical procedure employed by any of these groups, (3) of the exegetical patterns that arise from a study of a particular writing or group of writings stemming from any of these groups, or (4) of the exegetical phenomena that occur within a particular passage or cluster of passages within these writings. All these investigations are of great significance, for only as the individual units of a question are understood can anything approaching an adequate comprehension of the whole be attained. On the other hand, research could be undertaken along more comprehensive lines, attempting to integrate the knowledge gained from the more restricted investigations into something of a portrayal of relationships and patterns on a broader scale. Here one could work either "vertically," tracing relationships and patterns from perhaps as early as the Pentateuch through the Church Fathers, or "horizontally," dealing with such relationships and patterns as they appear during the span of one epoch or more limited period. Of course, if the mind doesn't boggle and time, energy or space permit, one could work both vertically and horizontally in the development of a more complete picture. Yet with the ever increasing amount of data available and the resultant growing complexity of the subject, probably no one person will ever be able to deal with all the issues at hand. Each can offer only what he is able, and must leave the rest to others.

It is my purpose in the pages that follow to treat the biblical quotations that occur in the New Testament in a more comprehensive and horizontal fashion, studying the relationships that exist between Jewish and Christian exegetical procedures during the first Christian century and tracing out the development of exegetical patterns in the New Testament. As a Christian, I am, of course, vitally interested in the exegetical phenomena of the New Testament. But as an historian, I am concerned to have an accurate understanding of both Jewish and Christian hermeneutics during the period under study, believing that each must be seen in its relation to the other. In addition to the New Testament, therefore, we must give close attention to the Talmud, the Jewish apocryphal (particularly apocalyptic) writings, the Dead Sea Scrolls, the Targums, and Philo. While fuller introductions to each of these bodies of literature will appear at the appropriate places in the discussion, it can at least be said here that the Talmud (broadly consisting of the Mishnah, Palestinian and Babylonian Gemaras, Midrashim, Tosephta, and the various "Sayings" collections from individual rabbis) represents the Pharisaic schools and later rabbinic explications, the apocalyptic writings of the Jewish apocryphal materials represent speculative authors living on the margin of ordinary Jewish life, the Dead Sea Scrolls represent one sectarian movement within Judaism, the Targums represent various interpretive traditions from the synagogues, and Philo represents a Jew heavily indebted to the categories of Grecian philosophy. Precise dating of the materials, especially with regard to the Talmud and the Targums, is a major issue that must be faced in each instance. But assuming for the moment the presence of certain traditional elements even in later codifications, the very range of material available for comparative study provides a number of intriguing possibilities for tracing out relationships and patterns in the area of biblical interpretation.

Raphael Loewe has warned that "the historical study of biblical exegesis, both Jewish and Christian, is a field in which generalisation is perilous, and any patterns that the investigator may discern he will, if he is wise, postulate but tentatively."[2] The warning is pertinent, and certainly must be seriously heeded. The evidence relating to first-century Jewish and Christian exegetical procedures is both voluminous and partial, requiring on the one hand a mastery of subject matter such as no one person can accomplish fully, and on the other, a realization that further evidence (as the discovery of the Dead Sea texts illustrates) will undoubtedly be forthcoming. Furthermore, later developments in the history of thought have often colored the data, thereby imposing extraneous nuances upon earlier ideas and termi-

[2] R. Loewe, "The 'Plain' Meaning of Scripture in Early Jewish Exegesis," *PIJSL*, I (1964), p. 140.

nology. And every interpreter, whether ancient or modern, tends to view earlier circumstances and practices in terms of his own situation and perspectives, no matter how hard he may try to divorce himself from his own understanding in his historical research.

There is, nevertheless, a need for a more comprehensive treatment of the exegetical procedures of the earliest Christians during the apostolic period of the Church, which will seek to relate itself to the presuppositions and practices of the various elements of Judaism then roughly contemporaneous and is prepared to deal seriously with both similarities and differences. And though there are difficulties regarding provenance and interpretation, there is a sufficient body of material available to draw up something of a precis of the evidence to date and the conclusions to which that evidence points. Geza Vermes has rightly insisted:

> In inter-testamental Judaism there existed a fundamental unity of exegetical tradition. This tradition, the basis of religious faith and life, was adopted and modified by its constituent groups, the Pharisees, the Qumran sectaries and the Judeo-Christians. We have, as a result, three cognate schools of exegesis of the one message recorded in the Bible, and it is the duty of the historian to emphasize that none of them can properly be understood independently of the others.[3]

And Vermes is right again when he says, "for those neither too timid to venture into these unknown fields, nor too gullible, there is promise of wider horizons and a denser background against which to set the message of the New Testament."[4]

In the following pages, we therefore intend first of all to deal with "Jewish Hermeneutics in the First Century" (Chapter I), then to explicate the exegetical procedures and patterns in the various strata of the biblical quotations in the New Testament (Chapters II-VII), and finally to speak to the question of "The Nature of New Testament Exegesis" (Chapter VIII). The treatment of these matters will be essentially descriptive, though their significance for personal faith, theology and proclamation will be suggested at times and should be obvious throughout.

[3] G. Vermes, "The Qumran Interpretation of Scripture in its Historical Setting," *ALUOS*, VI (1966-68), p. 95.
[4] *Ibid.*, p. 94.

BIBLICAL EXEGESIS IN THE APOSTOLIC PERIOD

I: JEWISH HERMENEUTICS IN THE FIRST CENTURY

Jewish interpreters, no matter how different their exegetical methods, were agreed on four basic points. In the first place, they held in common a belief in the divine inspiration of the Scriptures. This meant for them that the words of the Bible had their origin in God and were in fact the very words of God—a doctrine qualitatively different from all Greek notions about a divine possession or an inspirational factor seizing the poets and seers, whose words, while lofty, remained purely human. Secondly, they were convinced that the Torah (whether the Written Torah alone, or both Written and Oral) contained the entire truth of God for the guidance of man. The transmitted texts, therefore, for the Jew of the first century, were extremely rich in content and pregnant with many meanings.[1] Thirdly, because of the many possibilities of meaning in the texts, Jewish interpreters viewed their task as one of dealing with both the plain or obvious meanings and the implied or deduced meanings. And finally, they considered the purpose of all biblical interpretation to be the translating into life of the instruction of God—that is, to make the words of God

[1] From the school of R. Ishmael (second-generation Tannaim, c. A.D. 90-130) we have the maxim: "Just as the rock is split into many splinters, so also may one biblical verse convey many teachings" (b. Sanh. 34a). Bemidbar Rabbah, the most recent of the pentateuchal Midrashim, dating no earlier than the eleventh or twelfth century A.D. in its codified form, expands this to insist, based on the numerical value of ודגלו ("standard") in Cant. 2:4, that the Torah "can be expounded in forty-nine different ways" (Num. R. 2.3), and, based on the value of יין ("wine"), that "there are seventy modes of expounding the Torah" (Num. R. 13.15f.). Philo (cf. De Prof. 458) and the men of Qumran indicate their agreement that there are multiple meanings in the words of Scripture.

meaningful and relevant to the people in their present situations. These are matters that were axiomatic to all Jewish exegetes no matter what other allegiances they may have espoused or whatever interpretive procedures they may have employed, and they will be repeatedly illustrated in the discussion that follows.

SOURCES

The work of interpreting the Bible within Judaism proceeded on many fronts and in various ways. The translation of the Hebrew Scriptures into Greek (the Septuagint, LXX) during the two centuries or so before Christ was an enterprise in interpretation, for every translation inevitably involves interpretation and reflects the translators' understanding of the text. The doctrines of resurrection and angelology, for example, were rising to prominence during this time and find explicit expression in the translation. The addition to Job 42:17 in the LXX is an instance of this: "And it is written, he [Job] will rise again with those whom the Lord raises up"; as are also the clarifications felt necessary in the cases of Isa. 26:19, reading in the LXX "they shall live," and Dan. 12:2, reading "they shall awake."[2] An emphasis upon angels is evident in the LXX's wording of "the angels of the nations" for the Hebrew's "the children of Israel" in Deut. 32:8, and "at his right hand were his angels with him" for "at his right hand was a fiery law for them" in Deut. 33:2; as well as in the transposition of "angels" (ἀγγέλους) for the possibly enigmatic "God/gods" (אלהים) of Ps. 8:6. Anthropomorphisms, as might be expected, are also recast in the translation, and alterations are made to avoid difficulties.[3] Likewise, the titles of the books of the Pentateuch in the LXX, the grouping of Samuel-Kings into the four Books of the Kingdom, the retitling of Chronicles ("Things Omitted") and Lamentations, and the reclassification of the books of the Old Testament into a chronological sequence "show at least an

[2] In Isa. 26:19, ἀναστήσονται translates יחיו, and in Dan. 12:2, ἐξεγερθήσονται translates יקיצו.

[3] Cf. E. J. Bickermann, "The Septuagint as a Translation," *PAAJR*, XXVIII (1959), pp. 1-39.

incipient attempt at interpretation which seems to have originated with the translators of the Pentateuch, and to have been carried on by their successors."[4] But that the LXX should be looked upon as a theological commentary, as has sometimes been suggested, and thereby employed as a primary source for a knowledge of the hermeneutical procedures of the day, is an overstatement of the facts. As Jellicoe points out in speaking of the various "translational units" in the LXX and their respective philosophies of translation:

> Style and method vary considerably, but this is no more than would be expected in a production which extended over some decades and which was the work of different hands. Liberties are taken at times, more so with the later Books, but here literary rather than theological interests seem to be the governing principle.[5]

For our purposes, therefore, the LXX will not be considered of major significance in determining the exegetical practices of first-century Judaism. Nor, for similar reasons, will the Greek translation of the Old Testament by Aquila, produced at the close of our period of interest. While the distinctive tendencies of each of these translations can be established, the translators did not provide us with prefaces setting forth their principles of interpretation nor are their productions so free as to allow deductions regarding the exegetical methodologies of their day.

The Targums, however, are important in the determination of early Jewish exegetical practice, for their purpose in rendering the Hebrew into Aramaic was not just to give a vernacular translation of the Bible, but, as the Levites of Neh. 8:8, "to give the sense and make the people understand the meaning." In giving "the sense," the Targumists attempted to remain as faithful as possible to the original text and yet to bring out the meaning of what the text had to say for their hearers. The Targums, therefore, "lie halfway between straightforward translation and free retelling of the biblical narrative: they were clearly attached to the Hebrew text, and at times translated it in a reasonably

[4] S. Jellicoe, *The Septuagint and Modern Study* (1968), p. 316.
[5] *Ibid.*

straightforward way, but they were also prepared to introduce into the translation as much interpretation as seemed necessary to clarify the sense."[6] As interpretive paraphrases or explanatory translations, they frequently incorporated later theological concepts and their own haggadoth for purposes of clarification and edification.[7]

The Synagogue was the home of the Targums, for there a reader read from the Hebrew Scriptures and an interpreter paraphrased the text into Aramaic to bring out its meaning and explicate its significance for the congregation. The process is described in Mish. Meg. 4:4:

> He who reads in the Law may not read less than three verses. He may not read to the interpreter more than one verse at a time [from the Law], or, in the Prophets, not more than three verses. But if these three are three separate paragraphs, he must read them out one by one. They may leave out verses in the Prophets, but not in the Law.

While Targums exist for all the biblical books, except those which already contain sizeable Aramaic portions (Ezra, Nehemiah and Daniel), they appear in five different collections (Neofiti I, the Fragment Targum, the Cairo Geniza Targum Fragments, Onkelos, and Pseudo-Jonathan), none of which can with certainty be dated to pre-Christian or Christian times and all of which evidence varying textual traditions both between them and within them. A great deal of work remains to be done in dating, collating and interpreting targumic materials—and, to this date, Neofiti I still remains to be published. Nonetheless, informed opinion believes that the targumic traditions that have been codified into our existing written Targums represent Palestinian and Babylonian Jewish hermeneutics of a very early time, possibly coming from various pre-Christian synagogues. As such, they are of great significance to the discussion of early Jewish exegesis. Perhaps, as Miss Bloch suggested, it was the

[6] J. Bowker, *The Targums and Rabbinic Literature* (1969), p. 13.

[7] On the Targums generally, see Bowker, *ibid.*, pp. 3-28; on the Fragment Targum and so-called Pseudo-Jonathan (both Palestinian, as is probably also Neofiti I), see M. McNamara, *The New Testament and the Palestinian Targum to the Pentateuch* (1966).

synagogue targumim that provided the basis for the later rabbinic haggadah.[8]

Rabbinic, or talmudic, literature is an extensive and varied body of traditional Pharisaic material that was codified, in the main, during the period from the end of the second century through the sixth century A.D. It is divided by subject matter into either halakah, having to do with behavior and the regulation of conduct, or haggadah, which concerns the illustration of the biblical texts and edification; though the distinctions are not always clearly in evidence, for halakic pronouncements colored the expression of haggadah and haggadic exegesis often embodied considertions pertinent for halakah.[9] The literature exists in a few main collections, with a number of peripheral codifications in addition.[10] The Mishnah is the basic halakic document, containing sixty-three tractates (*Massektoth*) of material not necessarily attached to a text of Scripture and organized under six major headings (*Sedarim*). It was codified by Rabbi Judah "the Prince" (*ha Nasi*), who, according to tradition, was born the year Rabbi Akiba died at the hands of the Romans, in A.D. 135. All of the later halakic developments in Judaism were built upon or related to the Mishnah. The Tosephta closely resembles the Mishnah in its organization and content, and, as its name implies ("addition"), has traditionally been regarded as a supplement to the Mishnah. Its authorship is ascribed to Rabbi Ḥiyya, a pupil of Judah the Prince, though various features in its manner of treatment have left the question of provenance unresolved in many minds. The Gemaras, Palestinian and Babylonian, are built directly upon the Mishnah, and seek, verse by verse, to relate its halakic pronouncements to Scripture, to support them by Scripture, and to illustrate

[8] R. Bloch, "Note méthodologique pour l'étude de la littérature rabbinique," *RSR*, XLIII (1955), pp. 194-227. Cf. also G. Vermes, *Scripture and Tradition in Judaism* (1961), pp. 9ff.; M. McNamara, *New Testament and the Palestinian Targum*, pp. 35ff.

[9] Cf. R. Loewe, "The 'Plain' Meaning of Scripture," *PIJSL*, I (1964), p. 150.

[10] For introductory discussions of rabbinic literature, see H. L. Strack, *Introduction to the Talmud and Midrash* (ET 1931), and J. Bowker, *Targums and Rabbinic Literature*, pp. 40-92.

them by both Scripture and the teachings of the rabbis. The name Gemara denotes "teaching," and thus the Gemaras contain, in addition to legal discussions on every aspect of Jewish life, "homiletical exegesis of Scripture; moral maxims, popular proverbs, prayers, parables, fables, tales; accounts of manners and customs, Jewish and non-Jewish; facts and fancies of science by the learned; Jewish and heathen folklore, and all the wisdom and unwisdom of the unlearned."[11] The Palestinian Gemara is the earlier, the shorter (though treating more tractates), and generally the simpler; the Babylonian Gemara was codified during the fourth through the sixth centuries, is longer (though omitting discussion on a number of tractates), and generally more ingenious in its exegesis of Scripture.[12]

The Midrashim are writings dealing principally with the exegesis of Scripture, as distinct from the Mishnah where the material is recorded independently of Scripture for the most part. The Tannaitic Midrashim are largely halakic in nature, though not entirely; the Homiletic Midrashim are made up of a number of synagogue sermons; and the Midrash Rabbah, meaning the "great" Midrash, is a complete commentary on the Pentateuch and the five Megilloth (Song of Songs, Ruth, Lamentations, Ecclesiastes and Esther). In addition to these larger codifications of traditional halakic and haggadic material, rabbinic literature includes a number of more individual and somewhat peripheral writings. Pirke de Rabbi Eliezer, a narrative midrashic treatment, and Aboth de Rabbi Nathan, a haggadic tractate similar to the famous Pirke Aboth ("Sayings of the Fathers"), are two of the most illustrious.

A major problem in the use of rabbinic materials for the elucidation of first-century practice is, of course, the lateness of the codifications. Yet we are dealing with a religious mentality that took great pride in the preservation of the traditional; and while changes due to development or differ-

[11] J. H. Hertz, *The Babylonian Talmud: Neziḳin I* (1935), p. xviii.

[12] The term "Talmud" is employed in a number of ways. In its narrowest sense it refers to the Gemaras, Palestinian or Babylonian. Frequently, however, it designates both the Mishnah and its respective Gemara together, as distinct from the Midrashim; though it can be used synonymously with "talmudic literature" generally.

ing circumstances cannot be denied, this desire to preserve the traditional—barring other considerations—minimizes the severity of the problem. Four strands of rabbinic material, in fact, are particularly relevant for our consideration here:[13]

1. Practices and rules deemed by Johanan b. Zakkai and his followers to be very ancient, or, as George F. Moore spoke of them, to be "customs the origin of which was lost in antiquity."[14] Often these are introduced by such a phrase as "Our rabbis taught," or "It has been taught," though the context must be noted in each case as well.

2. Actions and teachings of certain named teachers who lived before the first destruction of Jerusalem, or who personally had their roots in that earlier period.[15] The chief representative here is Pirke Aboth, with its haggadic statements attributed to teachers up to A.D. 70 in chapter one and to Johanan b. Zakkai and his disciples, whose roots were firmly planted in the predestruction period, in chapter two. Yet there are other passages of this type scattered throughout the rabbinic materials.

3. Passages and portions which have no reason to be a reaction to either religious opposition (particularly Christianity) or political oppression, and which do not seem to have been influenced by a particular local situation or passing fancy but have parallels elsewhere in the literature. It is at this point that the subjective factor in interpretation enters most. Yet here are portions that must not be overlooked.

4. Ancient liturgies, confessions and prayers: the Shema, the Shemoneh Esreh ("Eighteen Benedictions" or "Prayers"), and, perhaps, the broad outlines of the 613 Commandments.[16]

[13] Cf. my *Paul, Apostle of Liberty* (1964), pp. 1-6.

[14] G. F. Moore, *Judaism in the First Centuries of the Christian Era* (1927), I, p. 29; cf. III, pp. 6ff.

[15] While it may never be proved, there seems little reason to doubt that "the authorities in whose names statements are quoted are a help, if not an infallible index, to fixing their date" (L. Finkelstein, "The Book of Jubilees and the Rabbinic Halaka," *HTR*, XVI [1923], p. 39).

[16] My debt to A. Lukyn Williams, *Talmudic Judaism and Christianity* (1933), pp. 38-43, is clearly evident at points 1, 2 and 4 above.

The apocalyptic writings of Judaism that were composed in the century (or so) before Christ and the century immediately following have some bearing on the question of early Jewish exegesis,[17] for in their interpretive retelling of the biblical stories and their extensions of the biblical teachings they reflect some of the nonconformist exegetical principles of the day. I refer particularly to such works as Jubilees, I Enoch,[18] Assumption of Moses, IV Ezra and II Baruch. Though a few of the writings may have been composed by Pharisaic authors (principally IV Ezra), most must now be seen to have been within an Essene cycle of influence, whether originally written by Essenes (or "proto-Essenes") or taken over by them.

A kindred body of writings, and of greater significance for the history of interpretation, are the Dead Sea Scrolls. Together with the vast majority of scholars in the field, I take the distinctive literature of Qumran to reflect one segment of the Essene mentality in Palestine and to have been written during the first century B.C. and early first century A.D.[19] About one-fourth of the approximately six hundred identifiable manuscripts (a few relatively intact, though most fragmentary) are biblical texts, with all of the Hebrew canon represented except Esther. This is important material for dealing with the transmission of the Hebrew text and tracing out variant readings during the first Christian century. Of more importance for our purposes, however, are the commentaries: principally on portions of

[17] For introductions to the Jewish apocalyptic literature, see R. H. Charles, *The Apocrypha and Pseudepigrapha of the Old Testament* (1913), vol. I.

[18] On the "Similitudes of Enoch" (I Enoch 37–71) and the Testaments of the Twelve Patriarchs as probably not being pre-Christian in their present form, see my *The Christology of Early Jewish Christianity* (1970), pp. 12-14, 83-85.

[19] For an early, brief, and altogether reliable discussion of the evidence, see W. F. Albright, "Postscript," *BASOR—Supplementary Studies*, Nos. 10-12 (1951), pp. 57-60. Note also such authors as M. Burrows, *The Dead Sea Scrolls* (1955); J. T. Milik, *Ten Years of Discovery in the Wilderness of Judaea* (ET 1959); F. M. Cross, *The Ancient Library of Qumran* (1958). The points raised in opposition to this view are probably most clearly highlighted and pertinently demolished in R. de Vaux's review of G. R. Driver's book in "Essenes or Zealots? Some Thoughts on a Recent Book," *New Blackfriars*, XLVII (1966), pp. 396-410.

Habakkuk, Isaiah, Hosea, Micah, Nahum, Zephaniah and Psalm 37, together with such treatments of scattered passages as found in 4QFlorilegium and 11QMelchizedek. In the commentaries we have a glimpse into the nature of the biblical text as it then existed among a certain group in that part of Palestine and the Qumran sectaries' distinctive cluster of ideas and exegetical procedures. The testimonia fragment from Cave 4 is also of textual and hermeneutical significance, as, undoubtedly, will be the recently recovered Temple Scroll when it is published.[20] In addition, the Manual of Discipline and the Damascus Document (Zadokite Fragments) take us into the structure and very heart of the community's *raison d'être*, the Psalms of Thanksgiving reflect (evidently) something of the piety and self-consciousness of their founder, the War Scroll and various other apocalyptic fragments deepen our understanding of their eschatological expectations, and the Prayer for Intercession and Liturgy of the Angels enable us to appreciate something of their liturgy. In all, we have material here which has given a fresh impetus to the study of both early Judaism and early Christianity, and is particularly significant in the study of nonconformist Jewish exegesis in the first Christian century.

Philo of Alexandria is also an important source in the study of early Jewish exegesis, though it is difficult to ascertain the degree of his importance for it is uncertain just how representative he was of hellenistic Judaism generally or of hellenistic Jews in Palestine in particular. Even his dates of birth and death are uncertain. We know he was alive in A.D. 39-40, for he was part of the Jewish delegation from Alexandria to Gaius at Rome of that time. Very roughly, we can speak of Philo as living from 20 B.C. to A.D. 50. Of the thirty-eight extant titles confidently attributed to him, four are treatises on special problems in philosophy, three deal with contemporary Jewish events in Alexandria, and thirty-one are in the form of either a running commentary on certain books of the Pentateuch or discussions of certain topics selected from the Pentateuch. While there are scattered references to Scripture in the nonbiblical discussions, it is in his detailed and extensive treatments of

[20] See Y. Yadin, "The Temple Scroll," *BA*, XXX (1967), pp. 135-39.

the Fentateuch that his exegetical methodology is spelled out.[21]

LITERALIST INTERPRETATION

Jewish exegesis of the first century can generally be classified under four headings: literalist, midrashic, pesher and allegorical. Admittedly, such a fourfold classification highlights distinctions of which the early Jewish interpreters themselves may not have always been conscious. In dealing with a system that thinks more wholistically, functionally and practically than it does analytically—and stresses precedent more than logic in defense of its ways[22] —any attempt at classification must inevitably go beyond that system's explicit statements as to its own principles. Nevertheless, as we will attempt to show in what follows, the Jewish treatment of Scripture falls quite naturally into one or the other of these four categories.

It need not be argued at any length that Judaism often took the words of the Old Testament quite literally. Rabbinic literature contains a number of examples of where the Scriptures were understood in a straightforward fashion, resulting in the plain, simple and natural meaning of the text being applied to the lives of the people—particularly in the application of deuteronomic legislation. Frequently, in fact, the interpretation is woodenly literal; as, for example, the teaching of the School of Shammai that "in the evening all should recline when they recite [the Shema], but in the morning they should stand up, for it is written, 'And when thou liest down and when thou risest up'."[23] The School of Hillel is recorded as countering this by insisting, "they may recite it every one in his own way, for it is written, 'And when thou walkest by the way'."[24] The Hillelian interpreta-

[21] On Philo, see the almost classic treatments by J. Drummond, *Philo Judaeus*, 2 vols. (1888), and H. A. Wolfson, *Philo*, 2 vols. (1947). A briefer and reliable summary of Philo's life and work can be found in S. G. Sowers, *The Hermeneutics of Philo and Hebrews* (1965).

[22] Cf. R. Loewe, "The 'Plain' Meaning of Scripture," *PIJSL*, I (1964), p. 153.

[23] Mish. Ber. 1.3, on Deut. 6:7.

[24] *Ibid.*

tion, of course, is favored in the passage. But even here, the rebuttal is based on almost as wooden an employment of the biblical text. Again, on the treatment of the "stubborn and rebellious son" of Deut. 21:18ff., a hyperliteralism comes to the fore:

> If either of them [his parents] was maimed in the hand, or lame or dumb or blind or deaf, he cannot be condemned as a stubborn and rebellious son, for it is written, 'Then shall his father and his mother lay hold on him'—so they were not maimed in the hand; 'and bring him out'—so they were not lame; 'and they shall say'—so they were not dumb; 'this our son'—so they were not blind; 'he will not obey our voice'—so they were not deaf.[25]

Literalist interpretation, it is true, is not as prominent in the talmudic literature as is what will later be identified as midrashic exegesis. Rabbi Simeon Lowy suggests that "the reason for this may be that this type of commentary was expected to be known by everyone; and since there were no disputations about it, it was not recorded."[26] It is, however, in evidence to a reasonable extent in the writings—principally in the earlier tannaitic halakah—and was considered basic to all further exegetical developments. As Lowy further points out, "the Rabbis considered the plain interpretation of the laws, based mainly upon a literal understanding, as being of equal value with 'things which even the Sadducees agree upon', and that these should therefore be learned in the elementary school."[27]

Philo, too, while most known for his allegorical interpretations, understood certain biblical passages in a literalist fashion. Most familiar in this regard is his insistence that though allegorical exegesis is proper, it must not set aside the literal practice of the Law.[28] He believed, for example, that circumcision should be allegorically understood, yet practiced literally;[29] he insisted upon the eternality of the Law,[30] and rebuked those who did not keep it.[31] In his

[25] Mish. Sanh. 8.4, on Deut. 21:19f.
[26] S. Lowy, "Some Aspects of Normative and Sectarian Interpretation of the Scriptures," *ALUOS*, VI (1966-68), p. 99.
[27] *Ibid.*, p. 131, n. 10, citing b. Sanh. 33b and b. Hor. 5a, b.
[28] De Migrat. Abr. 89-94.
[29] De Migrat. Abr. 92.
[30] De Vita Mos. 44.
[31] De Exsecrat. 138f.

treatment of the biblical accounts of creation, a curious disparity of attitude seems to appear. While he usually felt free to reject their literal meaning entirely, asserting that God's planting a garden in Eden, the creation of Eve from a rib of Adam, and the speaking of the serpent are "mythical nonsense,"[32] "incurable folly,"[33] and "of the nature of myth,"[34] in *Quaestiones et Solutiones in Genesin* he accepts the stories in their literal sense that God put man into the garden of Eden to tend it, that Adam gave names to the various animals and that the serpent spoke,[35] and he advances as equally valid both a literal and an allegorical interpretation of God's planting a garden in Eden, his creation of Eve, and his making of garments for Adam and Eve.[36] Philo's attitude in the *Quaestiones et Solutiones* may be apologetically motivated in view of the different type of reader there addressed, as Wolfson suggests,[37] or may reflect more truly his thought regarding "the parallel legitimacy of literal and allegorical exegesis, the peaceful coexistence of which he can countenance," as Loewe believes.[38] With regard to the historical events in the Pentateuch, the one qualification of their literal truth made by Philo is that their literalness must be rejected whenever such an acceptance of the words of God compels one "to admit anything base or unworthy of their dignity"; which, as Wolfson comments, "leaves a great deal to the reader"—and to Philo—"to decide for himself if a story in its literal sense is base and unworthy of the dignity of the words of God."[39]

The situation is somewhat similar in the Dead Sea Scrolls, where preoccupation with one distinctive type of interpretive procedure (pesher, in this case) so overshadows all

[32] Leg. All. I. 14, 43.
[33] De Plant. 8, 32.
[34] Leg. All. I. 7, 19.
[35] Quaes. et Sol. Gen. I. 14, 20-22, 32.
[36] Quaes. et Sol. Gen. I. 6, 25, 53.
[37] H. A. Wolfson, *Philo*, I, p. 122.
[38] R. Loewe, "The 'Plain' Meaning of Scripture," *PIJSL*, I (1964), p. 148. Loewe cites Philo's use of παρεμφαίνειν ("to indicate alongside") in allegorical contexts (e.g., De Abr. 36, 200; Quis Rer. Div. Heres 23, 112; De Somn. II. 29, 195, 324) in support of his thesis of parallel legitimacy.
[39] H. A. Wolfson, *Philo*, I, p. 123.

others that one could easily get the impression that the men of Qumran never understood the Old Testament literally. Yet in the opening lines of the Manual of Discipline, the members commit themselves not only to "the rule (order, *serek*) of the community" but also "to do what is good and right before him [God], as he commanded through Moses and through all his servants the prophets."[40] It is perhaps not without significance that the pesher commentaries from Qumran are, to date, only on prophetic material: the "former prophets," the "latter prophets," and the Psalms. Evidently deuteronomic legislation, while having to be necessarily adapted somewhat to their unique situation, was taken for the most part quite literally—if not hyperliterally.[41]

Since at least the fourth century A.D., the word *peshaṭ* has been associated with literalist interpretation as opposed to any more elaborate type of exegesis. The word comes from the verb פשט, which in the Old Testament means "to strip off" (a garment), "flatten," or "to make a dash" (either "from" or "against"). The War Scroll from Qumran uses it in a manner closely parallel to the biblical, to mean "stripping" the slain and "deploying into battle order."[42] In association with Aramaic, it came to mean in the late Hebrew of the tannaitic Mishnah and Gemara "to stretch out, extend, make plain," and as such was employed more or less synonymously with the verb דרש to mean "to interpret." At times, the term "peshaṭ" is employed in the tannaitic writings with a more straightforward and natural explanation than any alternative with which it may be associated,[43] but this is not always the case. Even when more literal alternatives to early allegorical expositions are given they are not stated to be "peshaṭ" interpretations.[44] Evidently, the earlier rabbis felt that their exegesis, what-

[40] 1QS 1.1-3.
[41] Josephus' comment about the Essenes, of which the men of Qumran were probably a part, is: "They are stricter than any other of the Jews" (War II. 147).
[42] 1QM 7.2; 8.6.
[43] Even the Babylonian Talmud, when based upon tannaitic materials, sometimes continues this employment; cf. Kidd. 80b, on Deut. 13:6.
[44] Cf. R. Loewe, "The 'Plain' Meaning of Scripture," *PIJSL*, I (1964), p. 177.

ever their methods might be later called and however we might classify them, was a setting forth of the essential meaning of the biblical texts, and therefore to be identified as either "peshaṭ" or "midrash," the two terms being considered roughly equivalent.[45] It is not, however, their nomenclature so much as their practice that is of importance here. And in regard to their practice, it must be concluded that early Jewish exegesis employed a literalist treatment of Scripture as well as more developed and elaborate forms of interpretation.

MIDRASHIC INTERPRETATION

The central concept in rabbinic exegesis, and presumably in that of the earlier Pharisees as well, was "midrash." The word comes from the verb דרש ("to resort to," "seek"; figuratively, "to read repeatedly," "study," "interpret"), and strictly denotes an interpretive exposition however derived and irrespective of the type of material under consideration. The expositions of the Gemaras and the Midrashim, therefore, while employing various exegetical methods, are referred to as either "midrash halakah" or "midrash haggadah"; the one term covering the full range of hermeneutical devices involved, with the second having reference to the type of material treated.

It is in the Babylonian Talmud, and during the early part of the fourth century A.D., that midrashic exegesis is consciously distinguished from literalist interpretation, and questions are raised regarding their relationship.[46] From this later perspective and employing the more fully developed definition of this period, "midrash" designates "an exegesis which, going more deeply than the mere literal sense, attempts to penetrate into the spirit of the Scriptures,

[45] Cf. W. Bacher, *Die exegetische Terminologie der jüdischen Traditions-literatur,* Vol. I: Tannaiten (1889), Vol. II: Amoräer (1905); J. Z. Lauterbach, "*Peshaṭ,*" *The Jewish Encyclopedia,* IX (1905), pp. 652f.; R. Loewe, "The 'Plain' Meaning of Scripture," *PIJSL*, I (1964), pp. 157-185.

[46] See b. Sanh. 100b; b. Hul. 6a; b. Erub. 23b; b. Yeb. 24a. Bacher proposes that it was Abbaye b. Kahana (a third-generation Palestinian Amoraite of the fourth century) who first distinguished "midrash" from "peshaṭ" (*Exegetische Terminologie*, II, pp. 112f.), as b. Sanh. 100b represents him doing.

to examine the text from all sides, and thereby to derive interpretations which are not immediately obvious."[47] But for the tannaitic period (through Judah the Prince), the distinction between "peshaṭ" as the literal sense and "derash" as a derivative exposition of hidden meanings seems not to have been consciously invoked. In the Mishnah, the Palestinian Gemara and the earlier Midrashim the verbs פשט and דרש are used in roughly synonymous fashion, for, as Lauterbach points out, "the Tannaim believed that their Midrash was the true interpretation and that their 'derash' was the actual sense of Scripture, and therefore 'peshaṭ'."[48]

But while acknowledging that *midrash* probably had a more comprehensive meaning in the tannaitic period than it later acquired in contradistinction to *peshaṭ*, and that earlier rabbis were not as conscious of distinctions in methodology as their later counterparts, it yet remains possible to postulate a basic continuity of practice between the earlier Tannaim and the Amoraim. That there were developments in methodology as well as in terminology is certainly true, and nowhere better illustrated than in the progression from the seven rules of exposition attributed to Hillel, to Rabbi Ishmael's thirteen *middoth*, to the much later thirty-two associated with the name of Rabbi Eliezer ben Jose ha-Galili.[49] But in discussing an earlier situation it is often necessary to employ terminology that has become refined through many years of experience. And this is legitimate, so long as we do not assume that the fulness of later developments was present in the earlier prototypes or try to foist such back.

It is to Hillel, whose teaching antedates the rise of Christianity by a generation or so,[50] that the Talmud attributes

[47] S. Horovitz, "Midrash," *Jewish Encyclopedia*, VIII (1904), p. 548. For a good treatment of "midrash," though entirely from this later perspective, see A. G. Wright, "The Literary Genre Midrash," *CBQ*, XXVIII (1966), pp. 105-138, 417-457.

[48] J. Z. Lauterbach, "Peshaṭ," *Jewish Encyclopedia*, IX (1905), p. 653.

[49] For listings of these three sets of *middoth*, see H. L. Strack, *Introduction to the Talmud and Midrash*, pp. 93-98.

[50] For the view that Hillel was the father of Gamaliel, who was the teacher of Saul of Tarsus (the apostle Paul), see E. Schürer, *The*

the seven basic rules of rabbinic exegesis. Coming from Babylonia, Hillel studied in Palestine under Shemaiah and Abtalion, whom posterity remembered as great in exegetical ability and of whom we are told that they were proselytes.[51] Once, when it could not be decided by the religious authorities ("the Bene Bathyra") whether Passover, the fourteenth of Nisan, should take precedence over the weekly sabbath or the sabbath over Passover, when both came on the same day, Hillel was called in for his advice. He so impressed and convinced the authorities of the precedence of Passover over the sabbath, employing in the process two (or perhaps three) logical arguments in the treatment of the biblical texts (i.e., *qal waḥomer* and *gezerah shawah*), that they made him "the Prince" (*ha Nasi*) over the assembly.[52] And, evidently based on this account, rabbinic tradition has ascribed all seven of the following *middoth* to him:

1. *Qal waḥomer*: what applies in a less important case will certainly apply in a more important case.
2. *Gezerah shawah*: verbal analogy from one verse to another; where the same words are applied to two separate cases it follows that the same considerations apply to both.
3. *Binyan ab mikathub 'eḥad*: building up a family from a single text; when the same phrase is found in a number of passages, then a consideration found in one of them applies to all of them.
4. *Binyan ab mishene kethubim*: building up a family from two texts; a principle is established by relating two texts together; the principle can then be applied to other passages.
5. *Kelal upherat*: the general and the particular; a general principle may be restricted by a particularisation of it in another verse; or conversely, a particular rule may be extended into a general principle.

Jewish People in the Time of Jesus Christ (ET 1890), Div. II, vol. I, p. 363 and n. 164; H. L. Strack, *Introduction to the Talmud and Midrash*, p. 109; that Hillel was Gamaliel's grandfather, R. T. Herford, "Pirke Aboth," *Apocrypha and Pseudepigrapha of the Old Testament*, ed. R. H. Charles, II, p. 694; W. Bacher, "Gamaliel I," *Jewish Encyclopedia*, V (1903), pp. 558f.

51 B. Pes. 70b. David Daube has proposed that their hellenistic background may well explain certain features in rabbinic exegesis ("Rabbinic Methods of Interpretation and Hellenistic Rhetoric," *HUCA*, XXII [1949], pp. 239ff.).

52 There are three slightly different versions of the story in j. Pes. 6.1, Tos. Pes. 4.1-3, and b. Pes. 66a, with the Babylonian Gemara speaking of two arguments and the Tosephta and Palestinian Gemara of three.

6. *Kayoze bo bemaqom 'aḥer*: as is found in another place; a difficulty in one text may be solved by comparing it with another which has points of general (though not necessarily verbal) similarity.
7. *Dabar halamed me'inyano*: a meaning established by its context.[53]

Obviously, some of these rules are a matter of common sense and sound judgment, while others are pregnant with possibilities for abuse. Whether Hillel originated any or all of them, or whether he merely transmitted them, cannot be determined. But with these *middoth* of Hillel the distinctive exegetical features of Pharisaic Judaism come clearly into view.

In the first part of the second century, Rabbi Ishmael ben Elisha, in opposition to the innovations in exegesis of Rabbi Akiba, developed Hillel's *middoth* into thirteen rules.[54] Probably much later, the thirty-two rules attributed to Rabbi Eliezer ben Jose ha-Galili were formed.[55] In so doing, rabbinic Judaism developed on the basis of Hillel's original seven exegetical norms "an atomistic exegesis, which interprets sentences, clauses, phrases, and even single words, independently of the context or the historical occasion, as divine oracles; combines them with other similarly detached utterances; and makes large use of analogy of expressions, often by purely verbal association."[56] In halakic matters, where tradition was more firmly rooted to an earlier period, the rules were applied quite moderately. But in haggadic exegesis, which was more dependent upon later developments and which had less to fear about the consequences of its explanations for practical living, excesses were frequent. Probably the most fanciful treatments are

[53] Quoted from J. Bowker, *Targums and Rabbinic Literature*, p. 315. For a more extensive explication, citing numerous examples, see J. W. Doeve, *Jewish Hermeneutics in the Synoptic Gospels and Acts*, pp. 66-75. The listing of the seven *middoth* is found in Aboth de R. Nathan 37, Tos. Sanh. 7.11, and the introduction to Sifra 3a, though some texts of Sifra omit the fourth.

[54] A.D. 110-130.

[55] R. Eliezer b. ha-Galili ("the Galilean") is dated between A.D. 130 and 160, though for references pointing to a late date of the thirty-two *middoth* see R. Loewe, "The 'Plain' Meaning of Scripture," *PIJSL*, I (1964), p. 152.

[56] G. F. Moore, *Judaism*, I, p. 248.

those stemming from the final four *middoth* attributed to Rabbi Eliezer:

29. *Gematria*: (a) computation of the numeric value of letters; (b) secret alphabets or substitution of letters for other letters.
30. *Notriḳon*: breaking up a word into two or more, exposition of the single letters to stand for just as many words which commence with them.
31. *Muḳdam shehu' me'uḥar ba-'inyan*: something that precedes which is placed second.
32. *Muḳdam u-me'uḥar shehu' beparashioth*: many a biblical section refers to a later period than the one which precedes, and vice versa.[57]

Doeve is quite right in saying that "the liberty obtaining in haggadic exegesis is often so great and the method of going to work so dependent on the ingenuity of the exegetist, that it is out of the question to attempt to give a consistent system of norms for this exegesis."[58]

It is also pertinent to note that not only did these exegetical *middoth* affect the manner of interpreting the biblical texts, but they also at times had an effect upon the wording of the texts themselves. As Asher Finkel points out,[59] the Babylonian Talmud contains instances of where the rabbis employed dual readings of a text and dual meanings of a word for exegetical purposes: (1) by reading different vowels with the consonants;[60] (2) by inserting or omitting a weak consonant;[61] (3) by the transposition and change of gutturals;[62] (4) by the alteration of letters that sound alike or look alike;[63] and (5) by even allowing the

[57] Cf. H. L. Strack, *Introduction to the Talmud and Midrash*, pp. 97f.

[58] J. W. Doeve, *Jewish Hermeneutics in the Synoptic Gospels and Acts*, p. 64.

[59] A. Finkel, "The Pesher of Dreams and Scriptures," *RQ*, IV (1963), pp. 368f.

[60] E.g., b. Ber. 64a, on Isa. 54:13, reading *bonayikh* ("your builders") for *banayikh* ("your sons"); b. Ber. 48b, on Exod. 23:25, reading *ubarekh* (imperative of "to bless") for *uberakh* (perfect waw-consecutive).

[61] E.g., b. Meg. 13a, on Esth. 2:7, reading *lebayith* ("housewife") for *lebath* ("daughter"); b. Shab. 119b, on Isa. 26:2, reading *se'omer* ("the one who reads") for *somer* ("keeper").

[62] E.g., b. Ber. 32a, on Num. 11:2, reading *'al* instead of *'el*; b. Ber. 30b, on Ps. 29:2, reading *beḥerdath* ("with trembling of") for *behadrath* ("in the splendor of").

[63] E.g., b. Ber. 57a and b. Meg. 15b, where the diacritical point over S and s is altered to suit the exegete's purpose; b. Yoma 75a, on Num.

Greek reading to determine the Hebrew text.[64] While pesher interpretation at Qumran, as we shall see, had its effect upon the biblical text, it is significant to note here that midrashic exegesis did as well.

Midrashic interpretation, in effect, ostensibly takes its point of departure from the biblical text itself (though psychologically it may be motivated by other factors) and seeks to explicate the hidden meanings contained therein by means of agreed upon hermeneutical rules in order to contemporize the revelation of God for the people of God. It may be briefly characterized by the maxim: "That has relevance to This"; i.e., What is written in Scripture has relevance to our present situation. Or, as the late Renée Bloch described it:

1. Its point of departure is Scripture; it is a reflection or meditation on the Bible.
2. It is homiletical, and largely originates from the liturgical reading of the Torah.
3. It makes a punctilious analysis of the text, with the object of illuminating obscurities found there. Every effort is made to explain the Bible by the Bible, as a rule not arbitrarily but by exploiting a theme.
4. The biblical message is adapted to suit contemporary needs.
5. According to the nature of the biblical text, the midrash either tries to discover the basic principles inherent in the legal sections, with the aim of solving problems not dealt with in Scripture (*halakhah*); or it sets out to find the true significance of events mentioned in the narrative sections of the Pentateuch (*haggadah*).[65]

Or again, as Birger Gerhardsson defines it:

> Midrash is normally composed out of already-existing material, accepted as authoritative because it comes from the Scripture or the tradition. Using this raw material, the new is evolved. Naturally new terms, new phrases, new symbols and new ideas are introduced but the greater part is taken from that which already exists in the authoritative tradition. Midrash starts from a text, a phrase or often a single word; but the text is not simply explained—its

11:32, reading *wayyisḥatu* ("they slaughtered") for *wayyistehy* ("they spread").

[64] E.g., b. Suk. 35a, on Lev. 23:40, reading ὕδωρ for *hadar*.

[65] Reproduced by G. Vermes, *Scripture and Tradition*, p. 7. Point two of the listing, of course, assumes the validity of Bloch's understanding of the synagogue targumim as the basis for rabbinic haggadah; cf. *supra*, pp. 22f.

> meaning is extended and its implications drawn out with the help of every possible association of ideas.[66]

In days when the Sadducees (until their demise) rejected the validity of the Oral Law and the faithful required guidance for living in an alien milieu, it was considered necessary to establish the Pharisaic traditions on a solid footing in Scripture and to explicate Holy Writ to cover every situation of life. And this halakic concern extended over into haggadic matters, so that the same exegetical methods were followed there as well. The purpose of rabbinic midrash was often noble, and its practice at times moderate—more so in the earlier period than later. But in that its *middoth* both allowed and later encouraged imaginative as well as truly creative treatments of the biblical text, its interpretations often went beyond the bounds of what would today be identified as proper.

PESHER INTERPRETATION

The exposition in the materials from Qumran is usually introduced by the term "pesher," a word meaning "solution" or "interpretation" and coming from the Aramaic פשר. There are also instances where *midrash* is employed in the texts, most significantly for our purpose in the first lines of the commentaries on Psalms 1:1 and 2:1-2,[67] though in these cases the word seems to have the nontechnical meaning found in earlier rabbinism. The Dead Sea sectarians considered themselves to be the divinely elected community of the final generation of the present age, living in the days of "messianic travail" before the eschatological consummation. Theirs was the task of preparing for the coming of the Messianic Age and/or the Age to Come. And to them applied certain prophecies in the Old Testament which were considered to speak of their situation and circumstances. While it is true in general that "the members of the community conceive[d] of themselves as repeating in a later age the experience of their remote forefathers in the days of Moses,"[68] it must also be recognized, as F. F. Bruce

[66] B. Gerhardsson, *The Testing of God's Son* (ET 1966), p. 14.
[67] 4QFlor 1, 14; see also 1QS 6.24; 8.15; 8.26; CDC 20.6.
[68] T. H. Gaster, *The Dead Sea Scriptures* (1964), p. 4; cf. W. D. Davies, *The Setting of the Sermon on the Mount* (1964), pp. 26n., 33.

has pointed out, that they did not think of the particular prophecies in question as the message of God which was significant in an earlier period and now, *mutatis mutandis*, also relevant to them. Rather, they looked upon these selected passages as being exclusively concerned with them.[69] And therefore, following a large number of the prophetic statements cited, there is the recurrence of the expression פשרו על, which may be variously translated "the interpretation of this is," "this refers to," or "this means."

In an early study of Qumran's exegetical practices, W. H. Brownlee distilled the essence of the exegesis in the Habakkuk Commentary to thirteen propositions,[70] which have been found to be generally representative of the other commentaries as well. Brownlee's first point, that "everything the ancient prophet wrote has a *veiled, eschatological meaning*," has reference to the community's understanding of itself as God's righteous remnant in the period of eschatological consummation. Here Qumran distinguishes itself from rabbinic interpretation, for while in the talmudic literature there is a contemporizing treatment of Holy Writ that seeks to make God's Word relevant to the present circumstances and on-going situations, among the Dead Sea covenanters the biblical texts were looked upon from the perspective of imminent apocalyptic fulfilment. Brownlee's second point regarding "*forced, or abnormal construction of the Biblical text*" concerns 1QpHab's more than fifty deviations from the MT (apart from the purely orthographic), of which several vary from all known versions of the LXX and Targums as well,[71] and the four cases where the Old Testament text is read as though it were multiform—i.e., not only as though each word had several meanings but also as if the text itself had more than one wording, one

[69] F. F. Bruce, *Biblical Exegesis in the Qumran Texts* (1960), pp. 16f. On the selected nature of the passages treated at Qumran, see C. Roth, "The Subject Matter of Qumran Exegesis," *VT*, X (1960), pp. 52, 56, though without accepting the implications drawn from this for his first-century-A.D. Zealot identification.

[70] W. H. Brownlee, "Biblical Interpretation among the Sectaries of the Dead Sea Scrolls," *BA*, XIV (1951), pp. 60-62.

[71] For a tabulation of the "Principal Variants," see W. H. Brownlee, *The Text of Habakkuk in the Ancient Commentary from Qumran* (1959), pp. 108-113.

appearing in the quotation and the other in the commentary following.[72]

The problem of textual variations and dual readings at Qumran is a difficult one. And in the present state of uncertainty regarding the history of the MT, the early recensions of the LXX, and the relation of the various Targumic traditions to each other, a final solution seems for the present out of the question. Stendahl, for example, tends to favor *ad hoc* creations in many of these cases;[73] while Brownlee is more cautious in saying: "Though deliberate alteration may have played a part in the formation of the Hab. text utilized in DSH, it is probably resorted to but rarely. Many divergent texts were current from which one might well select the reading most advantageous to the purpose at hand."[74] Until further evidence is forthcoming on the state of the Hebrew, Greek and Aramaic texts in this early period, we do well to withhold final judgment on the matter. It may well be that in some cases 1QpHab reflects *ad hoc* textual creations or deliberate corrections of existing versions by an expositor or group of expositors within the community. Or the phenomenon may be entirely one of selection among variants. All that can be said with certainty at the time is that pesher interpretation has affected the form of the biblical text upon which it bases itself, however that text came about.

In the remaining eleven characteristics of his listing, Brownlee has clearly demonstrated that the mode of exegesis employed at Qumran is strikingly similar to that of

[72] On the dual readings of Hab. 1:8; 1:11; 1:15f. and 2:16, see *ibid.*, pp. 118-123; also K. Stendahl, *The School of St. Matthew* (1954), pp. 186-89.

[73] Stendahl's reaction, while favoring *ad hoc* creations, is rather mixed in saying: "The relation between DSH, the M.T. and the Versions is of great interest. In many cases DSH appears to be created *ad hoc*. What is more remarkable is that some of these readings are supported by one or more of the Versions" (*School of St. Matthew*, p. 189). Stendahl later builds on this *ad hoc* understanding in his treatment of Matthew's formula quotations, though he concludes his section on the textual variations in 1QpHab by stating: "We must rather presume that DSH was conscious of various possibilities, tried them out, and allowed them to enrich its interpretation of the prophet's message, which in all its form was fulfilled in and through the Teacher of Righteousness" (*ibid.*, p. 190).

[74] W. H. Brownlee, *Text of Habakkuk*, pp. 117f.

rabbinic midrash. And thus many have followed him in labelling the interpretive procedure of the Qumran commentaries a "midrash pesher," considering it comparable to rabbinic "midrash halakah" and "midrash haggadah" and to be distinguished from them only in regard to literary form and content.[75]

But though it is often done, it is not sufficient to define "pesher" as midrashic exegesis which displays a greater audacity in its handling of the text, coupled to an apocalyptic orientation.[76] Such a characterization is true as far as it goes, but it does not touch upon the vital factor in Qumran hermeneutics. Central in the consciousness of the covenanters of Qumran was what might be called the *rāz* (mystery)-*pesher* (interpretation) revelational motif, which is found explicitly stated in the commentary on Hab. 2:1-2:

> God told Habakkuk to write the things that were to come upon the last generation, but he did not inform him when that period would come to consummation. And as for the phrase, "that he may run who reads," the interpretation (*pesher*) concerns the Teacher of Righteousness to whom God made known all the mysteries (*rāzīm*) of the words of his servants the prophets.[77]

And this is echoed in the treatment of Hab. 2:3:

> The last period extends beyond anything that the prophets have foretold, for "the mysteries of God are destined to be performed wondrously."[78]

Furthermore, to read the Dead Sea Hymns of Thanksgiving not only as an expression of the Teacher of Righteousness himself, whether written directly by him or derived from his oral teaching,[79] but also with the *rāz-pesher* motif in mind, is illuminating. Repeatedly there occurs the idea of having been given the interpretation of divine mysteries, which are

[75] Cf. W. H. Brownlee, "Biblical Interpretation," *BA*, XIV (1951), p. 76; K. Stendahl, *School of St. Matthew*, p. 184. M. Black's comment is apropos: "*midrash-pesher* is a modern invention probably best forgotten" ("The Christological Use of the Old Testament in the New Testament," *NTS*, XVIII [1971], p. 1).

[76] E.g., Stendahl, *School of St. Matthew*, p. 193; Brownlee, "Biblical Interpretation," pp. 54-76.

[77] 1QpHab 7.1-5.

[78] 1QpHab 7.7-8, accepting T. H. Gaster's literal rendering of the maxim (*Dead Sea Scriptures*, p. 280, n. 25).

[79] Cf. J. T. Milik, *Ten Years of Discovery*, p. 40.

then shared with the people. Representative of this theme is 1QH 4.26-29:

> Through me hast Thou illumined the faces of full many, and countless be the times Thou hast shown Thy power through me. For Thou hast made known unto me Thy deep, mysterious things, hast shared Thy secret with me and so shown forth Thy power; and before the eyes of full many this token stands revealed, that Thy glory may be shown forth, and all living know of Thy power.[80]

The men of Qumran seem not so much conscious of following a rabbinic mode of exegesis as recreating the Danielic pattern of interpretation. In Dan. 9:24-27, Jeremiah's prophecy of seventy years is reinterpreted by the angel Gabriel to mean seventy heptads of years,[81] and in Dan. 11:30 Balaam's prophecy regarding the "ships of Kittim" is employed to denote a Roman fleet.[82] In the Aramaic portion of Daniel (2:4–7:28) there are thirty occurrences of the word פשר; and the greater part of the material contained therein can appropriately be classed as "Theme and Variations on the *Rāz-Pesher* Motif": Nebuchadnezzar's dream of the metalic human image, and Daniel's interpretation (ch. 2), Nebuchadnezzar's dream of the gigantic tree and its fall, and Daniel's interpretation (ch. 4), the writing on the wall at Belshazzar's banquet, and Daniel's interpretation (ch. 5), and Belshazzar's dream of the composite animal, and Daniel's interpretation (ch. 7). "In the Book of Daniel it is clear that the *rāz*, the mystery, is divinely communicated to one party, and the *pesher*, the interpretation, to another. Not until the mystery and the interpretation are brought together can the divine communication be understood."[83] And, as Bruce comments further:

> This principle, that the divine purpose cannot be properly understood until the *pesher* has been revealed as well as the *rāz*, underlies the biblical exegesis in the Qumran commentaries. The *rāz* was

[80] Cf. also 1QH 1.21; 2.13.
[81] See Jer. 25:11f.; 29:10.
[82] See Num. 24:24.
[83] F. F. Bruce, *Biblical Exegesis in the Qumran Texts*, p. 8. Cf. also A. Finkel, "The Pesher of Dreams and Scriptures," *RQ*, IV (1963), p. 357, who cites also the nine uses of *pesher* in Gen. 40-41 (the stories of Joseph's interpretation of the dreams of the butler, the baker, and of Pharaoh himself).

communicated by God to the prophet, but the meaning of that communication remained sealed until its *pesher* was made known by God to His chosen interpreter. The chosen interpreter was the Teacher of Righteousness, the founder of the Qumran community.[84]

Extensive consideration has been given to whether "pesher" interpretation as found in the Scrolls is to be classed as "commentary" or as "midrash." But the discussions have usually been carried on solely in categories pertinent to either a commentary form or a mode of exegesis, and largely ignore the factor wherein the Dead Sea community felt itself to be distinctive. In fact, Qumran's pesher interpretation of the Old Testament is neither principally "commentary" nor "midrashic exegesis." "It does not," as Cecil Roth points out, "attempt to elucidate the Biblical text, but to determine the application of Biblical prophecy or, rather, of certain Biblical prophecies: and the application of these Biblical prophecies in precise terms to current and even contemporary events."[85] The crucial question in defining pesher interpretation has to do with the point of departure. In contradistinction to rabbinic exegesis which spoke of "That has relevance to This," the Dead Sea covenanters treated Scripture in a "This is That" fashion. Or as Karl Elliger put it as early as 1953: "Seine Auslegung gründet sich also nicht auf den Text allein, sondern in noch stärkerem Masse und im entscheidenden Punkte auf eine besondere Offenbarung."[86]

Biblical interpretation at Qumran, then, was considered to be first of all revelatory and/or charismatic in nature. Certain of the prophecies had been given in cryptic and

[84] F. F. Bruce, *Biblical Exegesis in the Qumran Texts*, p. 9.

[85] C. Roth, "The Subject Matter of Qumran Exegesis," *VT*, X (1960), pp. 51f.

[86] K. Elliger, *Studien zum Habakuk-Kommentar vom Toten Meer* (1953), p. 155; cf. also pp. 154-164. Elliger's main point is paralleled in the treatments of F. F. Bruce, *Biblical Exegesis in the Qumran Texts*, pp. 7-19; J. A. Fitzmyer, "The Use of Explicit Old Testament Quotations in Qumran Literature and in the New Testament," *NTS*, VII (1961), p. 310; and G. Vermes, "The Qumran Interpretation of Scripture in its Historical Setting," *ALUOS*, VI (1966-68), pp. 90-97; though the sharp dichotomy which Elliger draws between a revelational perspective and a midrashic mode of exegesis may be legitimately questioned.

enigmatic terms, and no one could understand their true meaning until the Teacher of Righteousness was given the interpretive key. In a real sense, they understood the passages in question as possessing a *sensus plenior* which could be ascertained only from a revelational standpoint,[87] and they believed that the true message of Scripture was heard only when prophecy and interpretation were brought together. The understanding of the Teacher in regard to certain crucial passages and the guidelines he laid down for future study were to be the touchstones for all further exegesis,[88] and members were strictly forbidden to incorporate extraneous opinion "in any matter of doctrine or law."[89] We need not suppose that interpretation ceased with the Teacher himself, or that the Dead Sea texts preserve only interpretations given explicitly by him. He sounded the keynote and set the paradigms in his treatment of certain prophecies, and the membership met in study cells and communal sessions to carry on investigations along the lines set out for them by their teacher. In such meditations on the text, of course, exegetical methods at hand were employed.

We cannot deny midrashic modes of treatment at Qumran. But we must not allow them to take ascendancy in our definition of pesher interpretation. If we must use the term "midrash" of the Qumran procedures, perhaps such a term as "charismatic midrash" should be employed to distinguish it from the "scholastic midrash" of the rabbis.[90] As in Dan. 5, where the interpretation is understood to be a divine revelation given through Daniel to the king and yet is explicated in terms of a midrash on the cryptic מנא מנא תקל ופרסין, so with the community on the shores of the

[87] Cf. J. A. Fitzmyer, "Use of Explicit Old Testament Quotations," *NTS*, VII (1961), p. 332. On the *sensus plenior* in Catholic theology, see R. E. Brown, *The "Sensus Plenior" of Sacred Scripture* (1955).

[88] 1QH 2.11-13: "Thou hast set me as a banner in the vanguard of Righteousness, as one who interprets with knowledge deep, mysterious things; as a touchstone for them that seek the truth, a standard for them that love correction."

[89] 1QS 5.15f.

[90] Brownlee mentions H. L. Ginsberg's reference to the Teacher of Righteousness as a "charismatic exegete" ("Biblical Interpretation," *BA*, XIV [1951], p. 60n).

Dead Sea. Exegesis at Qumran stands between Daniel and the rabbis, and is a matter of both revelatory stance and midrashic mode—though, it must be insisted, in that order.

ALLEGORICAL INTERPRETATION

The most prominent Jewish allegorist of the first century was Philo of Alexandria, whose expositions of Scripture were produced during the life of Jesus and the earliest day of the Church. While a Jew, Philo was the inheritor of Stoic and Platonic ideas. And while a severe critic of the content of these philosophies, he (consciously or unconsciously) employed their basic categories in the presentation of what he believed to be the truth of the Jewish Torah. From Stoicism he inherited a tripartite division of philosophy which assigned the lowest place to logic and the more noble places to physics and ethics.[91] Philo, of course, had little interest in the thoroughly immanent God of Stoicism, and therefore had little interest in developing the Stoic category of physics. He assigned theology to the category of ethics, though he defined ethics as not only a knowledge of right conduct but a knowledge of the transcendent Maker of the world as given in the Torah revealed to Moses and as immanent in the Logos. From Platonism he inherited the "fundamental contrast between (a) the external world of passing sensation with its unreliable flux of 'opinion' based thereon, and (b) the inner world of unchanging reason and harmony, the realm of the eternal 'ideas' of goodness, truth, and beauty."[92]

Philo's attitude toward allegorical and literalist exegesis appears in a number of passages throughout his writings. He entirely rejected a literal interpretation where anthropomorphism is at issue, insisting that Num. 23:19 makes it clear that "God is not as man" (*οὐχ ὡς ἄνθρωπος ὁ θεός*)[93]

[91] Cf. H. A. Wolfson, *Philo*, I, p. 146.
[92] F. C. Grant's characterization of Platonism, "Plato, Platonism," *Dictionary of the Bible*, rev. & ed. F. C. Grant and H. H. Rowley (1963), p. 777.
[93] Quod Deus Immut. 13, 62; De Somn. I. 40, 237. Cf. Wolfson, *Philo*, I, pp. 116f.

and endeavoring to safeguard the transcendence of God against the anthropopathisms that follow a literal treatment of the anthropomorphisms.[94] Likewise, he was prepared to interpret allegorically anything that might derogate the dignity of the inspired words of God: anything that is nonsensical in the creation accounts, that is reprehensible in the legal portions, or that is trivial in the historical narratives of the Pentateuch.[95] In his endeavor to vindicate Jewish theology before the court of Grecian philosophy,[96] and in his desire to contemporize the sacred writings so as to make them relevant to present circumstances and experience,[97] Philo usually treated the Old Testament as a body of symbols given by God for man's spiritual and moral benefit, which must be understood other than in a literal and historical fashion. The *prima facie* meaning must normally be pushed aside—even counted as offensive—to make room for the intended spiritual meaning underlying the obvious;[98] though, as noted above, at times he seems willing to consider literal and allegorical exegesis as having "parallel legitimacy."[99] In the main, however, exegesis of Holy Writ was for him an esoteric enterprise which, while not without its governing principles,[100] was to be disassociated from literal interpretation. And that this dichotomy was both conscious and deliberate with Philo is expressly indicated by his repeated distinctions between literal and

[94] De Post. Cain. 4; Quod Deus Immut. 59; De Sacrif. Ab. et Cain. 95. Cf. S. Sowers, *Hermeneutics of Philo and Hebrews*, pp. 22f.
[95] Cf. R. Loewe, "The 'Plain' Meaning of Scripture," *PIJSL*, I (1964), p. 147.
[96] Quis Rer. Div. Heres 214; Quod Omnis Prob. Liber 57; De Mutat. Nom. 167f.; De Migrat. Abr. 128; De Spec. Leg. IV. 61; Quaes. et Sol. Gen. II. 6, III. 5, IV. 152.
[97] S. Sowers, citing S. Sandmel and G. Kuhlmann, speaks of Philo's work as "a religious existentialism somewhat like the kind of interpretation fashionable because of Kierkegaard" (*Hermeneutics of Philo and Hebrews*, p. 32, n. 9).
[98] For Philo, "der buchstäbliche Sinn ist lediglich der Körper, der den allegorischen als die Seele umschliesst" (O. Michel, *Paulus und seine Bibel* [1929], p. 106). Cf. C. Siegfried, "Philo Judaeus," *Jewish Encyclopedia*, X (1906), p. 7.
[99] *Supra*, p. 30.
[100] Philo speaks of "canons of allegory" (De Somn. I. 73, De Spec. Leg. I. 287) and "laws of allegory" (De Abr. 68); cf. C. Siegfried, *Philo von Alexandria* (1875), pp. 165-68.

allegorical interpretation,[101] his running debate with the literal interpreters of Alexandria,[102] and his references to those who rejected his work as being "pedantic professors of literalism."[103]

Philo, it is true, was not universally admired; and he may not be representative of the entirety of hellenistic Judaism in many ways. But his exegetical methods were not unique to himself. C. Siegfried and H. A. A. Kennedy have shown that "there can be little question that Philo stood in a long succession of allegorical interpreters of the Old Testament. The practice had been reduced to a kind of science."[104] Clement of Alexandria mentions a second-century-B.C. Alexandrian Jew by the name of Aristobulus who employed allegorical exegesis in a series of works on the Mosaic law.[105] The Letter of Aristeas includes one instance of a mild allegorical treatment in its portrayal of the High Priest Eleazer's defense of the Jewish dietary laws,[106] which, judging from Josephus' extensive paraphrase of the Letter and his specific references to Aristeas,[107] was probably widely known. Jacob Lauterbach has identified two groups of Palestinian Pharisees active prior to the time of Rabbi Judah "the Prince," the *Dorshe Reshumot* and the *Dorshe Hamurot*, who employed a mild allegorical exegesis in their treatment of Scripture—and whose work was gradually repudiated, though not entirely purged, in the tightening up of Judaism at the end of the second century A.D.[108] And Joseph Bonsirven and David Daube have presented signifi-

[101] E.g., De Spec. Leg. II. 147; Quaes. et Sol. Exod. II. 71; De Plant. 74; De Fuga 181; De Somn. I. 15.

[102] De Fuga 179f.; Quod Det. Pot. Insid. 22; De Somn. I. 39, II. 301. Cf. M. J. Shroyer, "Alexandrian Jewish Literalists," *JBL*, LV (1936), pp. 261-284.

[103] De Somn. I. 102; De Cherub. 42.

[104] H. A. A. Kennedy, *Philo's Contribution to Religion* (1919), p. 32; cf. also pp. 32-34. C. Siegfried, *Philo von Alexandria*, pp. 16-37.

[105] Strom. V. 14. 97.

[106] Letter of Aristeas 150-170. See esp. 150: "For the division of the hoof and the separation of the claws are intended to teach us that we must discriminate between our individual actions with a view to the practice of virtue."

[107] Antiq. XII. 11-118.

[108] J. Z. Lauterbach, "Ancient Jewish Allegorists," *JQR*, I (1911), pp. 291-333, 503-531.

cant papers in support of the thesis of an early Pharisaic allegorical exegesis within Palestine itself.[109] In addition, the Dead Sea Scrolls include a number of examples of allegorical interpretation, representative of which is the treatment of Hab. 2:17 in 1QpHab 12.3-4: " 'Lebanon' stands here for the Communal Council, and 'wild beasts' for the simple-minded Jews who carry out the Law."[110] But though allegorical exegesis was widespread amongst Jews of the first century, it was not dominant in Palestine.

SUMMATION

Our survey of Jewish hermeneutics in the first Christian century has brought us to the point of summation. What can be concluded from this mass of varying opinions and differing strands of tradition?

In the first place, it is important to emphasize the areas and points of agreement, whatever differences might also have existed. All Jewish interpreters believed in the divine inspiration of the Scriptures, that they were dealing with the very words of God, and that these words were pregnant with meaning for the people in their present circumstances. As to interpretive methodologies, there was, in Palestine at least, a commonality of exegetical tradition which each group adopted and modified for its own purposes. Both the Pharisaic teachers and the nonconformist exegetes em-

[109] Bonsirven cites several cases of allegorical treatment of biblical legislation in the talmudic materials that fly in the face of prohibitions against allegorical interpretation of halakic passages ("Exégèse allégorique chez les rabbins tannaites," *RSR*, XXIII [1933], pp. 522-24); Daube develops a thesis that the whole system of rabbinic exegesis initiated by Hillel about 30 B.C. was based on hellenistic models ("Rabbinic Methods of Interpretation and Hellenistic Rhetoric," *HUCA*, XXII [1949], pp. 239-264), and argues that "in the eyes of the Rabbis, the Bible, since it enshrined the wisdom of God, contained various layers of meaning. . . . A word might have an ordinary sense and one or two allegorical senses at the same time" ("Alexandrian Methods of Interpretation and the Rabbis," *Festschrift Hans Lewald* [1953], p. 38). Particularly noted for its mild allegorical treatment is Song of Songs Rabbah.

[110] Cf. also 1QpMic 8-10; CDC 6.2-11; 7.9-20. "Lebanon" stands for the Communal Council: *Laban* means white; the Council dressed in white.

ployed literalist interpretation, particularly in halakic concerns. This may also have been true of Philo, though the evidence is not as certain. Both the Pharisaic teachers and the nonconformist exegetes employed midrashic modes in interpreting the biblical texts, usually, in the period of our interest, following the more restrained procedures of the seven *middoth* attributed to Hillel rather than those rules codified later; though Philo seems not to be conscious of such procedures. And both Pharisaic teachers and the nonconformist exegetes employed, at times, a mild allegorical exegesis,[111] as distinguished from the excesses of Philo in this area.

On the other hand, it is possible to view in first-century Judaism a number of distinguishable strands of developing and developed exegetical tradition. Broadly speaking, Pharisaic Judaism, from a practical need to tie the oral tradition more closely to Scripture and from a theoretic recognition of various layers of meaning implicit in the biblical texts, rather unself-consciously built upon its midrashic inheritance and continued the process of developing midrash exegesis into something of a science. The covenanters of Qumran, convinced that they were God's righteous remnant preparing the way for the Lord in these days of final travail and that God had revealed the interpretation of the pro-

[111] Determination of the extent of allegorical interpretation depends largely on how one defines "allegorical exegesis," and how one relates it to "allegory" and to what I prefer to call "poetic symbolism." Sidney Sowers, for example, finds allegorical exegesis in Wisdom of Solomon (*Hermeneutics of Philo and Hebrews*, p. 16), but because of the presence of what I believe to be "poetic symbolism." James Barr disputes the criterion of history in distinguishing between allegorical and typological exegesis, and argues that allegorical interpretation was more widespread and more indeterminate from typology than is usually considered. But his definition equates "allegory" and "allegorical exegesis" (*Old and New in Interpretation* [1966], pp. 103-111). Rudolf Bultmann, together with a number of other scholars, lumps "allegory," "typology," and the "fulfilment motif" under the heading "allegorical exegesis" (*Theology of the New Testament*, I [ET 1952], pp. 116f.), which I believe to be an extreme of imprecision and confusion. I propose that "allegory" be understood simply as an extended metaphor (as a parable is an extended simile), whose intent is different from that of historical narrative, and that "allegorical exegesis" be understood as a reworking of a portion that is *prima facie* historical in order to bring out its hidden layer of symbolic meaning.

phetic mysteries to their Teacher, consciously and overtly based their interpretations on a revelational perspective.[112] They continued to employ midrashic exegesis in their treatment of some of the texts, as was their earlier practice, but subsumed this under their more charismatic approach. Philo, building upon an Alexandrian Jewish exegetical tradition and incorporating large doses of Grecian categories into his thought, developed allegorical exegesis to the point where it became almost his exclusive passion. Each of these, Pharisees, sectarians, and Philo alike, worked from distinctive doctrinal and ideological commitments, which produced distinctive features in their exegetical methodologies. In addition, for the Pharisees and the Dead Sea covenanters, their commitments and methods had an effect upon the form of the biblical texts upon which they expended their energies—more so at Qumran than for the Pharisees, though nevertheless a factor for both. In effect, textual criticism to some extent proceeded on a theological basis.

[112] G. Vermes has aptly characterized the interpretation of Scripture at Qumran: "Firstly, the words of the prophets are full of mystery; they have a hidden significance which must be discovered by means of further revelation. Secondly, this hidden meaning alludes to what is to take place at the end of the world. Thirdly, the end of the world is near; the prophecy consequently applies to the writer's own generation. Fourthly, and most important of all, the person to whom all these mysteries were revealed was the Teacher of Righteousness himself" ("The Qumran Interpretation of Scripture," *ALUOS*, VI [1966-68], p. 91).

II: JESUS AND THE OLD TESTAMENT

"What is the principal impression of Christ which we get, and which the Evangelist meant that we should get, from a continuous reading of the Gospel according to St Mark?" That was the question posed by E. G. Selwyn in his presidential address of 1956 to the Studiorum Novi Testamenti Societas.[1] Selwyn answered his question with one word, "authority"; and then illustrated his point by a brief survey of the Synoptic Gospels.

The authority of Christ undergirds the doctrine and practice of the earliest Christians, and is reflected throughout the New Testament. Convinced of his Messiahship and Lordship, the early believers began with Jesus as the "certain and known quantity."[2] And in him they witnessed a creative handling of the Scriptures which became for them both the source of their own understanding and the paradigm for their own exegesis of the Old Testament.[3] The maxim that

[1] E. G. Selwyn, "The Authority of Christ in the New Testament," *NTS*, III (1957), pp. 83-92.

[2] Quoting J. Barr, *Old and New in Interpretation* (1966), p. 139, though in opposition to his point. On Messiahship and Lordship in early Christian conviction, see my *The Christology of Early Jewish Christianity*, chs. III-IV, pp. 63-147.

[3] There is a similar approach taken in the papers and the statement on "general consensus" from the 1949 Oxford conference on hermeneutics (*Biblical Authority for Today*, ed. A. Richardson and W. Schweitzer [1951]), though the explication of this approach will inevitably vary among given interpreters. In the statement of "Guiding Principles," the point is made: "It is agreed that the unity of the Old and the New Testaments is not to be found in any naturalistic development, or in any static identity, but in the ongoing redemptive activity of God in the history of one people, reaching its fulfilment in Christ. Accordingly it is of decisive importance for hermeneutical method to interpret the Old Testament in the light of the total revelation in the

"in Palestinian Christianity, Jesus of Nazareth and the redemptive significance of his person is the creative element"[4] is true in the area of biblical interpretation as well.

A REALISTIC APPRAISAL OF THE DOCUMENTS

Contemporary New Testament historiography is in large measure in reaction to nineteenth-century historicism. Controlled by a positivistic view of history, many scholars of the past century believed that by means of an "objective" (i.e., secular, devoid of supernaturalistic conditioning) view of the data, one could reconstruct the events of biblical history as they actually happened without being compelled to accept them as they are presented. The result of this so-called "neutral" reading of the life of Jesus and the course of apostolic history was a product so innocuous and so minimal in content that it was difficult to see how the phenomenon of Christianity could have had any impact on the ancient world or have any significance for men today.

But with a profound consciousness of the living quality of New Testament proclamation—coupled with a deep respect for the negative conclusions of nineteenth-century criticism—Karl Barth claimed to have solved the problem by asserting that redemptive occurrences take place in a realm inaccessible to historical or scientific inquiry, Paul Tillich constructed a system of metaphysics that could not be disturbed by any historical consideration, and Rudolf Bultmann averred that the meaning of history (*Geschichte*) lay not in historical events (*Historie*) but in man's understanding of himself and his predicament.[5] Scholarship in the twentieth century, therefore, came to be concerned almost exclusively with the *kerygma* of the New Testament, and, by means of demythologizing the symbols of that proclamation, the faith to which the symbols bore witness. In so

---

person of Jesus Christ, the Incarnate Word of God, from which arises the full Trinitarian faith of the church" (*ibid.*, p. 241).

[4] K. G. Kuhn, "The Lord's Supper and the Communal Meal at Qumran," *The Scrolls and the New Testament*, ed. K. Stendahl (1957), p. 86.

[5] Cf. A. Richardson, *History, Sacred and Profane* (1964), pp. 125-153.

doing, many took an agnostic position—frequently even a hostile position—toward questions of historicity and facticity, denouncing all attempts to view history as a prolegomenon for faith. It is true that Bultmann, Martin Dibelius and Karl Schmidt, for example, as distinct from Barth in this regard, developed an historical methodology in support of their philosophical positions. But that methodology, which generally is labelled the "New Hermeneutic" as to its overall thrust, is built upon the revolutionary principle that documents tell us more about the people who wrote them than about the events they purport to relate. It asserts the antithetical relation of proclamation and historical events, and through Bultmann, whose influence has been dominant, holds presuppositions hostile to the New Testament's own understanding of itself and attitudes that are extremely negative toward matters of historical reliability.

Bultmann's historical radicalism elicited a reaction on the part of many of his former students, which found its voice in Ernst Käsemann's 1953 Marburg address on "The Problem of the Historical Jesus."[6] But the so-called "New Quest," while modifying the negativism of its teacher and seeking to bridge the gap between the Church's message and the historical Jesus, still bases itself upon the sharp distinction between *Historie* and *Geschichte* (understanding the former in only a positivistic manner) and still labors, though not always as extremely, under its heritage of the depreciation of facticity. In its historical criticism, the New Quest has developed Bultmann's explicit *Formgeschichte* and his implicit *Redactionsgeschichte*, employing, in the process, at least four tests for the authenticity of any element in the Gospels' portrayal of Jesus: (1) the criterion of dissimilarity, (2) the criterion of multiple attestation, (3) the criterion of eschatological context, and (4) the criterion of coherence. The first eliminates from the accounts all features of Jesus that "are paralleled in the Jewish tradition on the one hand (apocalyptic and Rabbinic) and those which reflect the faith, practice and situations of the post-Easter

[6] E. Käsemann, "Das Problem des historischen Jesus," *ZTK*, LI (1954), pp. 125-153. For a summation of the program of and prospects for the "New Quest," see J. M. Robinson, *A New Quest of the Historical Jesus* (1959).

church as we know them from outside the gospels."[7] The second suggests that "material may be accepted which is found in a multiplicity of sources or forms of tradition, provided always that this multiple attestation is not due to the influence of some widespread church practice such as the Eucharist."[8] The third demands that authentic representations of Jesus be rooted inextricably in an eschatological context, on the supposition that Jesus was "thoroughgoing" or entirely "proleptic" in his own understanding of eschatology.[9] And the fourth proposes that "material which is consistent with or coheres with material established as authentic by other means may also be accepted."[10] In addition, some form critics and redaction critics employ the criteria of language and style;[11] though among the more radical, language and style seemingly have little effect upon conclusions derived from the application of the criteria of dissimilarity, multiple attestation, eschatological context and coherence.

But while we empathize with Bultmann's desire to translate essential Christianity into modern terms, and must acknowledge that he and many of his disciples are motivated by a pastoral concern, we cannot believe that a true faith or a sound scholarship can long survive the drastic Bultmannian disparagement of history. As Stephen Neill says:

> Though some scholars, and many Christians, are impatient in the face of such assertions, it seems to be the case that the faith of the Church stands or falls with the general reliability of the historical evidence. . . . 'What really happened?' This is the naive but inevitable question of the theologically unsophisticated.[12]

[7] R. H. Fuller, *The Foundations of New Testament Christology* (1965), p. 18. Cf. R. Bultmann, *The History of the Synoptic Tradition* (ET 1963), p. 205; E. Käsemann, *Essays on New Testament Themes* (ET 1964), pp. 34-37; N. Perrin, *Rediscovering the Teaching of Jesus* (1967), pp. 39-43; *idem*, *What is Redaction Criticism?* (1970), p. 71.

[8] N. Perrin, *ibid.*, p. 71.

[9] Note, particularly, Bultmannian treatments of the "Son of man" in the Gospels, accepting as authentic only the eschatological references to a coming personage distinct from Jesus.

[10] N. Perrin, *What is Redaction Criticism?*, p. 71.

[11] Most distinctly and effectively, J. Jeremias, *New Testament Theology*, I (1971), pp. 3-41.

[12] S. Neill, *The Interpretation of the New Testament* (1964), p. 221.

To ignore or to discredit such a question is to engage in an "avoiding-action,"[13] which, while it insulates faith from the onslaughts and fluctuations of criticism, also isolates faith from the world of human experience and thereby cuts the cord of communication that links the Church with the world it is endeavoring to address. Worse yet, such a disparagement of the historical strikes at what is intrinsic and vital to the Christian faith, and not merely secondary: God's redemptive activity in and self-revelation through human history.[14] The faith of the New Testament must be made accessible to the modern mind, but not at the sacrifice of the heart of the biblical message.

Likewise, while criteria of dissimilarity, multiple attestation, eschatological context, coherence, and (to include just as important a category) language and style are all important in the historian's criticism of the Gospel portrayals, none of them should be used as a straitjacket to conform the material to our expectations, or be employed in any ham-fisted manner. M. D. Hooker is quite right in pointing out:

> Use of the principle of dissimilarity, it is claimed, gives us what is distinctive in the teaching of Jesus. But the English word 'distinctive' can have two senses—it can mean 'unique' (what makes it distinct from other things, the German *verschieden*), or it can mean 'characteristic' (the German *bezeichnend*). In what sense is it being used here? Clearly the method is designed to give us the former—but what we really want is the latter; and the two are by no means necessarily the same.[15]

And Joachim Jeremias speaks to the point in saying:

> Indeed, it has to be said that the way in which the 'criterion of dissimilarity' is often used today as a password is a serious source

[13] A. Richardson, "Second Thoughts—III. Present Issues in New Testament Theology," *ExpT*, LXXV (1964), p. 110; also *idem*, *History, Sacred and Profane*, p. 134.

[14] Cf. O. Cullmann, *Heil als Geschichte* (1965), pp. 80-96. Cullmann also points out: "Das Skandalon des Kreuzes und der Auferstehung als Zentrum allen Geschehens war damals—wie heute—eine 'Torheit'. Nicht Heil über den Weg der 'Entweltlichung', sondern Heil in der Bindung an die Geschichte—das ist das Skandalon für die Philosophen des 1. Jahrhunderts wie für die Philosophen unserer Zeit" (*ibid.*, p. 295).

[15] M. D. Hooker, "Christology and Methodology," *NTS*, XVII (1971), p. 481.

of error. It foreshortens and distorts the historical situation, because it overlooks the continuity between Jesus and Judaism.[16]

In similar fashion, care must be taken in the application of the other criteria as well. The criterion of eschatological context, for example, assumes a thoroughly futuristic eschatology in the thought of Jesus, which assumption is more imposed upon the data than derived from the data. And the criterion of coherence can very easily become coherence with the critic's preconceived idea of the state of affairs, and little more.

This is not to deny a legitimate place to criticism. The Evangelists each had their own interests, their own theological perspectives, and their own purposes. To a great extent, as in any writing, these affected their selection, arrangement and shaping of the material. And it is incumbent upon the historian to make distinctions among the various strands of tradition. Here source criticism, form criticism and redaction criticism all have a proper place. But it is a *non sequitur* to argue that therefore the Evangelists' portrayal of Jesus must be viewed historically with scepticism.[17]

All of this has an important bearing on the investigation of Jesus' use of the Old Testament. If, of course, we believe that the Old Testament quotations attributed to Jesus reflect the biblical interpretation of the churches in which the Gospels emerged, and not of Jesus himself, then our investigation must focus entirely on those churches, leaving aside the question of Jesus' own use. The evidence would just not be there for the study of Jesus and the Old Testament. On the other hand, if we believe that "while we must frequently note points where interpretation has obviously affected the form of the text," it is our "primary task to interpret the Gospels as they stand as credible reports of Jesus and his preaching,"[18] then we are interested in both Jesus' own employment of the Old Testament as recorded in the Gospels and each of the Evangelists' own

[16] J. Jeremias, *New Testament Theology*, I, p. 2.
[17] Cf. B. Reicke, "Incarnation and Exaltation. The Historic Jesus and the Kerygmatic Christ," *Interp*, XVI (1962), esp. p. 159; G. E. Ladd, "History and Theology in Biblical Exegesis," *Interp*, XX (1966), pp. 54-64.
[18] G. E. Ladd, *Jesus and the Kingdom* (1964), p. xiii.

biblical exegesis as distinguishable from that of Jesus. It is this latter position which I believe to be realistic and true, and which I believe the patterns of dissimilarity and of continuity as traced out in what follows will demonstrate.

THE PHENOMENA OF THE QUOTATIONS

The study of Jesus' use of the Old Testament must focus, in the first place, upon the explicit Old Testament quotations attributed to him in the Gospels. The distinction between a direct quotation and an allusion is, of course, notoriously difficult, and any listing of one apart from the other will inevitably be somewhat arbitrary in areas where they overlap. Nonetheless, for purposes of analysis, such distinctions must be made. The present study of Jesus' usage, therefore, will base itself upon the following thirty-nine quotations attributed to him:[19]

I. Quotations occurring in Mark and the double or triple synoptic tradition:

A. With introductory formulae:

1. Mark 7:6f.; Matt. 15:8f. (Isa. 29:13).
2. Mark 7:10; Matt. 15:4 (Exod. 20:12; 21:17 [LXX=21:16]; Deut. 5:16).
3. Mark 11:17; Matt. 21:13; Luke 19:46 (Isa. 56:7; Jer. 7:11).
4. Mark 12:10f.; Matt. 21:42; Luke 20:17 (Ps. 118:22f. [LXX=117:22f.]).
5. Mark 12:26; Matt. 22:32; Luke 20:37 (Exod. 3:6).
6. Mark 12:36; Matt. 22:44; Luke 20:42f. (Ps. 110:1 [LXX=109:1]).
7. Mark 13:14; Matt. 24:15 (Dan. 9:27; 12:11).
8. Mark 14:27; Matt. 26:31 (Zech. 13:7).

B. Without introductory formulae:

9. Mark 10:7f.; Matt. 19:5 (Gen. 2:24).
10. Mark 10:19; Matt. 19:18f.; Luke 18:20 (Exod. 20:12-16; Deut. 5:16-20).
11. Mark 12:29f.; Matt. 22:37; Luke 10:27 (Deut. 6:4f.).

[19] Only the major source or sources are listed, without the inclusion of possible parallels.

12. Mark 12:31; Matt. 22:39; Luke 10:27 (Lev. 19:18).
13. Mark 15:34; Matt. 27:46 (Ps. 22:1 [MT=22:2; LXX=21:2]).

II. Quotations occurring in Matthew and Luke, but not in Mark:

A. With introductory formulae:

14. Matt. 4:4; Luke 4:4 (Deut. 8:3).
15. Matt. 4:7; Luke 4:12 (Deut. 6:16).
16. Matt. 4:10; Luke 4:8 (Deut. 6:13).
17. Matt. 11:10; Luke 7:27 (Mal. 3:1).

B. Without introductory formulae:

18. Matt. 23:39; Luke 13:35 (Ps. 118:26 [LXX=117:26]).

III. Quotations occurring in Matthew alone:

A. With introductory formulae:

19. Matt. 5:21 (Exod. 20:13; Deut. 5:17).[20]
20. Matt. 5:27 (Exod. 20:14; Deut. 5:18).
21. Matt. 5:31 (Deut. 24:1).
22. Matt. 5:33 (Ps. 50:14 [LXX=49:14]).
23. Matt. 5:38 (Exod. 21:24; Lev. 24:20).
24. Matt. 5:43 (Lev. 19:18).
25. Matt. 13:14f. (Isa. 6:9f.).
26. Matt. 21:16 (Ps. 8:2 [MT & LXX=8:3]).

B. Without introductory formulae:

27. Matt. 9:13 (Hos. 6:6).
28. Matt. 12:7 (Hos. 6:6).
29. Matt. 18:16 (Deut. 19:15).

[20] D. Daube, following S. Schechter, points out the close relation between the introductory formulae in the Sermon on the Mount and rabbinic formulae to the effect, "Ye have understood literally"—i.e., superficially (*The New Testament and Rabbinic Judaism* [1956], pp. 55-62), and M. McNamara proposes on the basis of this that "the formula may then introduce not a biblical citation, but rather a false, narrow, understanding of it" (*The New Testament and the Palestinian Targum to the Pentateuch*, p. 127n). It may be that "we have here a reference to the current Jewish paraphrasis of some OT text on the sanction attached to the crime of murder rather than to any OT text in particular. The unlearned audience of Christ would have listened to such a paraphrase in the school or synagogue; hence Our Lord's words: 'You have *heard* that it was said . . .' " (*ibid.*, pp. 127f.). Nonetheless, the synagogue tradition being based on biblical portions, Jesus' usage here would still be something of a biblical quotation: the quotation of a conflation of Scripture and various Jewish traditions.

30. Matt. 19:19 (Lev. 19:18).

IV. Quotations occurring in Luke alone:

A. With introductory formulae:

31. Luke 4:18f. (Isa. 61:1f.; 58:6).
32. Luke 22:37 (Isa. 53:12).

B. Without introductory formulae:

33. Luke 23:30 (Hos. 10:8).
34. Luke 23:46 (Ps. 31:5 [MT=31:6; LXX=30:6]).

V. Quotations occurring in John alone, with introductory formulae:

35. John 6:45 (Isa. 54:13; Jer. 31:33).
36. John 7:38 (Isa. 12:3; 43:19f.; 44:3; 58:11).
37. John 10:34 (Ps. 82:6 [LXX=81:6]).
38. John 13:18 (Ps. 41:9 [MT=41:10; LXX=40:10]).
39. John 15:25 (Ps. 35:19 [LXX=34:19]; 69:4 [MT=69:5; LXX=68:5]).

Jesus' allusive use of the Old Testament is also of importance to our study, particularly where the language comes close to being a quotation or where there appears something distinctive in his employment of the language. The following instances are of particular pertinence:

1. Mark 4:12; Matt. 13:13; Luke 8:10 (Isa. 6:9f.), where the language of Jesus is almost a paraphrase of Isaiah; though Matthew's manner of first alluding to the passage (13:13) and then quoting it quite exactly from the LXX (13:14f.) indicates that this earlier employment should be understood more as an allusion than a quotation.

2. Mark 12:1; Matt. 21:33; Luke 20:9 (Isa. 5:1f.), where Jesus picks up the well-known Isaian parable of the vineyard and applies it allusively to himself and to his ministry.

3. Matt. 11:5; Luke 7:22 (Isa. 35:5f.; 61:1), where in his answer to the messengers from John the Baptist Jesus vindicates his authority in terms allusively drawn from the promised kingdom blessings of Isaiah.

In addition, it is profitable to note some of Jesus' comments on situations and personages of the biblical narrative (e.g., "the days of Noah," "the days of Lot," Moses' raising the brass serpent, David's eating bread of the Presence, Jonah's entombment in the fish) and some of the instances where he says "as it is written," "that the Scripture might be fulfilled," or the like, without actually quoting or even alluding to any particular Old Testament passage (e.g., Mark 9:12; 14:21, 49; Matt. 26:24, 54; Luke 18:31; 21:22; John 17:12).

Immediately apparent in any survey of the quotations of Jesus is the wide variety of introductory formulae employed. In twenty-seven of the thirty-nine attributed to him, such formulae occur. Most common is the expression "it is written," employing the verb *γέγραπται* (see one or more of the passages cited above in numbers 1, 3, 8, 14, 15, 16, 17) or the participle *γεγραμμένος* (see numbers 31, 32, 35, 37, 39). Frequently a prophet is identified as speaking: Isaiah (1, 25, 31), Moses (2, 5), David (6), or Daniel (7). And once, in Matthew, God is directly credited (2). "Have you not read" is also used by way of introduction (4, 5, 26); and in the Matthean "Sermon on the Mount," the expression "you have heard it has been said" appears repeatedly in the conflation of Scripture and various Jewish traditions (19, 20, 22, 23, 24). The content of the quotations is identified variously as "scripture" (4, 36, 38), "the book of Moses" (5), "the book of Psalms" (6), "the prophets" (35), "the law" (37, 39), the words of one of the prophets (1, 2, 5, 6, 7, 25, 31), and the statement of God (2). And in four cases the introductory formula contains an explicit note of fulfilment, in Matthew and John by the use of *πληρόω* (25, 38, 39) and in Luke by the use of *τελειόω* (32). The other twelve quotations have no introductory formulae. But the presence or absence of such formulae and the differences in wording between them—except for the fulfilment formulae, of which we must speak later[21] —signal little if anything of consequence, and they were evidently employed principally for stylistic and literary reasons, whether strictly dominical in their present form or having been shaped to some extent by the Evangelists.

Of greater interest in reviewing the form of the quotations attributed to Jesus in the Gospels is that the great majority are septuagintal in character. In most cases, of course, this is of no importance, for the LXX is a fair translation of the MT and Jesus could have made his point

[21] *Infra*, pp. 135f., 143-152. Also, perhaps, the introductory formulae of the Matthean Sermon on the Mount (see note 20).

from either. In a few cases, however, it is the LXX reading, as against the reading of the MT or known Targums, that provides Jesus with the wording and the application which he makes. Mark 7:6f. and Matt. 15:8f., for example, quoting Isa. 29:13, follow the LXX's translation of *μάτην* ("in vain," "to no end"), and thereby read the passage "in vain do they worship me, teaching as doctrines the commandments of men" rather than the masoretic and targumic rendering "their fear of me is a commandment of men learned by rote." In Matt. 21:16, quoting Ps. 8:3, the LXX translation of *αἶνον* ("praise") is followed rather than the masoretic עז or targumic עושנא ("strength," "stronghold"), thereby allowing Jesus to connect the children's praise of him in the temple with Isaiah's words that "out of the mouth of babes and sucklings you have established praise."[22] And in Luke 4:18, quoting Isa. 61:1, the LXX's *τυφλοῖς ἀνάβλεψιν* ("recovering of sight to the blind") is employed rather than the MT's reading of פקח-קוח ("opening of the prison to those who are bound").[23]

But the nature of the data is not sufficiently grasped in highlighting only the septuagintal character of Jesus' quotations. Despite their heavy reliance on the wording of the LXX, there are also a few instances (1) where they differ from all known Old Testament versions, whether Greek, Hebrew, or Aramaic, and (2) where they agree with the MT against the LXX. Cases of the first are best represented in the following:

1. Mark 10:19; Matt. 19:18f.; Luke 18:20, quoting Exod. 20:12-16 and Deut. 5:16-20, where the placing of the fifth commandment at the end of the listing is different than in all known versions and Mark's addition of the phrase "do not defraud" (*μὴ ἀποστερήσῃς*) is a further variation.

2. Mark 12:36; Matt. 22:44; Luke 20:42f., quoting Ps. 110:1, where Mark and Matthew read "under (*ὑποκάτω*)

[22] Though עז could be understood to connote "praise," for the acclamation of "strength" in the mouth of babes carries something of this idea.

[23] The quotation of Isa. 61:1 in Luke 4:18, while generally making use of LXX wording, also evidences a rather mixed text: here it is distinctly septuagintal as against the MT, elsewhere (see below) it is against both LXX and MT, and yet again (see below) it agrees with the MT against the LXX.

your feet," which is a literal translation of MT's הדום (cf. כביש of the Targums); though Luke agrees with the LXX's "a footstool (*ὑποπόδιον*) for your feet."

3. Mark 14:27 and Matt. 26:31, quoting Zech. 13:7, where "I will strike" (*πατάξω*) is a unique reading; all known versions have the imperative.

4. Luke 4:18f., quoting Isa. 61:1f., where, despite the quotation's generally septuagintal features,[24] Luke omits the line about healing the broken-hearted[25] and adds from Isa. 58:6, "to set at liberty those who are bruised" (*ἀποστεῖλαι τεθραυσμένους ἐν ἀφέσει*), neither of which alterations has a parallel in the versions.

Instances where Jesus' quotations agree in their wording with the MT against the LXX are fewer, and, generally speaking, suggest that a traditional testimonia reading is being employed or are of the nature of a more incidental variation. Representative are the following:

1. Matt. 11:10 and Luke 7:27, quoting a conflation of Mal. 3:1 and Isa. 40:3, where Matthew and Luke correctly translate the MT's ופנה-דרך as a Piel, rendering it ὃς *κατασκευάσει* ("who shall prepare"), against the LXX's *καὶ ἐπιβλέψεται*, which takes it as a Qal. Mark 1:2 also reads it as the other synoptists do, though not as a quotation of Jesus. Probably the reading that appears in the Gospels reflects a traditional conflation of messianic testimonia, which in turn rested upon Hebrew and/or Aramaic wording.[26]

2. Matt. 18:16, quoting Deut. 19:15, reads *ἤ*, corresponding to the masoretic and targumic או against the LXX's *καί*.

3. Luke 4:19, quoting Isa. 61:2, renders לקרא by *κηρῦξαι* ("to preach") rather than by the LXX's *κάλεσαι* ("to call"). Reference could also be made to instances where Jesus' wording corresponds to LXX^A against LXX^B, and vice versa. But that is an intra-septuagintal issue and such cases would do nothing to alter the picture of the

[24] See above, note 23.
[25] Though included in the Byzantine collection of texts.
[26] Cf. J. Mann, *The Bible as Read and Preached in the Old Synagogue*, I (1940), pp. 6f., 11-15, 479f.

dominance, with but few exceptions, of the LXX in the quotations of Jesus.

The septuagintal character of Jesus' quotations from the Old Testament, of course, poses a problem, which James Barr aptly highlights in saying:

> One of the peculiarities of Christianity is that the words of Jesus have not been preserved in the language in which they were originally spoken. Even from the earliest days there was no great effort—perhaps there was no effort at all—to ensure that his sayings should be kept alive in the original tongue. The tradition of his teaching was carefully cultivated and was set forth in the various versions of the different Gospels, but it was a tradition in translation.[27]

Why, if Jesus spoke and taught in Aramaic, is it that not only are his words recorded in Greek but his biblical quotations are based upon the LXX, and not upon a Hebrew or Aramaic version?

It will not do to say, as is commonly asserted today, that Jesus' LXX quotations indicate that they are part-and-parcel of the early hellenistic *Gemeindetheologie*, and therefore probably not dominical. This may be argued for the Fourth Gospel, where the difference in form between the Evangelist's own citations and those included in his narrative is not that distinct, or in the cases of Mark and Luke, who record the use of the Old Testament by others but do not themselves directly quote Scripture. But it will hardly serve as an explanation for the phenomena of the First Gospel, where the Evangelist's own eleven fulfilment-formulae quotations, though mixed in text-form, are dominantly semitic in character,[28] while those of Jesus, though also mixed in form (though to a more limited extent), are strongly septuagintal. Employing the criteria of dissimilarity and of multiple attestation (the pattern is consistent in Matthew throughout a large number of samples), the sharp distinction between these two groups of text-forms prohibits any such easy equation. Nor can it be said, for basically the same reason, that the Evangelists have simply assimilated Jesus' citations

[27] J. Barr, "Which Language did Jesus Speak?—Some Remarks of a Semitist," *BJRL*, LIII (1970), p. 9.
[28] Cf. *infra*, pp. 136f.

to the LXX for the sake of their Greek-speaking readers. If Matthew made no attempt to assimilate his own fulfilment-formulae quotations to the LXX, but allowed his hebraic sources to evidence themselves quite clearly, why should it be supposed that he did this for those of Jesus? Editorial assimilation may be an explanation for the text-forms of the quotations in certain other New Testament writings, particularly in Acts and the so-called "Catholic Epistles,"[29] but it is inadequate as a solution for the form of Jesus' quotations in the Gospels.

Whatever hypothesis is formed in explanation of the data in the Gospels, at least four considerations must be taken into account: (1) the bi- or probably tri-lingual nature of first-century Palestine generally, and on the part of Jesus and his hearers in particular;[30] (2) the lack of standardization in the various Hebrew, Aramaic and Greek versions of the biblical text current in the first century;[31] (3) the pesher treatment of certain passages by Jesus, which in-

[29] Cf. *infra*, pp. 87-89, 198.

[30] The questions regarding the languages of first-century Palestine and of those employed by Jesus have come to the fore in New Testament research of late. For recent treatments advocating the supremacy of Hebrew (Mishnaic or biblical) in the day and on the lips of Jesus, see H. Birkeland, *The Language of Jesus* (1954); J. M. Grintz, "Hebrew as the Spoken and Written Language in the Last Days of the Second Temple," *JBL*, LXXIX (1960), pp. 32-47; I. Rabinowitz, " 'Be Opened' = Ἐφφαθά (Mark 7:34): Did Jesus Speak Hebrew?" *ZNW*, LIII (1962), pp. 229-238. For recent treatments advocating the importance of Greek in the day (not always its supremacy, though often on the lips of Jesus), see A. W. Argyle, "Did Jesus Speak Greek?" *ExpT*, LXVI (1955), pp. 92f., LXVII (1956), p. 383; R. H. Gundry, "The Language Milieu of First-Century Palestine," *JBL*, LXXXIII (1964), pp. 404-8; *idem*, *The Use of the Old Testament in St. Matthew's Gospel* (1967), pp. 174-78; J. N. Sevenster, *Do You Know Greek?* (1968). For recent treatments stressing the supremacy of Aramaic in the day and on the lips of Jesus, though acknowledging that Mishnaic Hebrew and Greek were probably also colloquial, see M. Black, *An Aramaic Approach to the Gospels and Acts*, 3rd ed. (1967), *passim*; *idem*, "The Recovery of the Language of Jesus," *NTS*, III (1957), pp. 305-313; J. A. Emerton, "Did Jesus Speak Hebrew?" *JTS*, XII (1961), pp. 189-202; J. Barr, "Which Language did Jesus Speak?" *BJRL*, LIII (1970), pp. 9-29.

[31] Cf. F. M. Cross, Jr., "The History of the Biblical Text in the Light of Discoveries in the Judean Desert," *HTR*, LVII (1964), pp. 281-299; *idem*, "The Contribution of the Qumran Discoveries to the Study of the Biblical Text," *IEJ*, XVI (1966), pp. 81-95; P. W. Skehan, "The Biblical Scrolls from Qumran and the Text of the Old Testament," *BA*, XXVIII (1965), pp. 87-100.

volved him to some extent in textual criticism;[32] and (4) the possible early compilation in Greek of the sayings of Jesus (which would include his quotations) by the Church.[33] A great deal of work remains to be done in all of these areas before anything resembling a final assessment can be made. Yet it seems, taking into account both the internal data and the external probabilities, that the form of Jesus' quotations is rooted in a very early period or source, and not just a product of *Gemeindetheologie* or assimilation by the Evangelists. It may be that an early Greek sayings compilation (or compilations), which not only translated Aramaic into Greek but also assimilated hebraic quotes to their septuagintal forms, circulated widely in the Church and gained a status of quasi-sanctity because stemming from Jesus. The Evangelists could have employed such a compilation(s) in their reproduction of the citations of Jesus without disturbing the LXX form of the quotations—even Matthew, though he preferred to work from a more semitic base in his own biblical citations. Or it may be that in his applications of the Old Testament, Jesus, who normally spoke in Aramaic but could also use Greek and Mishnaic Hebrew to some extent,[34] at times engaged himself in

[32] Cf. *infra*, pp. 70-75.

[33] E. G. Selwyn, citing M. Dibelius (*From Tradition to Gospel* [ET 1934], pp. 233-265), summarizes the position by pointing out that there are "reasons for believing that the words of Jesus were collected at an early date explicitly as words of the Lord, and therefore inspired; that these collections were definite as regards both their authority and their limits; and that they were almost certainly in Greek; for no trace has been found of any written Aramaic tradition, unless we suppose that Papias had such a collection in mind in what he wrote (about A.D. 140) about St. Matthew's Gospel. If the document known as Q existed, then it was such a collection, perhaps the most authoritative of several" ("The Authority of Christ in the New Testament," *NTS*, III [1957], p. 83). In his commentary on I Peter, Selwyn has pertinently added: "Q was a collection of Christ's sayings compiled for hortatory purposes, and these would have operated at a very early date to create a demand for as complete a collection of His words as possible. Partial collections may well have been in use before that date; others may have been excerpted from the full collection after it; but the authoritative collection itself which is represented for us by Q—though of course Q may have contained many sayings that are not recorded in St. Matthew or St. Luke—need be dated no later than the middle of the first century" (*The First Epistle of St. Peter* [1946], p. 24).

[34] Cf. the works of Emerton and Barr cited in note 30, *supra*.

textual selection among the various Aramaic, Hebrew and Greek versions then current, and some of the septuagintal features in the text-forms attributed to him actually arise from him. The very mixed form of Isa. 61:1f. in Luke 4:18f. would seem to support such a thesis in at least this one case, for the text-form of the quotation defies all explanations based on assimilation whenever employed. Or it may be that the solution to the septuagintal form of Jesus' quotations in the Gospels lies in postulating both (1) a use of an early Greek compilation(s) of the sayings of Jesus by the Evangelists, and (2) a degree of textual selection from among existing versions by Jesus himself.

LITERALIST AND MIDRASHIC TREATMENTS

A number of times in the Gospels, Jesus is portrayed as interpreting the Old Testament in a literalist manner, particularly in matters concerned with basic religious and moral values. In answer to the scribe, for example, who asked regarding the greatest of the commandments, Jesus quoted Deut. 6:4f. (the *Shema*) quite straightforwardly: "Hear, O Israel, the Lord our God is one Lord. And you shall love the Lord your God with your whole heart, and with your whole soul, and with your whole mind, and with your whole strength."[35] Then, lest it be thought that God's commandments apply only to man's vertical relationship and not also to his attitudes and actions on the horizontal level, he quoted Lev. 19:18: "You shall love your neighbor as yourself."[36] The unusual features in Jesus' quotation of the *Shema* are the introduction in all of the synoptic accounts of the expression "and with all your mind" (*καὶ ἐξ ὅλης τῆς διανοίας σου*) and the fourfold listing in Mark and Luke against the threefold in Matthew.[37] But the *Shema* was widely employed in Judaism liturgically,[38] with the result

[35] Mark 12:29f.; Matt. 22:37; Luke 10:27.
[36] Mark 12:31; Matt. 22:39; Luke 10:27.
[37] All, that is, except the Western text of Mark and Luke, and the old Syriac of Matt. In Matt., however, *διανοία* replaces *ἰσχύς* rather than being added to the listing.
[38] Its antiquity is attested by its inclusion in the Nash Papyrus (probably first century B.C.), which has it in conjunction with the Decalogue, and on a phylactery found at Wadi Murabbaat, where Deut. 6:4-9 follows Exod. 13:1-16 and Deut. 11:13-21.

that it easily acquired slightly different forms. And, as Stendahl points out, "the wealth of variants indicates that there was no authorized Greek form of that part of the Jewish liturgy in the days of the evangelists or that there were different forms, which influenced the N.T. texts in different ways."[39] Likewise, in countering the devil's suggestions in the wilderness, Jesus based his replies on a literal rendering of three deuteronomic passages: Deut. 8:3, "Man does not live by bread alone, but by every word which proceeds from the mouth of God"; 6:16, "You shall not tempt the Lord your God"; and 6:13, "You shall worship the Lord your God, and him only shall you serve."[40]

In his teachings on human relationships, Jesus is represented as employing the Scriptures in a straightforward manner as well, with only minor variations in the texts cited. In rebuke of the Pharisees, for example, he quoted Exod. 20:12, "Honor your father and your mother," and 21:17, "Whoever curses father or mother, let him die the death."[41] In support of the indissolubility of marriage, he quoted Gen. 2:24, "For this reason shall a man leave his father and his mother and be faithfully devoted (*προσκολληθήσεται*) to his wife, and the two shall be one flesh."[42] And on settling disputes between brothers, he advises that the wronged party confront the other in the presence of one or two others, for, quoting Deut. 19:15, "by the mouth of two or three witnesses shall every word be established."[43] Like Judaism generally—whether Pharisaic, nonconformist, or even hellenistic—on matters having to do with man's basic orientation to God, man's basic moral values, and man's basic human relations, Jesus inter-

[39] K. Stendahl, *School of St. Matthew*, p. 76.

[40] Following Matt.'s order in Matt. 4:4, 7, 10 (cf. Luke 4:4, 8, 12). The addition of *μόνῳ* in Matt. 4:10 and Luke 4:8 is distinctive to the Gospels. The reading of *προσκυνήσεις* follows LXX^{A}, not *φοβηθήσῃ* of LXX^{B}.

[41] Mark 7:10; Matt. 15:4. The text of Exod. 21:17 in the Gospels follows LXX^{A} in reading *θανάτῳ τελευτάτω* rather than *τελευτήσει θανάτω*.

[42] Mark 10:7f.; Matt. 19:5. Mark probably follows LXX^{B} in reading *πρὸς τὴν γυναῖκα αὐτοῦ*, whereas Matt. follows LXX^{A} in reading *τῇ γυναικὶ αὐτοῦ*.

[43] Matt. 18:16. Matt. reads *ἤ*, which corresponds to the masoretic and targumic או, rather than the *καί* of the LXX.

preted the Scriptures quite literally. These are matters of foundational importance upon which God had spoken plainly, and therefore they were taken by Jesus and his contemporaries in Judaism without further elaboration.

Midrashic syllogism also played a part in the teaching of Jesus. In the Sermon on the Mount, for example, he is presented as employing Hillel's first exegetical rule of *qal waḥomer* (light to heavy) in saying, "If you then, being evil, know how to give good gifts to your children, how much more (*πόσῳ μᾶλλον*) shall your Father who is in heaven give good things to those who ask him."[44] In sending out the Twelve into Galilee, he warned, "If they have called the master of the house Beelzebub, how much more (*πόσῳ μᾶλλον*) them of his household."[45] And in applying the parable of the foolish rich man, he illustrated by saying, "If God so clothes the grass in the field, which today exists and tomorrow is cast into the oven, how much more (*πόσῳ μᾶλλον*) you, O you of little faith."[46]

In a few instances, Jesus is portrayed as confounding the Sadducees and the Pharisees on their own exegetical grounds. To the Sadducees, who believed that every word of the written Torah possessed validity—though they rejected the oral traditions of the Pharisees and their exegetical *middoth*—but who denied doctrines of personal resurrection and the afterlife, Jesus quoted Exod. 3:6, "I am the God of Abraham, and the God of Isaac, and the God of Jacob."[47] And from this he concluded that a living, personal relationship with God continues beyond death, for God is the God of the living. "The real authority for the conclusion," as C. F. D. Moule rightly observes, "is the conviction that if God establishes contact with a man and is willing to be called his God, then that relationship is such that death cannot break it: the appeal, beneath and behind the words of scripture, is to an otherwise known quality in the character of God and

[44] Matt. 7:11; Luke 11:13.
[45] Matt. 10:25.
[46] Luke 12:28.
[47] Mark 12:26; Matt. 22:32; Luke 20:37. Mark and Luke follow LXX[A] in adding the article before *θεὸς* *Ἀβρααμ*, though Matt. extends the use of the article to all three instances of *θεός*.

therefore of his relations with men."[48] But the exegetical point upon which Jesus hung his demonstration to the Sadducees was the present tense of the declaration: "I *am* the God of Abraham, and the God of Isaac, and the God of Jacob." The tense of Exod. 3:6, where no copula is used, must be the present; it does not say, "I *was* the God of Abraham, etc."

With the Pharisees, Jesus is represented as employing Scripture in both a *qal waḥomer* and a *gezerah shawah* (analogy) fashion. When they objected to his disciples plucking and eating grain on the sabbath, for example, he first alluded to the incident of David eating bread of the Presence in the house of God, an act unlawful yet permitted in this case because of the greater importance of the life of David, Israel's anointed king, and, on analogy, argued that "the Son of man is Lord of the sabbath."[49] Then he noted that the Law sanctions work for the priests on the sabbath, and, *a minore ad majorem*, his presence among them was greater than the cultic regulations.[50] Again, in debate with the Pharisees, the Fourth Gospel presents him as arguing *qal waḥomer:* "If a man receives circumcision on the sabbath, in order that the law of Moses not be broken [circumcision on the eighth day took precedence over the sabbath regulations], why are you angry with me because I made a man entirely whole on the sabbath?"[51] And this same exegetical principle appears in the report of Jesus' rather ingenious treatment of Ps. 82:6: "Is it not written in your law, 'I said, you are gods'? If he called them gods to whom the word of God came, and the scripture cannot be broken, can you say of him whom the Father sanctified and sent into the world, 'You blaspheme!' because I said, 'I am the Son of God'?"[52] On occasion, therefore, Jesus—if we can accept the synoptists' report of his use of Exod. 3:6 and John's of his use of Ps. 82:6—employed the verbal casuistry of the day in his exegetical discussions. But he evidently did so *ad hominem*,

[48] C. F. D. Moule, *The Birth of the New Testament* (1966), p. 65.
[49] Mark 2:25-28; Matt. 21:3f., 8; Luke 6:3-5.
[50] Matt. 12:5-7.
[51] John 7:23.
[52] John 10:34-36.

for it is significant that his more atomistic and ingenious treatments of Scripture are in the context of polemical debate. Evidently, at times he was willing to outclass his antagonists on their own exegetical grounds.

PESHER INTERPRETATIONS

But while there are a number of instances recorded in the Gospels of Jesus' use of literalist and midrashic exegesis, his most characteristic employment of Scripture is portrayed as being a pesher type of interpretation. The "this is that" fulfilment motif, which is distinctive to pesher exegesis, repeatedly comes to the fore in the words of Jesus.

According to Luke's Gospel, Jesus began to expound the Scriptures in terms of a fulfilment theme very early in his ministry. In Luke 4:16-21, he enters the synagogue at Nazareth and is called upon to read the lesson from the prophet Isaiah. He reads Isa. 61:1f., rolls up the scroll, hands it to the attendant, sits down to speak, and proclaims: "Today this scripture is fulfilled in your ears." In John's Gospel the theme of fulfilment is just as explicitly stated in the denunciation of the Pharisees by Jesus in John 5:39-47. The passage begins with a rebuke of his opponents' false confidence, proceeds to give an unfavorable verdict on their attitudes and interpretations, and climaxes in the assertion: "If you believed Moses, you would have believed me; for he wrote of me." If we had only these two passages, it would be possible to claim that it was Jesus himself who gave the impetus to the explication of the fulfilment theme and to a pesher approach to Scripture in the early Church.

But the demonstration of Jesus' use of a fulfilment theme and of a pesher approach to the biblical texts does not depend on these two portions alone. In addition, the following instances should be noted:

1. In Mark 12:10f.; Matt. 21:42; Luke 20:17, Jesus concludes his allusion to the well-known parable of the vineyard (Isa. 5:1ff.) and his not-so-veiled rebuke of the people's rejection of the son with the quotation of Ps. 118:22f.: "The stone which the builders rejected has become the head of the corner. This was from the Lord, and it

is marvelous in our eyes." The text is an exact reproduction of the LXX, and his point obviously concerns fulfilment of the psalmist's words in his own rejection and exaltation.

2. In Mark 14:27; Matt. 26:31, after the Last Supper, he quotes Zech. 13:7 in regard to his approaching death and the disciples' reactions: "I will strike down the shepherd and the sheep (of the flock) will be scattered."[53] The citation is introduced by Jesus with the formula "it is written" (γέγραπται) and directly invokes the "this is that" pesher motif. In application of the passage, the tenses, number and vocabulary of the LXX are somewhat altered from "strike down (πατάξατε) the shepherds (plural) and draw out (ἐκσπάσατε) the sheep" to "I will strike down (πατάξω) the Shepherd and the sheep (of the flock) will be scattered (διασκορπισθήσονται)." Here, obviously, Jesus' application to himself has affected the form of the passage itself.

3. In Matt. 11:10; Luke 7:27 (cf. Mark 1:2f.), Jesus applies the conflated texts of Mal. 3:1 and Isa. 40:3 to John the Baptist: "Behold, I will send my messenger before your face who will prepare your way before you." In Matthew's Gospel he is represented as employing a typically pesher formula, saying by way of introduction: "This is he of whom it is written" (οὗτός ἐστιν περὶ οὗ γέγραπται). The text-form of the passages has also been affected, with Mal. 3:1 reading "I will send (ἀποστέλλω) my messenger before your face who will prepare (κατασκευάσει) your (σου) way before you (σου)" for the LXX "I will send (ἐξαποστέλλω) my messenger and he will survey (ἐπιβλέψεται) the way before my (μου) face," and Isa. 40:3 being simplified in its final phrase from "the paths of our God" (τὰς τρίβους τοῦ θεοῦ ἡμῶν) to "his paths" (τὰς τρίβους αὐτοῦ).[54] But here, textually, we might only have a common variant of a widely used messianic testimonia conflation.

4. In Matt. 13:14f., Jesus quotes Isa. 6:9f. in explanation of his employment of parables. However difficult it may be to understand his teaching on the "negative" purpose of

[53] Matt. adds τῆς ποίμνης.

[54] Though only Mark 1:3 (cf. Matt. 3:3) has the final phrase, this is probably to be understood in Matt. 11:10 and Luke 7:27.

parables, it must not be overlooked that Jesus is here presented as introducing the quotation with the words "in them is fulfilled the prophecy of Isaiah, which says" (*ἀναπληροῦνται αὐτοῖς ἡ προφητεία Ἠσαΐου ἡ λέγουσα*), and of applying in pesher fashion the words of the prophet to his own ministry.

5. In Matt. 15:8f., he paraphrases Isa. 29:13 (possibly also collating Ps. 78:36f.) in rebuke of the scribes and Pharisees from Jerusalem. Again, it is to be noted that he introduces the quotation by a fulfilment motif, "Isaiah prophesied concerning you, saying" (*ἐπροφήτευσεν περὶ ὑμῶν Ἠσαΐας λέγων*), and applied the passage in pesher fashion to the Jewish leaders' rejection of himself.

6. In Luke 22:37, Jesus applies the phrase "he was numbered among the transgressors" of Isa. 53:12 directly to himself,[55] altering only the LXX preposition *ἐν* to *μετά*. On either side of the citation he directly invokes a pesher theme, saying first that "it is necessary that that which is written be fulfilled in me" (*τοῦτο τὸ γεγραμμένον δεῖ τελεσθῆναι ἐν ἐμοί*) and then that "that concerning me [in Isaiah's prophecy] has fulfilment" (*τὸ περὶ ἐμοῦ τέλος ἔχει*).

7. In John 6:45, he alludes to the message of Isa. 54:13 and Jer. 31:33, making the point that the words "and they shall be taught of God"—as the prophets' message may be rather freely rendered—apply to his teaching and his ministry in particular.

8. In John 13:18, he applies the lament of David in Ps. 41:9 (LXX 40:10) to his betrayal by Judas: "He who ate

[55] The fact that this is the only direct quotation from Isa. 53 in a passion context in the reported sayings of Jesus, and that it is not included as such by Matthew or Mark, is not necessarily conclusive against its authenticity. While our assessment of the authenticity of any particular saying of Jesus can be heightened when that saying appears in more than one tradition or more than one Gospel, it is beyond the scope of the literary criterion of multiple attestation (or, "the cross section method") to rule negatively with any assurance just because a saying appears in only one Gospel. "After all," as C. F. D. Moule reminds us, "selection is often at work on the traditions; and I see no reason to reject a tradition merely because it appears in only one stream, provided it is not intrinsically improbable or contradicted by the other" (*The Phenomenon of the New Testament* [1967], p. 71).

my bread lifted up his heel against me." In the text itself, synonyms are employed for the LXX readings: ὁ τρώγων for ὁ ἐσθίων ("he who ate"), ἐπῆρεν for ἐμεγάλυσεν ("he lifted up"), and τὴν πτέρναν αὐτοῦ for πτερνισμόν ("his heel"). And Jesus introduces the quotation by the fulfilment formula: "in order that the scripture might be fulfilled" (ἵνα ἡ γραφὴ πληρωθῇ).

9. Again, in John 15:25, the lament of Ps. 35:19 and 69:4, "hated without a cause," is applied by Jesus to his own person and introduced by the statement "in order that the word which is written in their law might be fulfilled" (ἵνα πληρωθῇ ὁ λόγος ὁ ἐν τῷ νόμῳ αὐτῶν γεγραμμένος). The participle of the LXX is changed to a finite verb in the quotation, but obviously only to conform to sentence structure.

A further instance of a pesher treatment of Scripture on the part of Jesus, though more inferentially expressed, is his quotation of Ps. 110:1, "The Lord said to my Lord, 'Sit at my right hand, until I make your enemies your footstool,' "[56] as countering the dominant understanding of messiahship then current. It can be doubted that by his treatment of Ps. 110:1 Jesus intended to deny Davidic descent to the Messiah. Rather, he seems to be taking up a somewhat enigmatic passage which possibly had messianic relevance in certain circles of his day,[57] explicating the enig-

[56] Mark 12:36; Matt. 22:44; Luke 20:42f. Luke reads "footstool," while Mark and Matt. read "under your feet."

[57] Though the evidence for pre-Christian interpretations of Ps. 110 is sketchy and ambiguous, and though some early rabbis linked the psalm with Abraham, David and even Hezekiah, and only from the middle of the third century (c. A.D. 260) is a messianic interpretation clearly attested in rabbinic writings, "it seems fair to suppose that in the NT era a messianic interpretation of Ps 110 was current in Judaism, although we cannot know how widely it was accepted" (D. M. Hay, *Glory at the Right Hand* [1973], p. 30; cf. *Str.-Bil.*, IV, pp. 452-460). The absence of early rabbinic evidence for a messianic identification—particularly R. Ishmael's attribution to Abraham in b. Ned. 32b and Lev. R. 25:6—may have been due to anti-Christian polemic (cf. *Str.-Bil.*, IV, pp. 458-460), which was less a factor in later centuries as Judaism and Christianity went their separate ways in isolation from one another. If this general thesis be so, the originality of Jesus lay not in the designation of this passage as being messianically relevant but in his explication of its enigmatic element and his application to himself.

matic element in the passage and arguing on the basis of David's acclamation that the Messiah must be considered more than just a junior David, a David *redivivus*, or even the "Son of David"—with all the nationalistic overtones inherent to that term. But in the process, he is also inferring that he thought of himself as "David's Greater Son," the One to whom even David bowed. And as suggested by the reported reactions,[58] it seems evident that those who heard him—particularly his disciples—understood him to be engaged in a creative interpretation of Scripture which explicated the enigmatic and applied the import of the passage to himself in a pesher fashion.

Jesus is also recorded as pointing out correspondences between earlier events in redemptive history and circumstances connected with his person and ministry. Mention has been made already of his application of psalmic laments to his own situation. In three other instances as well he is represented as invoking a correspondence-in-history theme and applying it to himself in pesher fashion: (1) in Matt. 12:40, paralleling the experience of Jonah and his own approaching death and entombment; (2) in Matt. 24:37, drawing the relationship between the days of Noah and the days of "the coming of the Son of man"; and (3) in John 3:14, connecting the elevation of the brass serpent in the wilderness to his own approaching crucifixion. In each case, Jesus viewed these Old Testament events as typological, pointing forward to their fulfilment in his person and ministry—not just as analogies that could be employed for purposes of illustration.

Much more could be said in regard to Jesus' pesher approach to the Old Testament. Reference could be made, for example, to his reinterpretation and use of such terms as "Son of man," "Servant of Yahweh," and "Day of Yahweh," all of which have inferential bearing on the subject. Likewise, greater treatment could be given the question of textual deviation in Jesus' quotations; though that whole complex of issues must await, in large measure and for the present, further evidence regarding early masoretic, targumic and septuagintal textual traditions. In some cases the

[58] Mark 12:37b; Matt. 22:46.

text-form of Jesus' quotations may also be accounted for in part by his own consciousness of being God's promised Messiah (e.g., Zech. 13:7; Mal. 3:1), by his use of a common messianic formulation which has become varied through repeated use (e.g., Isa. 40:3; 54:13; Jer. 31:33; Mal. 3:1), or by a free rendering (e.g., Ps. 41:9; Isa. 29:13; 53:12). But enough has been given of a direct nature to indicate that all four Evangelists believed that Jesus viewed the Old Testament from the perspective of his own ministry, that the fulfilment theme was a definite element in his teaching, and that he often treated selected biblical texts in a fashion that we have learned of late to call pesher.

A PARADIGM FOR CONTINUED STUDY

At the conclusion of his "parables of the kingdom," the First Gospel reports that Jesus asked his disciples: "Have you understood these things?"[59] When they answered "Yes," he then gave them another parable: "Every scribe who is instructed in matters pertaining to the kingdom of heaven is like a man who is a householder, who brings out of his treasury things new and old."[60] The parable is notoriously difficult to interpret, and has often been either ignored or treated as a Matthean displacement of teaching originally relevant elsewhere. Nevertheless, the expression "therefore" (*διὰ τοῦτο*) by which Jesus introduced the parable directly connects it with the disciples' understanding of his teaching, and suggests that it has something to do with the exegesis of Scripture in view of Christ's redemptive ministry, his exegetical example and his living presence. Probably J. W. Doeve is correct in understanding Jesus' comparison to be signifying something of the following:

> The landowner has apparently old material, but also more modern material at his disposal. That is also the situation of the scribe who has been made a disciple of the Kingdom of Heaven. Beside the old, which he brought with him, he now finds himself master of new, disparate material, not previously taught or heard of. In other

[59] Matt. 13:51.
[60] Matt. 13:52.

> words, his exegesis of Scripture will lead to results different from those formerly obtained.[61]

In John 16:12f., Jesus is reported to have told his disciples: "I have yet many things to say to you, but you cannot bear them now. But when the Spirit of truth comes, he will guide you into all truth." And throughout chapters 14–16 of the Fourth Gospel there is an emphasis upon the Holy Spirit as shortly to take up a ministry among the apostles and early believers in Jesus which would be comparable to that carried on among them by Jesus himself.

That the ministry of the Spirit was understood by the earliest believers to include advances in the interpretation of Scripture is suggested in at least three places in John's Gospel. In each instance the disciples came to understand certain actions and statements of Jesus in light of the Old Testament only at a later time. And in each case there is no hint that an express interpretation of Jesus gave rise to their understanding—though, of course, they were thinking along general lines which stemmed from him. The first instance is in John 2:17, where, after the report of the cleansing of the temple, the rather bland comment is made: "His disciples remembered that it was written, 'The zeal of your house will consume me'." We wish we were told as to when they remembered, but we are given no more. The second instance is in John 2:22, where Jesus' statement about destroying and raising the temple is seen to refer to his own death and resurrection—and thereby gives rise to a deeper understanding of the Scriptures. The Evangelist's words are: "When therefore he was raised from the dead, his disciples remembered that he had said this; and they believed the scripture and the word which Jesus spoke." The third is in John 12:16, where it is expressly stated regarding Jesus' "triumphal" entry into and reception at Jerusalem: "These things his disciples did not at first understand; but when Jesus was glorified, then they remembered that these things were written of him and that they did these things to him." In each case there is a kind of delayed-action response to Jesus and understanding of Scripture, which ultimately

[61] J. W. Doeve, *Jewish Hermeneutics in the Synoptic Gospels and Acts*, p. 100.

found their source in Jesus himself but immediately resulted from the ministry of the Holy Spirit.

At those points where he explicitly "transformed the pre-messianic Torah into the messianic Torah,"[62] Jesus' expositions were undoubtedly preserved. But even here we need not insist that he simply schooled his disciples in verbal retention and that they reproduced his interpretations as memorized "Holy Words," going no further.[63] Louis Finkelstein has shown that much of the tannaitic tradition preserved in the Talmud was formulated around catch words or key phrases, which served as "pegs" on which the whole portion depended. The phrases or "pegged words" stabilized the tradition, yet the reproduction of the tannaitic discussions among the later amoraite scholars also evidences a degree of fluidity where the tradition was not "nailed down."[64] Even though it is undoubtedly true that Jesus was accorded at least as much respect by his disciples as that given a rabbi by his pupils, the parallel of rabbinic practice does not therefore necessitate a fixed wording of his expositions being preserved. Nor does the evidence drawn from the synoptic Evangelists' treatment of the words of Jesus allow such a rather wooden conclusion.

Perhaps most illuminating in this regard is the treatment of the Lord's Prayer in Matt. 6:9-13 and Luke 11:1-4, for here is an item of central significance in Christian tradition which is explicitly said to have been taught by Jesus to his

[62] B. Gerhardsson, *Memory and Manuscript: Oral Tradition and Written Transmission in Rabbinic Judaism and Early Christianity*, trans. E. J. Sharpe (1961), p. 327.

[63] While Riesenfeld and Gerhardsson have done theology a service in stressing the creative personality of Jesus behind all the New Testament tradition, and while they offer a more plausible solution for the literary forms in the Gospels based on relevant Palestinian materials than do the Bultmannians based on hellenistic resemblances, their theory of memorized "Holy Words" is an unjustified reading of the evidence—or, at least, has been more interested in the idealized portrayals of the rabbis than their actual practice—and neglects the New Testament emphasis upon the continuing ministry of the Spirit (cf. H. Riesenfeld, "The Gospel Tradition and its Beginnings," *Studia Evangelica*, I, ed. K. Aland [1959], esp. p. 59; B. Gerhardsson, *Memory and Manuscript*, esp. pp. 130-36 and 328f.).

[64] L. Finkelstein, "The Transmission of Early Rabbinic Tradition," *HUCA*, XVI (1941), pp. 115-135. Gerhardsson commends Finkelstein's article, but evidently only as to his references to memorization and the fixity of the text (cf. *Memory and Manuscript*, pp. 145-48).

disciples and which lends itself readily to verbal retention. In comparing the two accounts, there is no evidence of variation such as would go beyond the intent of Jesus. And, interestingly, even though the prayer is set in contexts that are dominantly Christological, there is no attempt to "Christianize" it to make it less "unitarian" or more Christocentric.[65] This is surely significant in questions having to do with the preservation of content. Yet the Lord's Prayer in the Gospels is preserved in two varying forms.[66]

The teaching and exegesis of Jesus became the direct source for much of the early Church's understanding of the Old Testament. But interpretation did not stop with him. The Fourth Gospel expressly speaks of biblical interpretation continuing after Jesus' ascension, and the New Testament writings throughout evidence it as well. Just as Paul acknowledged that Christian tradition had preserved no explicit teaching of Jesus on certain marital problems at Corinth, so the earliest Christians were conscious of lacunae in their Lord's own treatment of Scripture. But also, just as Paul worked from principles enunciated by Christ to a Spirit-directed and apostolic statement on the issues confronting believers at Corinth,[67] so the early believers seem to have taken Jesus' own interpretation of selected Old Testament passages as a paradigm for their continued exegetical endeavors.

The analogy of the practice at Qumran is pertinent here. It seems that the members of the Dead Sea community both passively retained interpretations of their Teacher on certain biblical portions and actively continued to study the Old Testament along lines stemming from him, either as directly laid out by him or as deduced from his practice. Likewise, the early Christians continued their study of the Scriptures under the immediate guidance of the Holy Spirit and according to the paradigm set by Jesus in his own explicit interpretations and exegetical practice.

[65] Cf. C. F. D. Moule, "The Influence of Circumstances on the Use of Christological Terms," *JTS*, X (1959), pp. 253f.
[66] Cf. G. W. H. Lampe, "Modern Issues in Biblical Studies: The Evidence in the New Testament for Early Creeds, Catechisms and Liturgy," *ExpT*, LXXI (1960), p. 361.
[67] I Cor. 7:10-12, 25.

III: EARLY CHRISTIAN PREACHING AND THE OLD TESTAMENT

The preaching of the early Christians focused upon the revelation and redemption of God in Jesus the Messiah. But it also was concerned with an apologetic based on the revelation of God in the Old Testament. Yet behind both Jesus and the Scriptures stood the witness of the Spirit. It was the Spirit who continued to testify to Jesus after his exaltation and who continued to guide the early Church in its Christocentric interpretation of the Old Testament. While explicit references to such a continuing ministry on the part of the Spirit are confined in the Gospels to the Fourth Gospel, the consciousness of such a ministry prevades the records of the earliest Christian proclamation.

SERMONIC AND CATECHETICAL MATERIALS

It is frequently argued today that the New Testament furnishes little if any direct evidence for the nature and content of the earliest Christian preaching, and that therefore we must confess our ignorance regarding both the preaching and the practices of this early period. Some, in fact, are prepared to consider New Testament theology as only truly beginning with hellenistic Christianity and Paul.[1] Nevertheless, there are sermonic and catechetical materials in the New Testament which reflect the essence of that early proclamation. And while they may appear in the canonical writings in a later literary or editorial form, they are nonetheless of great significance in studying the use of the Old Testament in early Christian preaching.

[1] E.g., H. Conzelmann, *An Outline of the Theology of the New Testament* (ET 1970).

The Speeches of Acts. The tone for contemporary critical study of the speeches in the Acts of the Apostles was set in 1922 by H. J. Cadbury in his discussion of Greek historiography:

> To suppose that the writers were trying to present the speeches as actually spoken, or that their readers thought so, is unfair to the morality of one and to the intelligence of the other. From Thucydides downwards, speeches reported by the historians are confessedly pure imagination. They belong to the final literary stage. If they have any nucleus of fact behind them it would be the merest outline in the ὑπομνήματα [remembrances].[2]

A number of studies have recently been presented in support of Cadbury's claim, arguing that (1) Luke indeed, as a Greek historian, followed the Thucydidean model, (2) the speeches of Acts fit too neatly into their redactional contexts to be material incorporated from the primitive Church, and (3) the theological content and vocabulary is that of Luke (as determined from his editorial material in Luke-Acts), and therefore not that of the earliest Christian preachers.[3] But critical study of the sermons and defenses in Acts has not moved in only one direction, for many have come to feel that such a judgment is extreme.

T. F. Glasson points out that "the parallel with the method of Thucydides is indeed apposite—as long as we pay heed to what Thucydides really said."[4] In the Peloponnesian War, I. 22, Thucydides writes regarding his historical method:

[2] H. J. Cadbury, "The Greek and Jewish Traditions of Writing History," *The Beginnings of Christianity*, ed. F. J. Foakes Jackson and K. Lake, II (1922), p. 13. It need be noted, however, that the implications arising from such a statement have been considerably modified by Cadbury himself in his later writings and addresses.

[3] Cf. P. Vielhauer, "On the 'Paulinism' of Acts," *Studies in Luke-Acts*, ed. L. E. Keck and J. L. Martyn (1966, trans. from 1950 article), pp. 33-50; E. Schweizer, "Concerning the Speeches in Acts," *Studies in Luke-Acts* (trans. from 1957 article), pp. 208-216; U. Wilckens, *Die Missionsreden der Apostelgeschichte* (1961); E. Haenchen, *Die Apostelgeschichte* (1968, from 1956 tenth edition), esp. pp. 93-99; *idem*, "The Book of Acts as Source Material for the History of Early Christianity," *Studies in Luke-Acts*, pp. 258-278; P. Schubert, "The Final Cycle of Speeches in the Book of Acts," *JBL*, LXXXVII (1968), pp. 1-16.

[4] T. F. Glasson, "The Speeches in Acts and Thucydides," *ExpT*, LXXVI (1965), p. 165.

> With reference to the speeches in this history, some were delivered before the war began, others while it was going on; it was hard to record the exact words spoken, both in cases where I was myself present, and where I used the reports of others. But I have used language in accordance with what I thought the speakers in each case would have been most likely to say, adhering as closely as possible to the general sense of what was actually spoken.

From this, Glasson aptly observed: "He does not claim to reproduce the precise words like a stenographer but in writing the speeches he keeps as closely as possible to 'the general sense of *what was actually spoken.*' . . . This is a very different matter from the imaginative composing of speeches suitable to the occasion."[5] And I. H. Marshall notes that while a comparison with the Greek historians has some legitimacy, Luke's indebtedness is plainly more to the Old Testament tradition of historiography; and therefore he "writes from a particular standpoint which traces the activity of God in historical events."[6]

That there is a striking similarity of structure between the speeches themselves and between the speeches and the narrative of Acts may be freely acknowledged without any necessary denigration of content.[7] To an extent, of course, all of the speeches in Acts must of necessity be paraphrastic in their present form, for certainly the original delivery contained more detail of argument and more illustrative material than presently included—as poor Eutychus undoubtedly could testify.[8] Stenographic reports they are not. And probably few ever so considered them. They have been restyled, as is required in every precis; and, furthermore, restyled in accordance with the styling of the narrative. But the recognition of a styling which produces speeches of others compatible with the narrative in which they are found should not be interpreted as a necessary declaration of either inaccuracy of reporting or a lack of traditional

[5] *Ibid.* (italics are Glasson's). Cf. A. W. Mosley, "Historical Reporting in the Ancient World," *NTS*, XII (1965), pp. 10-26.

[6] I. H. Marshall, *Luke: Historian and Theologian* (1970), p. 56.

[7] Schweizer speaks of a "far-reaching identity of structure" ("Concerning the Speeches in Acts," *Studies in Luke-Acts*, p. 210), but his expression overruns the evidence.

[8] Acts 20:7-12.

material, since one author is responsible for the literary form of the whole.

Comparing the Third Gospel with the First, it can be demonstrated that Luke did not invent sayings for Jesus. On the contrary, he seems to have been more literally exact in the transmission of the words of Jesus than in the recording of the events of his life. C. F. Evans believes that such a comparison is fallacious, since the discourses of Jesus and the speeches of Acts were two entirely different literary genre, the one presenting independent *logia* and the other composed of more rounded and carefully constructed sermons.[9] And M. Dibelius insisted that the comparison should not be taken as presumptive evidence for a similarity of treatment in Acts, for:

> When he wrote the Gospel, Luke had to fit in with a tradition which already had its own stamp upon it, so that he had not the same literary freedom as when he composed the Acts of the Apostles. On the other hand, unless we are completely deceived, he was the first to employ the material available for the Acts of the Apostles, and so was able to develop the book according to the point of view of an historian writing literature.[10]

But, as S. S. Smalley points out, the differences of structure which Evans has underscored, while impressive, are not surprising "if the teaching method of Jesus is taken properly into account."[11] And further, contra Dibelius, "because we are not able to confirm the reliability of Luke's use of sources in his second volume [in that there is no comparable "Matthew" for Acts], there is no *prima facie* reason why it should be assumed to differ widely from its character in the first."[12] There is, therefore, it must still be insisted, a presumption in favor of a similarity of treatment in Luke's recording of the words of Jesus and his recording of the addresses of Peter, Stephen, Philip, James and Paul. And though it is certainly true that his respect for the latter

[9] C. F. Evans, "The Kerygma," *JTS*, VII (1956), p. 27.

[10] M. Dibelius, *Studies in the Acts of the Apostles* (ET 1956), p. 185. Cf. W. G. Kümmel, *Introduction to the New Testament* (ET 1966), p. 116.

[11] S. S. Smalley, "The Christology of Acts," *ExpT*, LXXVIII (1962), p. 358.

[12] *Ibid.*, p. 359.

never rivaled his veneration of the former,[13] it is difficult to believe that such a difference would have appreciably affected his desire for accuracy of content, if not also of word, which he evidences in his Gospel.

In addition, that Luke actually strove for accuracy of content—or, at least, that he did not impose his own theology on the speeches to the perverting of their original character—has been suggested in significant articles by H. N. Ridderbos and C. F. D. Moule.[14] Ridderbos points to the lack of developed theology in the speeches of Peter as a mark of reliable historiography, and not inventive genius. And Moule convincingly argues that, contrary to frequent claims that it is so, the Christology of Acts is not uniform, either between the speakers represented or between Luke and his characters: that there are a "number of seemingly undesigned coincidences and subtle nuances" which indicate a retention of the essential character of the content presented.[15]

The problem as to why Luke portrays the earliest Christian apostles and leaders as quoting from the LXX (in the main), when their sermons and defenses must have had their origin (for the most part) in an Aramaic-speaking community, is a difficulty without a ready solution, though some suggestions will be offered later.[16] Nevertheless, it must still be insisted that the book of Acts—particularly in its first fifteen chapters—is of major importance for the study of the earliest Christian preaching. As Bo Reicke rightly says: "Luke may be assumed to have taken over material that was originally Jewish-Christian. This, accordingly, can for good reasons be traced back to the Jerusalem congregation."[17]

Incorporated Materials in the Epistles. That Paul's consciousness of uniqueness as to his ministry and message must not be understood to mean his disinterest in or igno-

[13] Cf. F. J. Foakes Jackson and K. Lake, "The Internal Evidence of Acts," *Beginnings*, II, pp. 121f.
[14] H. N. Ridderbos, *The Speeches of Peter in the Acts of the Apostles* (1962); C. F. D. Moule, "The Christology of Acts," *Studies in Luke-Acts*, pp. 159-185.
[15] C. F. D. Moule, *ibid.*, pp. 181-82.
[16] *Infra*, pp. 87-89.
[17] B. Reicke, "Incarnation and Exaltation," *Interp*, XVI (1962), p. 161; cf. *idem*, *Glaube und Leben der Urgemeinde* (1957), pp. 5-8.

rance of the Church's early preaching and catechetical formulae (confessions, hymns, catechisms, liturgies) has been a commonplace in criticism during the past quarter-century.[18] And of all the various incorporated formulae that have been identified in the Pauline letters, I Cor. 15:3-5 has the strongest claim to an early provenance and holds the most interest for a study of the use of the Old Testament among the earliest believers. The verbs Paul employs to introduce the material (*παραδίδωμι*, *παραλαμβάνω*) suggest the reception and transmission of an earlier formulation. The fourfold repetition of *ὅτι* seems to signal the presence of a formula; as does also the inclusion of references to Christ's death and burial, going beyond, as they do, the point of immediate and contextual relevance in the discussion of the resurrection. The expression "according to the scriptures" occurs nowhere else in Paul, and the term "the twelve" appears somewhat strange on his lips. The double reference to the Old Testament, the inclusion of the Aramaic "Cephas," and the mention of James, all suggest a Palestinian milieu. And, finally, Paul unequivocally states in verse 11 that what he has just cited is the common proclamation of all the apostles.[19] There are, probably, other catechetical portions incorporated into the Pauline corpus which have a bearing on the use of Scripture by the early Christian preachers, but their precise identification is extremely difficult. Perhaps Eph. 4:8 is one of them,[20] though of this and other similar passages we must speak later.

A case could also be made for the canonical James as having been first a homily or a sermon—perhaps extracts drawn from a number of James' sermons—and only later cast into the form of a letter and circulated more widely. This would be in keeping with the Jewish practice of com-

[18] Among English-speaking scholars, particularly since the first edition of A. M. Hunter's *Paul and his Predecessors* (1940, rev. ed. 1961).
[19] Cf. Hunter: "Where did this formula originate? Formerly, I took the view that 'Paul was here reproducing the baptismal creed of the Damascus church—a creed perhaps taught him by Ananias before his baptism.' I should now prefer to think that the tradition stemmed from the Jerusalem church" (*ibid.* [1961], p. 117). See also R. H. Mounce, "Continuity of the Primitive Tradition: Some Pre-Pauline Elements in I Corinthians," *Interp*, XIII (1959), p. 418.
[20] Cf. *infra*, pp. 124f.

piling characteristic teachings and distinctive maxims of prominent religious leaders, which may very well have carried over into early Jewish Christianity. The same could be postulated for I Peter, I John, and even Jude as well. I personally favor, for example, the view that the situation which called forth the writing of I Peter is reflected in the present tenses of 4:12–5:14, and that in addressing himself to the situation at hand the author incorporated sermonic and catechetical material (perhaps also a baptismal hymn, 3:18-22) between the opening salutation of 1:1f. and the concluding exhortations of 4:12ff.—material which he probably had a large part in developing and which was therefore known to be characteristic of him. But though these three or four writings may very well have originated as Jewish Christian compilations of sermonic and catechetical materials, the form in which they are preserved for us is genuinely epistolary. Furthermore, the time of their composition into their present form was probably somewhat later than that of our immediate interest. We may consider these Jewish Christian "tractates" to have some relevance for the question of the use of the Old Testament in early Christian preaching, but must employ them here in subsidiary fashion and with caution.

THE PHENOMENA OF THE QUOTATIONS

The study of the use of the Old Testament in early Christian preaching focuses upon the explicit quotations attributed to Peter, Stephen, Philip, James and Paul in the Acts of the Apostles. Again, as in the investigation of Jesus' quotations, it must be pointed out that the distinction between a direct quotation and an allusive employment of Scripture is notoriously difficult, and any listing of one apart from the other will inevitably be somewhat arbitrary in those areas where they overlap. Nevertheless, this study of the use of the Old Testament in early Christian preaching will base itself primarily upon the following twenty-seven quotations attributed to the early Christian leaders in the book of the Acts.[21]

[21] Only the major source or sources are listed, without the inclusion of possible parallels.

I. Quotations attributed to Peter:

1. Acts 1:20 (Ps. 69:25 [MT=69:26; LXX=68:26])—I.F.: "it is written (γέγραπται) in the book of Psalms."
2. Acts 1:20 (Ps. 109:8 [LXX=108:8])—I.F. "and" (covered by the preceding introductory formula).
3. Acts 2:17-21 (Joel 2:28-32 [MT & LXX=3:1-5])—I.F.: "this is that spoken (τοῦτό ἐστιν τὸ εἰρημένον) by the prophet Joel."
4. Acts 2:25-28, 31 (Ps. 16:8-11 [LXX=15:8-11])—I.F.: "David said concerning him."
5. Acts 2:34f. (Ps. 110:1 [LXX=109:1])—I.F.: "he [David] said."
6. Acts 3:22f. (Deut. 18:15, 18f.)—I.F.: "Moses indeed said."
7. Acts 3:25 (Gen. 12:3; 18:18; 22:18)—I.F.: "saying to Abraham."
8. Acts 4:11 (Ps. 118:22 [LXX=117:22])—I.F.: "this is" (οὗτός ἐστιν).

II. Quotations attributed to the Church generally:

9. Acts 4:25f. (Ps. 2:1f.)—I.F.: "sovereign Lord . . . who through the Holy Spirit, by the mouth of our father David, your servant, said."

III. Quotations attributed to Stephen:

10. Acts 7:3 (Gen. 12:1)—I.F.: "he [God] said to him."
11. Acts 7:6f. (Gen. 15:13f.)—I.F.: "God spoke in this manner."
12. Acts 7:7b (Exod. 3:12)—I.F.: "God said."
13. Acts 7:27f. (Exod. 2:14)—I.F.: "saying."
14. Acts 7:32 (Exod. 3:6)—I.F.: "the voice of the Lord came."
15. Acts 7:33f. (Exod. 3:5, 7-10)—I.F.: "the Lord said to him."
16. Acts 7:37 (Deut. 18:15)—I.F.: "Moses, who said to the sons of Israel."
17. Acts 7:42f. (Amos 5:25-27)—I.F.: "as it is written in the book of the prophets."
18. Acts 7:49f. (Isa. 66:1f.)—I.F.: "as the prophet said."

IV. Quotations attributed to Philip:

19. Acts 8:32f. (Isa. 53:7f.)—I.F.: "the place of the scripture which he [the Ethiopian Eunuch] read was this"; cf. v. 35, "from the same scripture he [Philip] preached to him Jesus."

V. Quotations attributed to James:

20. Acts 15:16-18 (Amos 9:11f.)—I.F.: "the words of the prophets, as it is written" (*γέγραπται*).

VI. Quotations attributed to Paul:

21. Acts 13:33 (Ps. 2:7)—I.F.: "as also it is written (*γέγραπται*) in the second psalm."
22. Acts 13:34 (Isa. 55:3)—I.F.: "thus he [God] said."
23. Acts 13:35 (Ps. 16:10 [LXX=15:10])—I.F.: "therefore also he [God] says in another place."
24. Acts 13:41 (Hab. 1:5)—I.F.: "which is spoken in the prophets."
25. Acts 13:47 (Isa. 49:6)—I.F.: "so the Lord commanded us."
26. Acts 23:5 (Exod. 22:28 [MT & LXX=22:27])—I.F.: "it is written" (*γέγραπται*).
27. Acts 28:26f. (Isa. 6:9f.)—I.F.: "truly spoke the Holy Spirit by the prophet Isaiah to our fathers, saying."

Also of significance for our study, though presented as quoting no specific passage in support, is Peter's affirmation in Acts 3:24 that, in addition to Moses, "all the prophets from Samuel, and those that follow after, as many as have spoken, have likewise foretold of these days." The double reference to "the scriptures" in the formula of I Cor. 15:3-5 is an additional important feature for our study, as well as are the more prominent allusions in Acts[22] and the quotations in the possibly earlier sermonic material of James and I Peter.[23]

It has usually been held that the source of the quotations in Acts, and in the letters of James and I Peter as well, is the LXX.[24] And on the basis of such an observation, it has often been concluded (1) that the phenomenon of Greek

[22] Acts 2:30; 3:13; 4:24; 7:5, 10f., 30, 40; 13:22 and 14:15.
[23] Jas. 2:8, 11, 23; 4:5, 6; I Pet. 1:16, 24f.; 2:6, 7, 8; 3:10-12; 4:18; 5:5; though these will be treated more fully in Chapter VII.
[24] Note, e.g., the detailed treatment of W. K. L. Clarke, "The Use of the Septuagint in Acts," *Beginnings*, II (1922), pp. 66-105.

citations in material credited to Aramaic-speaking preachers lies heavily against the authenticity of the accounts, or (2) that the LXX was the only Bible of the earliest Christians. But both the observation and the conclusions deduced from it fail to take into account a number of pertinent factors.

In the first place, while the quotations of Acts are fairly representative of the LXX in general, the LXX alone is not sufficient to explain all their textual phenomena. J. de Waard points out that the quotations of Acts 3:22f. (Deut. 18:15, 18f.); 7:43 (Amos 5:26f.); 13:41 (Hab. 1:5) and 15:16 (Amos 9:11) are prime examples of where "certain New Testament writings show affinities to the DSS as regards the Old Testament text."[25] Likewise, though we have rejected this as an explanation for the septuagintal form of Jesus' quotations in the Gospels (particularly the First Gospel),[26] there is the possibility in Acts of Luke having assimilated Aramaic or more hebraic text-forms to the text that was, to quote C. C. Torrey, "familiar to those for whom he wrote."[27] M. Wilcox has shown that while the citations in Acts are strongly septuagintal, the allusions, because they are less capable of exact identification and therefore less subject to special treatment, seem to have escaped a process of assimilation.[28] Perhaps, as well, some credit for the septuagintal features of the quotations should be given to a Greek testimonia of Old Testament passages circulating within the Church about the time of Luke's composition.[29] Or perhaps, in the cases of James and I Peter, an amanuensis has played a part.[30]

Whatever the final resolution of the problem, it seems that we are faced with at least two issues regarding the text-form of the quotations in Acts (as well as, possibly, of those in James and I Peter): (1) the variety of biblical versions in the first century, and (2) assimilation for the

[25] J. de Waard, *A Comparative Study of the Old Testament Text in the Dead Sea Scrolls and in the New Testament* (1965), p. 78.
[26] Cf. *supra*, pp. 63f.
[27] C. C. Torrey, *The Composition and Date of Acts* (1916), p. 58.
[28] M. Wilcox, *The Semitisms of Acts* (1965), pp. 20-55.
[29] *Ibid.*, pp. 181f.
[30] Cf. I Pet. 5:12; though, in opposition, see J. N. Sevenster, *Do You Know Greek?* pp. 3, 10-14.

sake of a Greek-speaking audience. In addition, the possible presence of a testimonia collection(s) and the activity of an amanuensis (in the case of the Epistles) add further complications. Until additional evidence is available, we are well advised to leave the questions of textual source and deviations in early Christian preaching open. We may suspect that the answer to our problem lies in one or more of the suggestions alluded to above, and may be able to build a reasonable case in defense. But all we really know, apart from further data, is that the quotations in Acts, James and I Peter are dominantly septuagintal in form, with a few parallels to the biblical texts at Qumran. None of this, however, necessarily impinges upon or supports authenticity.

TESTIMONIA PORTIONS AND COLLECTIONS

It has been frequently noted that the New Testament not only has a distinctive treatment of Old Testament passages, but also reflects a distinctive selection of biblical material. At times, passages that were accepted in Judaism as applying directly to the Messiah are cited (e.g., Deut. 18:15, 18f.; Isa. 11:1, 10; Mic. 5:2; Zech. 9:9; Mal. 3:1b). More frequently, however, passages are quoted which in Judaism were considered to have only tangential messianic relevance (without any direct application to the Messiah himself), or none at all. Quotations of this latter sort are well represented in the preaching of the earliest Christians as portrayed in the Acts of the Apostles.

In an attempted explanation of this phenomenon of selection, J. R. Harris proposed in 1916 that there existed in the early Church a "Book of Testimonies" which brought together particular verses of pertinence for an anti-Judaic polemic, antedated all of our New Testament writings, and upon which the New Testament writers drew for their quotations.[31] Adopting F. C. Burkitt's view of the character of the *λόγια* referred to by Papias,[32] he suggested that it was Matthew who composed this testimonia collection and

[31] J. R. Harris, *Testimonies*, I (1916), II (1920).
[32] Eusebius, Eccl. Hist. III. 39. 16.

that others translated it as best they could.[33] The theory gained ascendancy in the English-speaking world, and during the first half of the century provided the starting point for most considerations of the use of the Scriptures in the New Testament.

In the early fifties, however, C. H. Dodd proposed an alternative understanding of the problem.[34] While recognizing that there existed a common biblical basis in New Testament interpretation, he pointed out that an anthology of isolated proof-texts could not explain the phenomena of varied selection of verses within an Old Testament portion or of the varied treatment of the same verse on the part of different New Testament writers. He therefore suggested that the New Testament writers worked from selected blocks of Old Testament material, rather than selected verses, and that from these blocks of material particular verses were drawn as the need arose.[35] Often, he believed, a particular verse quoted in the New Testament was intended to evoke the whole passage from which it had been selected. Further, Dodd proposed that those larger portions of Old Testament material constituting "the substructure of all Christian theology" could, in the main, be grouped according to three kerygmatic themes: (1) "apocalyptic-eschatological Scriptures' (principally Joel 2–3; Zech. 9–14; Dan. 7 and 12); (2) "Scriptures of the New Israel" (principally Hosea; Isa. 6:1–9:7; 11:1-10; 40:1-11; Jer. 31:31-34; Hab. 2:3f.); and (3) "Scriptures of the Servant of the Lord and the Righteous Sufferer" (principally Isa. 42:1–44:5; 49:1-13; 50:4-11; 52:13–53:12; Pss. 22, 34, 69, 118). In addition, he noted some passages (e.g., Pss. 2, 8, 110) and certain isolated texts (e.g., Deut. 18:15, 18f.; II Sam. 7:14) which were employed with messianic significance, though they do not fit into such a threefold scheme.[36]

Dodd's thesis of the primacy of selected blocks of Old Testament portions which served as quarries for the mining

[33] On the nature of τὰ λόγια in Papias' remarks on the Gospels, see C. F. D. Moule, *Birth of the New Testament*, Excursus I, pp. 215ff.
[34] C. H. Dodd, *According to the Scriptures: The Sub-Structure of New Testament Theology* (1952).
[35] *Ibid.*, pp. 28-60.
[36] *Ibid.*, pp. 61-108.

of particular texts, while, of course, not universally accepted, has been generally regarded as explaining most adequately the data of selection in the New Testament's use of the Old. This is not to deny that testimonia collections of individual proof-texts on specific topics and for specific purposes may have been formulated. The bringing together of five such texts in 4QTest and of three passages in 4QFlor indicates that this was done by certain Jewish sectarians prior to the advent of Christianity.[37] But the acceptance of Dodd's hypothesis is to assert that "Testimony Books," if there were such, were secondary to and developed from an earlier selection and use of larger units of Old Testament material.[38]

The question naturally arises, however, as to how these biblical portions were selected, and by whom. Dodd has noted that while the common answer today is the collective community and processes inherent in its task of proclamation and polemic, "the New Testament itself avers that it was Jesus Christ Himself who first directed the minds of His followers to certain parts of the scriptures as those in which they might find illumination upon the meaning of His mission and destiny."[39]

Luke 24:27 recounts that in appearing to two from Emmaus, Jesus "interpreted to them in all the scriptures, beginning from Moses and from the prophets, the things concerning himself." Luke 24:45 says that he later met with his disciples and "opened their mind that they might understand the scriptures." And Acts 1:3 tells of Jesus teaching his disciples "things concerning the kingdom of God" dur-

[37] 4QTest contains Deut. 5:28f.; 18:18f.; Num. 24:15-17; Deut. 33:8-11; Josh. 6:26. On a date as early as 100-75 B.C., see J. T. Milik, *Ten Years of Discovery in the Wilderness of Judaea*, p. 61. 4QFlor contains II Sam. 7:10-14; Ps. 1:1 and 2:1f., together with pesher comments and supporting texts. On the marked texts of the Second Isaiah Scroll as Qumran testimonia, see G. R. Driver, *The Judaean Scrolls* (1965), pp. 527ff.

[38] Cf. J. A. Fitzmyer, "4Q Testimonia and the New Testament," *TS*, XVIII (1957), pp. 527-537; C. F. D. Moule, *Birth of the New Testament*, pp. 83f.

[39] C. H. Dodd, *According to the Scriptures*, p. 110. In agreement, A. M. Hunter, *Paul and his Predecessors*, pp. 133f.; while in disagreement, B. Lindars, *New Testament Apologetic* (1961), p. 30, and J. Barr, *Old and New in Interpretation*, pp. 139f.

ing a forty-day post-resurrection ministry. These verses, together with the post-resurrection ministry generally, are highly suspect in contemporary studies, due to modern theology's equation of Jesus' spiritual resurrection and his ascension, and therefore the denial of a physical resurrection and any post-resurrection ministry.[40] But at the very least, it must be said that in these passages Luke is relating what he believes to be the rationale for the distinctive Christian employment of Scripture, whether it originated in this specific period or not.

The selection of Old Testament testimonia portions reflects, indeed, a highly creative and original approach to the Scriptures. Dodd has pertinently observed: "Creative thinking is rarely done by committees, useful as they may be for systematizing the fresh ideas of individual thinkers, and for stimulating them to further thought. It is individual minds that originate."[41] And he concludes his discussion in words that cannot be improved upon: "To account for the beginning of this most original and fruitful process of rethinking the Old Testament we found need to postulate a creative mind. The Gospels offer us one. Are we compelled to reject the offer?"[42]

[40] Dodd expresses reservations on Luke 24:27 and 45, and the claim that Jesus "formally set before them a comprehensive scheme of biblical interpretation" (*According to the Scriptures*, p. 110). And E. Haenchen masks his real objection in the rather trifling criticism on Acts 1:3: "If anyone takes the words of 1:3 seriously as history—that Jesus talked about the kingdom of God with his disciples for forty days—he either makes Jesus a preposterously poor teacher who cannot clarify what he means in ever so long a period, or he makes the disciples appear incredibly foolish" ("The Book of Acts as Source Material for the History of Early Christianity," *Studies in Luke-Acts*, p. 260). That later gnostic writings generally attribute their teachings to instructions given by Jesus between the resurrection and the ascension need not discredit Luke's account. It may only indicate how widespread was the attitude regarding the source of the Christian reinterpretation of Scripture, and could just as well be used in support of Luke's tradition as against it. And though his thesis is taken to an unwarranted extreme, it yet remains true that Birger Gerhardsson's work on formal instruction in rabbinic Judaism (cf. *Memory and Manuscript*) is of considerable value in support of the thesis that some type of formal exegetical teaching must be attributed to Jesus.

[41] C. H. Dodd, *According to the Scriptures*, pp. 109f.

[42] *Ibid.*, p. 110. Cf. S. L. Edgar, "New Testament and Rabbinic Messianic Interpretation," *NTS*, V (1958), pp. 47-54.

EXEGETICAL PRESUPPOSITIONS

Behind the use of the Old Testament by the earliest Christians stood not only a body of testimonia portions, but also certain distinctive presuppositions. If we are to appreciate their exegetical practices, it is necessary to have an awareness of their basic hermeneutical outlooks and attitudes. It has been pertinently observed that "it is doubtful whether we can hope to understand the contents of any mind whose presuppositions we have not yet learned to recognize."[43] In what follows, therefore, four major exegetical presuppositions in early Christian preaching are indicated. The succeeding section of this chapter will illustrate these presuppositions more adequately in the treatment of individual biblical quotations.

Corporate Solidarity. In the first place, the concept of "corporate solidarity" or "corporate personality" had a profound effect upon the exegesis of early Jewish Christians. Since H. Wheeler Robinson's pioneer essay of 1935, this fact has been increasingly recognized.[44] The concept has been defined as "that important Semitic complex of thought in which there is a constant oscillation between the individual and the group—family, tribe, or nation—to which he belongs, so that the king or some other representative figure may be said to embody the group, or the group may be said to sum up the host of individuals."[45] The precise nature of the relationships involved is not always entirely clear from the literature of the Jews, nor from that of their semitic neighbors. Probably this is due in large measure to the fact that "ancient literature never does fit exactly into our categories."[46] But though there are uncertainties as to precisely how the idea expressed itself in ancient life generally and as to the degree of influence it exerted in specific

[43] L. S. Thornton, as quoted by G. W. H. Lampe, "The Reasonableness of Typology," *Essays on Typology* (1957), p. 18.
[44] H. W. Robinson, "The Hebrew Conception of Corporate Personality," now in *Corporate Personality in Ancient Israel* (1964), pp. 1-20. Cf. A. R. Johnson, *The One and the Many in the Israelite Conception of God* (1942).
[45] J. Reumann, "Introduction" to H. W. Robinson's *Corporate Personality in Ancient Israel*, p. v.
[46] *Ibid.*, p. 16.

instances in the literature, there seems to be little question of its presence in the structure of Jewish and early Jewish Christian thought.

In biblical exegesis, the concept of corporate solidarity comes to the fore in the treatment of relationships between the nation or representative figures within the nation, on the one hand, and the elect remnant or the Messiah, on the other. It allows the focus of attention to "pass without explanation or explicit indication from one to the other, in a fluidity of transition which seems to us unnatural."[47]

Correspondences in History. Stemming in part from the concept of corporate solidarity is the understanding of history—or, at any rate, of the history of the people of God—as evidencing a unity in its various parts which is there by divine ordination.[48] For both Jew and Jewish Christian, historical occurrences are "built upon a certain pattern corresponding to God's design for man His creature."[49] This is but one aspect of a larger Hebrew-Christian *Weltanschauung*, wherein the nature of man, the relations between man and man (contemporary, past and future), the interaction between man and the universe, and the relation of both to God, their Creator and Redeemer, are viewed in wholistic fashion. In such a view, history is neither endlessly cyclical nor progressively developing due to forces inherent in it. Nor can it be considered in a secular manner. Rather, in all its movements and in all its varied episodes, it is expressive of the divine intent and explicating the divine will. With such an understanding of history, early Christians were prepared to trace correspondences between God's activity of the past and his action in the present—between events then and events now, between persons then and persons now. Such correspondences were not just analogous in nature, or to be employed by way of illustration. For the early

[47] *Ibid.*, p. 15.
[48] "The corporate personality of the family, the clan, and the people was conceived realistically as a unity, a unity which made possible the all-important doctrine of election, and lent unity to the history itself" (*ibid.*, pp. 4f.). See also J. Daniélou, "The New Testament and the Theology of History," *Studia Evangelica*, I, ed. K. Aland (1959), pp. 25-34.
[49] C. H. Dodd, *According to the Scriptures*, p. 128.

Christians they were incorporated into history by divine intent, and therefore to be taken typologically. Their presence in the history of a former day is to be considered as elucidating and furthering the redemptive message of the present.

Eschatological Fulfilment. An obvious presupposition also affecting early Jewish Christian interpretation is the consciousness of living in the days of eschatological fulfilment. Peter's sermon on the day of Pentecost begins with the assertion that the "last days" are being actualized now.[50] And this theme is recurrent throughout the preaching of the earliest Christians. As with the covenanters of Qumran, early Jewish believers in Jesus understood their ancient Scriptures in an eschatological context. Unlike the Dead Sea sectarians, however, whose eschatology was mainly proleptic and anticipated, Christians were convinced that the coming of the Messianic Age was an accomplished fact. Messiahship had been realized in Jesus of Nazareth, and the last days inaugurated with him. While awaiting final consummation, their eschatology was rooted in and conditioned by what had already happened in the immediate past. The decisive event had occurred, and, in a sense, all else was epilogue.

Messianic Presence. In addition, as F. F. Bruce reminds us, "the New Testament interpretation of the Old Testament is not only eschatological but Christological."[51] For the earliest believers, this meant (1) that the living presence of Christ, through his Spirit, was to be considered a determining factor in all their biblical exegesis, and (2) that the Old Testament was to be interpreted Christocentrically. W. D. Davies has pointed out that at least in popular and haggadic circles within Judaism, there existed the expectation that with the coming of the Messiah the enigmatic and obscure in the Torah "would be made plain."[52] And such an expectation seems to have become a settled conviction among the early Christians, as evidenced by the exegetical practices inherent in their preaching.

[50] Acts 2:14ff.
[51] F. F. Bruce, *Biblical Exegesis in the Qumran Texts,* p. 77.
[52] W. D. Davies, *Torah in the Messianic Age and/or the Age to Come* (1952), esp. pp. 84-94.

EXEGETICAL PRACTICES AND PATTERNS

Immediately obvious in any scanning of the biblical quotations and allusions in Acts is that they are set entirely within Jewish contexts, and never, except for the similarity of language in the apostles' cry at Lystra,[53] in the context of a Gentile audience. The great bulk of quotations and allusions appear in the first fifteen chapters of Acts. And even though some citations are credited to Paul, they are even then set in the context of a Jewish audience: in the synagogue at Antioch of Pisidia (Acts 13:33-35, 41, 47), before the Sanhedrin at Jerusalem (23:5), and before the Jewish leaders at Rome (28:26f.). The apologetic of the earliest preaching, therefore, according to the patterns portrayed in Acts, seemingly expressed itself somewhat circumstantially even in its broad outlines; for while the earliest Christians understood themselves to be living in the days of biblical fulfilment and based their rationale in large measure upon the Old Testament, they quoted Scripture principally—if not exclusively—within their mission to Jews. Evidently it was only among Jews that such a direct appeal to the Old Testament would be appreciated, or even understood. Paul, on the other hand, in his desire to find a point of common ground with his hearers, seems to have been willing to employ other means in his initial proclamation among Gentiles.[54]

A literalistic employment of Scripture appears in several places and on the part of various persons in Acts. In speaking to the crowd in the temple precincts, Peter employed the covenant promise to Abraham quite literally, acknowledging that his hearers were "the sons of the prophets and of the covenant which God made with our fathers."[55] All of Stephen's quotations and allusions in his detailed tracing of Israel's history before the council adhere closely to the

[53] Acts 14:15. Barnabas and Paul may be expected, particularly in crisis situations, to revert at times to biblical language even among pagan Gentiles. The surprising thing is not that this occurred at Lystra, but that it is portrayed as happening so infrequently (only this once) in the Gentile mission.

[54] Cf. W. Barclay, "A Comparison of Paul's Missionary Preaching and Preaching to the Church," *Apostolic History and the Gospel*, ed. W. W. Gasque and R. P. Martin (1970), pp. 165-175.

[55] Acts 3:25 (Gen. 12:3; 18:18; 22:18).

plain meaning of the Old Testament text.[56] And his use of Deut. 18:15, while by implication applied to Jesus, is a straightforward treatment of a prophecy understood widely within Judaism to have direct reference to the coming Messiah.[57] Paul's recounting at Pisidian Antioch of God's dealings with his people takes the history of Israel, as recorded in the biblical narrative, quite literally.[58] And before the Sanhedrin, he quite readily took the warning of Exod. 22:28, "you shall not speak evil of the ruler of your people," as having direct moral application to the situation at hand, and accepted its rebuke.[59] Likewise in the possibly sermonic materials of James and I Peter, there are a number of literalist interpretations.[60]

A midrashic treatment of Scripture also appears in the Acts of the Apostles. The exegetical rule *qal waḥomer* (light to heavy) underlies the use of Ps. 69:25 (MT=69:26) and 109:8, allowing Peter to assert that what has been said of false companions and wicked men generally applies, *a minore ad majorem*, specifically to Judas, the one who proved himself uniquely false and evil.[61] In Peter's Pentecost sermon, Ps. 16:8-11 and 110:1 are brought together in support of the resurrection on the principle *gezerah shawah* (analogy), since both passages contain the expression "at my right hand" (*ἐκ δεξιῶν μου*) and therefore are to be treated together.[62] In Paul's sermon at Pisidian Antioch, Isa. 55:3 and Ps. 16:10 are brought together on the same basis, since both contain the adjective *ὅσιος*—which in substantival form can mean either "divine decrees" (*τὰ ὅσια*) as in Isa. 55:3 or "holy one" (*τὸν ὅσιον*) as in Ps. 16:10.[63]

[56] Acts 7:3 (Gen. 12:1); 7:6f. (Gen. 15:13f.); 7:7b (Exod. 3:12); 7:27f. (Exod. 2:14); 7:32 (Exod. 3:6); 7:33f. (Exod. 3:5, 7-10); 7:42f. (Amos 5:25-27); 7:49f. (Isa. 66:1).

[57] Acts 7:37. On early Jewish expectations regarding the "Eschatological Mosaic Prophet" and the employment of Deut. 18:15, 18f., see my *Christology of Early Jewish Christianity*, pp. 32-35.

[58] Acts 13:17-22.

[59] Acts 23:5.

[60] E.g., Jas. 2:8 (Lev. 19:18); 2:11 (Exod. 20:13f.); 4:6 (Prov. 3:34); I Pet. 1:16 (Lev. 19:2; 11:44); 3:10-12 (Ps. 34:13-17); 5:5 (Prov. 3:34). These will be treated later in Chapter VI.

[61] Acts 1:20.

[62] Acts 2:25-28, 34f.

[63] Acts 13:34f. Paul's sermon in the synagogue to Diaspora Jews was probably delivered in Greek, so that such a play on the word *ὅσιος* would be midrashically understandable and fitting.

Likewise, it is probable that we should understand the joining of II Sam. 7:14 and Ps. 2:7 in Acts 13 along the same lines. J. W. Doeve and E. Lövestam have pointed out that II Sam. 7:6-16 undoubtedly formed the biblical basis for Paul's historical résumé in Acts 13:17-22.[64] And in Acts 13:33, the first explicit citation following that recitation of God's dealings with his people, the apostle quotes from Ps. 2:7. These two passages, of course, are quoted together by the author of the Letter to the Hebrews at the very beginning of his homily.[65] They also appear in close proximity in Luke's account of Jesus' ministry and baptism.[66] And the evidence from Qumran has shown that they were possibly associated with messianic relevance prior to the advent of Christianity.[67] Probably their union was originally based on the fact that they both portray God as speaking of "my son," and on that basis (*gezerah shawah*) it was considered appropriate to treat them together. But while such a union of passages may have been made in pre-Christian Judaism, it was evidently brought over into the New Testament as being legitimate.

Literalist and midrashic modes of exegesis were indeed features in early Christian preaching. But what appears to be most characteristic in their treatment of Scripture is pesher interpretation. Addressing those gathered in the temple courts, Peter affirmed that, in addition to direct prophetic statements (e.g., Deut. 18:15, 18f.), "all the prophets from Samuel, and those that follow after, as many as have spoken, have likewise foretold these days."[68] Such a view of prophetic activity, when coupled with concepts of corporate solidarity and correspondences in history, opens up all

[64] J. W. Doeve, *Jewish Hermeneutics in the Synoptic Gospels and Acts,* p. 172; E. Lövestam, *Son and Savior: A Study of Acts 13. 32-37,* trans. M. J. Petry (1961), pp. 6-15.
[65] Heb. 1:5.
[66] Luke 1:32f. (II Sam. 7:12-16); 3:22 (Ps. 2:7).
[67] 4QFlor is a pesher commentary on II Sam. 7:10-14; Ps. 1:1 and Ps. 2:1f., with the remainder broken off. Whether the text originally went on to include a discussion of Ps. 2:7 is impossible to substantiate—or to refute. Ps. 2:7 is also found in 3Q2, although without an accompanying pesher treatment (cf. M. Baillet, J. T. Milik, R. de Vaux, eds., *Discoveries in the Judaean Desert of Jordan, III: Les 'Petites Grottes' de Qumran* [1962], p. 94).
[68] Acts 3:24.

the biblical message and history to a Christocentric interpretation. All that is now required is to identify those portions of pertinence to the Messianic Age (as Christians understood it) and to explicate them in accordance with the tradition and principles of Christ. On such a view, the earliest believers could declare, as Paul records their confession, that Christ's death "for our sins" and his resurrection "on the third day" were "according to the scriptures"[69] —either epitomizing the sum total of prophetic teaching, or, more likely, treating such passages as Isa. 53:5-12 and Hos. 6:2 in a corporate solidarity fashion and applying them to the experiences of Jesus.[70]

In the possibly sermonic portion of I Peter, there is a clear-cut pesher attitude expressed toward the nature of Old Testament prophecy, which attitude very likely reflects the conviction of the earliest believers as well:

> The prophets who spoke of the grace that was to come to you searched intently and with the greatest care concerning this salvation, trying to find out the time and circumstances to which the Spirit of Christ in them was pointing when he predicted the sufferings of Christ and the glories that would follow. It was revealed to them that they were not serving themselves but you, when they spoke of the things that have now been told you by those who have preached the gospel to you by the Holy Spirit sent from heaven—things into which angels long to look.[71]

While the terms "mystery" and "interpretation" are not employed, the thought is strikingly parallel to that of the *rāz-pesher* motif in the Dead Sea Scrolls.

The exegetical practice of Peter, as seen in the quotations credited to him in Acts and those in the possibly sermonic portion of I Peter, evidence as well the importance placed

[69] I Cor. 15:3-5.
[70] For the view that "according to the scriptures" refers only to the verb "he was raised" and not also to the statement "on the third day," see B. M. Metzger, "A Suggestion Concerning the Meaning of I Cor. xv. 4b," *JTS*, VIII (1957), pp. 118-123. H. K. McArthur, however, has convincingly shown that "Hos. vi. 2 was the outstanding, single scriptural passage behind the 'on the third day' tradition, although the phrase 'according to the Scriptures' in I Cor. xv. 4 may have been based on the general 'third day' motif which the Rabbis found in numerous passages and not exclusively in Hos. vi. 2" ("On the Third Day," *NTS*, XVIII [1971], pp. 81-86).
[71] I Pet. 1:10-12.

on a pesher interpretation of Scripture in early Christian preaching. In the majority of cases of Petrine preaching, the "this is that" pesher theme of fulfilment comes to the fore, as can be noted in the following examples:

1. The application of Joel 2:28-32 (MT=3:1-5) to the Pentecost outpouring of the Spirit in Acts 2:17-21, stating explicitly that "this is that spoken (*τοῦτό ἐστιν τὸ εἰρημένον*) by the prophet Joel." The aspect of fulfilment is heightened by Peter's alteration of the MT's and LXX's simple "afterwards" (אחרי-כן, *μετὰ ταῦτα*) to "in the last days, says God" (*ἐν ταῖς ἐσχάταις ἡμέραις, λέγει ὁ θεός*), and his breaking into the quotation to emphasize the fact of the restoration of prophecy (*καὶ προφητεύσουσιν*).

2. The "stone" citations of Acts 4:11 and I Pet. 2:7, quoting Ps. 118:22 and introducing the passage in Acts by the words "this is the stone" (*οὗτός ἐστιν ὁ λίθος*). The midrashic bringing together of Isa. 28:16; Ps. 118:22 and Isa. 8:14 in I Pet. 2:6-8 appears to be a later development, of which we must speak later.[72]

3. The statements applied to Judas in Acts 1:20, taken from Ps. 69:25 (MT=69:26) and 109:8. While Hillel's first exegetical rule is employed, arguing that that which is said about the unrighteous in general applies to the betrayer of the Messiah specifically, the aspect of fulfilment, employing the presupposition of correspondence in history, gives the treatment a pesher flavor as well.

4. The application of Ps. 16:8-11 and 110:1 to the resurrection and ascension of Jesus in Acts 2:25-36. While a midrashic understanding has brought the two passages together, it is a pesher understanding that evokes such an introduction as "David said concerning him" (*Δαυὶδ λέγει εἰς αὐτόν*) and applies the passages directly to Jesus.

5. The citation of Isa. 40:6-8 in I Pet. 1:24f. While there is an atomistic treatment of the expression "the word of our God remains forever" (*τὸ ῥῆμα τοῦ θεοῦ ἡμῶν μένει εἰς τὸν αἰῶνα*), a pesher application is also made in the assertion, "this is the word (*τοῦτο δέ ἐστιν τὸ ῥῆμα*) which is preached unto you."

There are also a number of instances in early Christian

[72] *Infra*, pp. 202-204.

preaching where passages that were understood to have direct reference to the Messiah, either in Judaism generally or by the earliest Christians alone, are employed once and sometimes again with something of a pesher force—though, evidently, simply repeating an earlier accepted view of the passage in question, not creating it. The stress on fulfilment lends a pesher flavor to the treatments; though they should probably be catalogued as "mild" pesher interpretations, since they are dealing with what were probably accepted as direct prophecies and working to explicit fulfilment.

Peter in Acts 3:22f. and Stephen in Acts 7:37, for example, are represented as quoting Deut. 18:15ff. as predictive of Christ. This is hardly surprising, for once Jesus was acclaimed as Messiah the employment of such a widely acknowledged messianic testimonium would be inevitable.[73] The early Christians are portrayed in Acts 4:25f. as quoting Ps. 2:1f. in their prayer, thereby alleging that opposition to Jesus was foretold by David. But, as E. Lövestam rightly points out, "in rabbinical literature there is plenty of evidence of the use of and allusions to Ps. 2:1f. in descriptions of the enemies' expected onslaught upon the Messiah and the Elect."[74] The early Christians, convinced concerning the Messiahship of Jesus and employing a corporate solidarity type of rationale, evidently did no more than apply the Lord's "anointed" of Ps. 2:2 directly to Jesus and think of themselves as "the Elect," thereby classing all opposition as the "heathen" spoken of in Ps. 2:1f.

Philip appears in Acts 8:32-35 preaching Jesus to the Ethiopian Eunuch on the basis of Isa. 53:7f., and I Pet. 2:22-25 employs a number of verses from Isa. 53 to explicate Christ's example of suffering. But such a use of Isaiah's

[73] On the acclamation of Jesus as Messiah in early Christian thought, see my *Christology of Early Jewish Christianity*, pp. 63-82, and on the attribution of categories drawn from Deut. 18:15ff. in early Christianity, see *ibid.*, pp. 35-38. On the correlation of the textually aberrant *τοῦ προφήτου ἐκείνου* of Acts 3:23 with the reading הנבי of 4QTest, see J. A. Fitzmyer, "4Q Testimonia and the New Testament," *TS*, XVIII (1957), p. 537, and J. de Waard, *A Comparative Study of the Old Testament Text*, p. 24.

[74] E. Lövestam, *Son and Saviour*, p. 17. See also pp. 17-19 for a compilation of talmudic passages to this effect, and p. 16 for the suggestion that the use of Ps. 2:1f. in 4QFlor should be understood in this light.

"Servant Song," while never accepted by Judaism to be applicable to the Messiah,[75] could very well have been fixed quite early in Christian thought, stemming from Jesus' own reinterpretation of the passage.[76] And if so reinterpreted, Isa. 53 could have been considered by the earliest believers to be a direct prophecy finding explicit fulfilment in Jesus' life and death—either as understood individualistically or as understood along the lines of corporate solidarity.

Likewise, Paul is presented in Acts as explicating a fulfilment theme; though, interestingly, many—if not all—of the passages he employs were probably earlier understood as messianic portions. In Acts 13:23 he alludes to Isa. 11:1 (perhaps also vs. 10) in speaking of Jesus as the "seed" of David, thereby making use of an acknowledged Jewish testimonium on the descent of the Messiah from David. In Acts 13:33 he quotes from Ps. 2:7 in biblical support of Jesus' resurrection (*ἀναστήσας Ἰησοῦν*).[77] The use of Ps. 2:7 in pre-Christian Judaism as a messianic prophecy is probably more inferential than obvious. Nevertheless, E. Lövestam has developed a plausible case drawn from Qumran and rabbinic materials for "a richer messianic application of the God's son proclamation" of Ps. 2:7 as existing in early Judaism before Christ.[78] And L. C. Allen has shown that Sir. 47:11 and 4QPatr on Gen. 49:10 are based on "the theme of God's effectual royal decree" of Ps. 2:7, and that in these passages the decree is taken as an eschatological promise.[79] It is therefore possible that in the apostle's use of Ps. 2:7, he was employing an enthronement psalm which

[75] For a reproduction of the Targum on Isa. 52:13–53:12, see W. Manson, *Jesus the Messiah* (1943), pp. 168-171.

[76] The one explicit passage is Luke 22:37. On Jesus' ministry as expressive of a suffering servant theme, see H. W. Wolff, *Jesaja 53 im Urchristentum* (1942), pp. 55-70; W. Manson, *Jesus the Messiah* (1943), pp. 110-13; J. W. Bowman, *The Intention of Jesus* (1945), pp. 32ff.; J. Jeremias (and W. Zimmerli), *The Servant of God* (ET 1957), pp. 83ff.; F. V. Filson, *The Gospel according to St. Matthew* (1960), p. 40.

[77] Cf. E. Lövestam, *Son and Saviour*, pp. 8ff., for a cogent defense of the view that Ps. 2:7 is employed here in support of the resurrection of Jesus from the dead, and not in connection with his presentation at his baptism.

[78] *Ibid.*, p. 17.

[79] L. C. Allen, "The Old Testament Background of (ΠΡΟ) ʽΟΡΙΖΕΙΝ in the New Testament," *NTS*, XVII (1970), pp. 104f. Allen also suggests that ὁρίζω and its compound προορίζω, which are possible

was understood in certain quarters to have messianic relevance. It may have been, therefore, that in his eyes he was applying a direct and explicit prophecy to the resurrection of Jesus. And such a direct application of an eschatological enthronement motif to the resurrection of Jesus would have been entirely fitting, for, as early Christian tradition testifies, by the resurrection "God made (*ἐποίησεν*) him both Lord and Christ"[80] and Jesus "was declared (*ὁρισθέντος*) to be the Son of God with power, according to the spirit of holiness."[81] Paul's quotation of Isa. 55:3, "I will give you the sure mercies of David," in Acts 13:34 reflects the covenant promise to David, which promise was certainly involved in traditional Jewish messianology. And his quotation of Ps. 16:10, "you will not give your holy one to see corruption," even though combined in midrashic fashion with Isa. 55:3 rather than Ps. 110:1, stems from the earliest Christian preaching at Pentecost.[82]

In the preaching of the early Christians, as recorded principally in the Acts of the Apostles, one looks almost in vain for any clear consciousness of employing varying modes of interpretation in quoting the Old Testament. For purposes of analysis, we may (rightly, I believe) catalogue their methods and trace out the respective patterns. But the first Christian preachers seem to have made no sharp distinctions between literalist treatments of the text, midrash exegesis, pesher interpretation, and the application of accepted predictive prophecies. All of these were employed, and at times there appears a blending and interweaving of methods. What they were conscious of, however, was interpreting the Scriptures from a Christocentric perspective, in conformity with the exegetical teaching and example of Jesus, and along Christological lines. In their exegesis there is the interplay of Jewish presuppositions and practices, on the one hand, and Christian commitments and perspectives on the other, which produced a distinctive interpretation of the Old Testament.

translations of the Hebrew חק employed in Ps. 2:7 (though the LXX translates it by *πρόσταγμα*), were possibly used in Acts 2:23; 9:25; 10:42; 17:31 and Rom. 1:4 with Ps. 2:7 in mind (*ibid.*, pp. 105-8).

80 Acts 2:36.

81 Rom. 1:4.

82 Cf. Acts 2:27.

IV: PAUL AND THE OLD TESTAMENT

It may be considered axiomatic that Paul shared generally the current Jewish exegetical presuppositions and the Jewish Christian attitudes toward Scripture. His own personal history would lead us to expect this,[1] and his writings evidence it.[2] Further, C. H. Dodd has shown that a common body of Old Testament material underlies the Pauline exegesis and that of other New Testament writers.[3]

But while there are broad areas of agreement between the Christian leaders at Jerusalem and Paul, there also appear differences of hermeneutical approach and practice. We must not magnify the variations into any dichotomous cleavage; though, on the other hand, we cannot merely equate Paul's exegetical habits with those of the earliest apostles.

Together with the earliest Jewish Christians, Paul understood the Old Testament Christologically. And he worked from the same two fixed points: (1) the Messiahship and Lordship of Jesus, as validated by the resurrection and as witnessed to by the Spirit; and (2) the revelation of God in the Scriptures of the Old Testament. But though in his own experience a true understanding of Christ preceded a proper understanding of Scripture, in his exegetical endeavors he habitually began with Scripture and moved on to Christ. As C. H. Dodd observed (even while constructing his important

[1] Cf. my *Paul, Apostle of Liberty*, pp. 21-64.

[2] Cf. H. St.J. Thackeray, *The Relation of St. Paul to Contemporary Jewish Thought* (1900); O. Michel, *Paulus und seine Bibel* (1929); W. D. Davies, *Paul and Rabbinic Judaism* (1955); E. E. Ellis, *Paul's Use of the Old Testament* (1957); J. Jeremias, "Paulus als Hillelit," *Neotestamentica et Semitica*, ed. E. E. Ellis and M. Wilcox (1969), pp. 88-94.

[3] C. H. Dodd, *According to the Scriptures*, esp. p. 23.

thesis regarding the common area of agreement underlying all New Testament interpretation), "Paul in the main tries to start from an understanding of the biblical text just as it stands in its context."[4] While the Jerusalem apostles placed the revelation of God in Jesus the Messiah "*neben dem Text*," so that both stood starkly side-by-side, Paul's treatment evidences not quite this rather wooden juxtaposition, but a placing of Scripture as central within a larger context of Christological awareness. And while the early Christian leaders at Jerusalem characteristically began with Jesus as the Messiah and moved on to an understanding of the Old Testament from this Christocentric perspective, Paul usually started with the text itself and sought by means of a midrashic explication to demonstrate Christological significance. There is an area of overlapping, of course. But whereas the exegesis of the Jerusalem apostles—and of Jesus himself—has its closest parallel known to date in the pesher interpretation of Qumran, Paul's treatment of the biblical texts is more closely related to that of Pharisaism.[5]

This is not to value one approach and methodology more highly than the other. Both Paul and the Christians of Jerusalem viewed the relations between the revelation of God in Jesus of Nazareth and the revelation of God in the Old Testament as complementary, as well as supplementary. And undoubtedly both would have acknowledged the legitimacy of the other's practice, as each seems to do unconsciously at those points where they overlap. It is only to point out that the Pauline approach to the Old Testament and Paul's own biblical apologetic varies to an extent from that practiced by the earliest Jewish Christians, and to suggest that such a difference is due in large measure to differences of training, ideological environment confronted in the missionary enterprise, and individual spiritual experience.

THE LETTERS OF PAUL

There is widespread agreement today that most, if not all, of the canonical missionary epistles of Paul and many of his

[4] *Ibid.*, p. 23.
[5] W. F. Albright, though here a bit extreme, is generally correct and stresses a point too often ignored in insisting that "St. Paul's inter-

canonical letters written from prison are authentic. Romans, I and II Corinthians, and Galatians are so strongly attested both internally and externally that few have ever questioned them. I Thessalonians has been generally accepted, although the apocalyptic nature of the second letter to the believers at Thessalonica caused some at an earlier time to question II Thessalonians. But with the realization that, though the apostle's eschatology was reoriented by his conversion to Jesus the Christ, it was not abandoned, the major argument against this epistle has been set aside. Colossians, Philemon and Philippians likewise have so commended themselves to scholars that none but the most radical have sought to oppose their authenticity, though questions have legitimately been raised regarding the exact locale for the composition of these letters.

The main current critical discussions as to Pauline authorship center on the letter to the Ephesians and the so-called Pastoral Epistles to Timothy and Titus. The rather general nature and style, the omission of the designation ἐν Ἐφέσῳ in the earliest extant manuscripts,[6] and the striking similarities to the letter to the Colossians have led many to view Ephesians as a summary of and introduction to the other letters of Paul which was written by a later disciple of the apostle.[7] But while Ephesians is often considered the product of a postapostolic Paulinist, the hypothesis that it was authored by Paul at the same time as the Colossian letter and meant to be something of a circular letter to Christians in Asia Minor is at least as good an explanation for these peculiarities of style, structure and content as any other. Of the canonical letters claiming Pauline authorship, the most problematic are I and II Timothy and Titus. These have been seriously questioned and discounted by many as being

---

pretation of the Old Testament follows the Greek hermeneutics of the Mishnah rather than the quite different type of interpretation found in the Essene commentaries of the books of the Bible" (*New Horizons in Biblical Research* [1966], p. 51).

[6] Eph. 1:1.

[7] In addition to J. Moffatt and the continental scholars he cited (*An Introduction to the Literature of the New Testament*, 3rd ed. [1918], pp. 373-394), see particularly: E. J. Goodspeed, *The Key to Ephesians* (1956); *idem*, *The Meaning of Ephesians* (1933); J. Knox, *Philemon Among the Letters of Paul* (1935); C. L. Mitton, *The Epistle to the Ephesians: Its Authorship, Origin and Purpose* (1951).

unauthentic, principally on the basis of their more formal tone and the high frequency of words not found elsewhere in the acknowledged writings of the apostle.[8] But taking into consideration a difference of topic in these letters, the altered situation of the apostle at the time of writing, and the probable use of an amanuensis in the actual composition, such factors need not be fatal to Pauline authorship. Scholarship of late, in fact, has begun to realize that its criticism of the Pastorals has been extreme, and is beginning to return to a consideration of the authenticity of these three letters as a live possibility.[9]

But while a precise determination of the Pauline corpus is of great significance for many historical and theological issues related to the apostle Paul, it is of lesser significance for a study of the apostle's use of the Old Testament. The great bulk of his biblical quotations are to be found in the so-called *Hauptbriefe* (Romans, I and II Corinthians, Galatians), with only six appearing elsewhere (four in Ephesians, one in I Timothy and one in II Timothy). It is, therefore, with these four great missionary epistles that we are here principally concerned.

THE PHENOMENA OF THE QUOTATIONS

The study of Paul's use of Scripture necessarily involves more than an investigation of his explicit Old Testament quotations. This, of course, as we have seen, is true as well for every interpreter, Jewish or Christian. Nevertheless, the biblical citations are of great importance, and it is with them that our study must begin. While it is possible to list and organize them in various ways, depending upon one's attitude toward conflated texts and one's understanding of the intention of a quotation as distinct from an allusion, the following eighty-three quotations will serve as the focus of our present study.[10]

[8] Cf. P. N. Harrison, *The Problem of the Pastorals* (1922).
[9] Cf. W. Michaelis, "Pastoralbriefe und Wortstatistik," *ZNW*, XXVIII (1929), pp. 69-76; B. M. Metzger, "A Reconsideration of Certain Arguments Against the Pauline Authorship of the Pastoral Epistles," *ExpT*, LXX (1958), pp. 91-94; J. N. D. Kelly, *The Pastoral Epistles* (1963), pp. 3-36.
[10] Only the major source or sources are listed, without the inclusion of possible parallels.

I. Quotations occurring in Romans:

1. Rom. 1:17 (Hab. 2:4)—I.F.: "as it is written."
2. Rom. 2:24 (Isa. 52:5)—I.F.: "as it is written."
3. Rom. 3:4 (Ps. 51:4 [MT=51:6; LXX=50:6])—I.F.: "as it is written."
4. Rom. 3:10-18 (Ps. 14:1-3 [LXX=13:1-3]; 5:9 [MT & LXX=5:10]; 140:3 [MT=140:4; LXX=139:4]; 10:7 [LXX=9:28]; Isa. 59:7f.; Ps. 36:1 [MT=36:2; LXX=35:2])—I.F.: "as it is written."
5. Rom. 4:3, 9, 22 (Gen. 15:6)—I.F.: "What does the scripture say?"
6. Rom. 4:7f. (Ps. 32:1f. [LXX=31:1f.])—I.F.: "as David also says."
7. Rom. 4:17 (Gen. 17:5)—I.F.: "as it is written."
8. Rom. 4:18 (Gen. 15:5)—I.F.: "according to that which was said."
9. Rom. 7:7 (Exod. 20:17; Deut. 5:21)—I.F.: "the law said."
10. Rom. 8:36 (Ps. 44:22 [MT=44:23; LXX=43:23])—I.F.: "as it is written."
11. Rom. 9:7 (Gen. 21:12)—I.F.: "but."
12. Rom. 9:9 (Gen. 18:10, 14)—I.F.: "this is the word of promise."
13. Rom. 9:12 (Gen. 25:23)—I.F.: "it was said to her."
14. Rom. 9:13 (Mal. 1:2f.)—I.F.: "as it is written."
15. Rom. 9:15 (Exod. 33:19)—I.F.: "to Moses he said."
16. Rom. 9:17 (Exod. 9:16)—I.F.: "the scripture said to Pharaoh."
17. Rom. 9:25f. (Hos. 2:23 [MT=2:25], 1:10 [MT=2:1])—I.F.: "as he [God] said also in Hosea."
18. Rom. 9:27f. (Isa. 10:22f.)—I.F.: "Hosea cried out concerning Israel."
19. Rom. 9:29 (Isa. 1:9)—I.F.: "as Isaiah said before."
20. Rom. 9:33 (Isa. 28:16; 8:14)—I.F.: "as it is written."
21. Rom. 10:5 (Lev. 18:5)—I.F.: "Moses wrote."
22. Rom. 10:6-8 (Deut. 30:12-14)—I.F.: "the righteousness which is by faith speaks in this manner."

23. Rom. 10:11 (Isa. 28:16)—I.F.: "the scripture says."
24. Rom. 10:13 (Joel 2:32 [MT & LXX=3:5])—I.F.: "for."
25. Rom. 10:15 (Isa. 52:7)—I.F.: "as it is written."
26. Rom. 10:16 (Isa. 53:1)—I.F.: "Isaiah says."
27. Rom. 10:18 (Ps. 19:4 [MT=19:5; LXX=18:5])—I.F.: "yes, indeed (*μενοῦνγε*)."
28. Rom. 10:19 (Deut. 32:21)—I.F.: "Moses says."
29. Rom. 10:20f. (Isa. 65:1f.)—I.F.: "Isaiah says."
30. Rom. 11:3 (I Kings 19:14)—I.F.: "the scripture says of Elijah."
31. Rom. 11:4 (I Kings 19:18)—I.F.: "What was the divine response to him?"
32. Rom. 11:8 (Isa. 29:10; Deut. 29:4 [MT=29:3])—I.F.: "as it is written."
33. Rom. 11:9f. (Ps. 69:22f. [MT=69:23f.; LXX=68:23f.])—I.F.: "David says."
34. Rom. 11:26f. (Isa. 59:20f.; 27:9)—I.F.: "as it is written."
35. Rom. 11:34f. (Isa. 40:13; Job 41:11 [MT & LXX=41:3])—I.F.: "for."
36. Rom. 12:19f. (Deut. 32:35; Prov. 25:21f.)—I.F.: "it is written . . . says the Lord."
37. Rom. 13:9 (Exod. 20:13-17; Deut. 5:17-21)—I.F.: "for this."
38. Rom. 13:9 (Lev. 19:18)—I.F.: "if there is any other commandment, it is summed up in this word."
39. Rom. 14:11 (Isa. 45:23)—I.F.: "it is written."
40. Rom. 15:3 (Ps. 69:9 [MT=69:10; LXX=68:10])—I.F.: "as it is written."
41. Rom. 15:9 (Ps. 18:49 [MT=18:50; LXX=17:50])—I.F.: "as it is written."
42. Rom. 15:10 (Deut. 32:43)—I.F.: "again he says."
43. Rom. 15:11 (Ps. 117:1 [LXX=116:1])—I.F.: "and again."
44. Rom. 15:12 (Isa. 11:10)—I.F.: "and again Isaiah says."
45. Rom. 15:21 (Isa. 52:15)—I.F.: "as it is written."

II. Quotations occurring in I Corinthians:

46. I Cor. 1:19 (Isa. 29:14)—I.F.: "it is written."
47. I Cor. 1:31 (Jer. 9:24 [MT=9:23])—I.F.: "as it is written."
48. I Cor. 2:9 (Isa. 64:4)—I.F.: "as it is written."
49. I Cor. 2:16 (Isa. 40:13)—I.F.: "for."
50. I Cor. 3:19 (Job 5:13)—I.F.: "it is written."
51. I Cor. 3:20 (Ps. 94:11 [LXX=93:11])—I.F.: "and again."
52. I Cor. 6:16 (Gen. 2:24)—I.F.: "for . . . said he."
53. I Cor. 9:9 (Deut. 25:4)—I.F.: "in the law of Moses it is written."
54. I Cor. 10:7 (Exod. 32:6)—I.F.: "as it is written."
55. I Cor. 10:26 (Ps. 24:1 [LXX=23:1])—I.F.: "for."
56. I Cor. 14:21 (Isa. 28:11f.)—I.F.: "in the law it is written."
57. I Cor. 15:27 (Ps. 8:6 [MT & LXX=8:7])—I.F.: "for."
58. I Cor. 15:32 (Isa. 22:13)—I.F.: none.
59. I Cor. 15:45 (Gen. 2:7)—I.F.: "so it is written."
60. I Cor. 15:54f. (Isa. 25:8; Hos. 13:14)—I.F.: "then shall come to pass the word which is written."

III. Quotations occurring in II Corinthians:

61. II Cor. 4:13 (Ps. 116:10 [LXX=115:1])—I.F.: "according to what is written."
62. II Cor. 6:2 (Isa. 49:8)—I.F.: "he [God] says."
63. II Cor. 6:16-18 (Lev. 26:11f.; Isa. 52:11f. and possibly II Sam. 7:14)—I.F.: "as God said."
64. II Cor. 8:15 (Exod. 16:18)—I.F.: "as it is written."
65. II Cor. 9:9 (Ps. 112:9 [LXX=111:9])—I.F.: "as it is written."
66. II Cor. 10:17 (Jer. 9:24)—I.F.: "but."
67. II Cor. 13:1 (Deut. 19:15)—I.F.: none.

IV. Quotations occurring in Galatians:

68. Gal. 3:6 (Gen. 15:6)—I.F.: "as."
69. Gal. 3:8 (Gen. 12:3)—I.F.: "the scripture . . . announced before to Abraham."
70. Gal. 3:10 (Deut. 27:26)—I.F.: "it is written."
71. Gal. 3:11 (Hab. 2:4)—I.F.: "because."
72. Gal. 3:12 (Lev. 18:5)—I.F.: "but."
73. Gal. 3:13 (Deut. 21:23)—I.F.: "it is written."

74. Gal. 3:16 (Gen. 13:15; 15:18; 17:8 and possibly 22:18)—I.F.: "he [God] did not say, . . . but."
75. Gal. 4:27 (Isa. 54:1)—I.F.: "it is written."
76. Gal. 4:30 (Gen. 21:10)—I.F.: "What does the scripture say?"
77. Gal. 5:14 (Lev. 19:18)—I.F.: "all the law is fulfilled in this one statement."

V. Quotations occurring in Ephesians:

78. Eph. 4:8 (Ps. 68:18 [MT=68:19; LXX=67:19])—I.F.: "therefore he [God] says."
79. Eph. 5:14 (Isa. 26:19; 60:1)—I.F.: "therefore he [God] says."
80. Eph. 5:31 (Gen. 2:24)—I.F.: none.
81. Eph. 6:2f. (Exod. 20:12; Deut. 5:16)—I.F.: none.

VI. Quotations occurring in the Pastoral Epistles:

82. I Tim. 5:18 (Deut. 25:4)—I.F.: "the scripture says."
83. II Tim. 2:19 (Num. 16:5)—I.F.: none.

There are also a number of allusions to the Old Testament which need to be considered as well, particularly: (1) the treatment in Rom. 5:12-14 of the entrance and reign of sin (Gen. 2:16ff.; 3:1ff., etc.); (2) the warnings in I Cor. 10:1-15 drawn from Israel's disobedience in the wilderness (Num. 11:1ff.; Exod. 32:1ff.; Num. 25:1ff.; 21:5ff.; 14:1ff.); (3) the contrasts in II Cor. 3:7-18 between the "ministry of death" and "condemnation" and the "ministry of righteousness" and "the Spirit" (Exod. 24:29-35, etc.); and (4) the lesson in Gal. 4:21-31 based on the relations between Hagar and Sarah, and their sons (Gen. 16:1ff.). In addition, it is of some interest to note that the apostle's quotations and allusions are not confined to biblical texts. Coupled with the Old Testament quotation in I Tim. 5:18 is the supporting statement that "the workman is worthy of his pay," which probably reflects the teaching of Jesus as later recorded in Matt. 10:10 and Luke 10:7. There are also a number of allusions to the words of Jesus, as, for example, in I Cor. 7:10; 9:14; 11:23ff. and Rom. 12–14.[11] And four times, either in his own letters or in material attributed to

[11] Cf. A. M. Hunter, *Paul and his Predecessors*, pp. 45-51, citing additional possibilities.

him, pagan authors are quoted with approval on a given point: I Cor. 15:33; Titus 1:12 and twice in Acts 17:28.

It is immediately apparent in any scanning of the Pauline quotations that (1) the overwhelming majority occur in the four *Hauptbriefe*, and (2) over half occur in the letter to the Romans. Such a dual observation can hardly be minimized by separating the conflated quotations (which we have treated as single units) into their component parts, for almost all of these appear in the letter to the Romans as well.[12] Allusive use of the biblical language, of course, is to be found in all of the apostle's letters, except Philemon. The Old Testament was for Paul "not only the Word of God but also his mode of thought and speech,"[13] and therefore parallels of language are inevitable. But where a conscious endeavor to refer to Scripture comes to the fore in the apostle's writings, it seems to be limited to only certain letters. Evidently, as with the pattern observed in the Acts of the Apostles,[14] this should be understood somewhat circumstantially. The letters to Christians at Rome, Corinth and Galatia may be understood to involve, in one way or another, audiences having some Jewish heritage or being affected (if not afflicted) by some type of Jewish teaching. Even I and II Timothy, if "Timothy" be the young man of Lystra referred to in Acts 16:1-3, and Ephesians, if it be postulated that the letter was originally intended for a wider audience than believers at Ephesus, could be so considered. But the letters to the churches at Thessalonica, Colosse (including Philemon) and Philippi were addressed, as far as we know, to Christians who were mainly, if not entirely, Gentile converts, and relatively unaffected by a Judaistic polemic. And in his pastoral correspondence with them, Paul evidently attempted to meet them on their own ideological grounds, without buttressing his arguments from the Old Testament.[15]

[12] Rom. 3:10-18; 9:25f.; 9:33; 11:8; 11:26f.; 11:34f.; I Cor. 15:54f.; II Cor. 6:16-18.
[13] E. E. Ellis, *Paul's Use of the Old Testament*, p. 10.
[14] Cf. *supra*, p. 96.
[15] Cf. A. Harnack's similar observations and circumstantial explanation in "Das alte Testament in den paulinischen Briefen und in den paulinischen Gemeinden," *Sitzungsberichte der Preussischen Akademie der Wissenschaften zu Berlin* (1928), pp. 124-141.

Of the approximately one hundred Old Testament passages quoted by Paul in his letters (disengaging the conflated texts and the possible dual sources, and treating each separately), over half are either absolute or virtual reproductions of the LXX, with almost half of these at variance with the MT. On the other hand, four are in agreement with the MT against the LXX (Job 41:11; 5:13; Ps. 112:9; Num. 16:5), and approximately forty vary from both the LXX and the MT to a greater or lesser degree.[16] The pattern here varies from the dominantly septuagintal form of the quotations in the teachings of Jesus and the preaching of the early Church, where "sayings" collections of the words of Jesus and assimilation by the author of Acts were possible factors influencing the text-forms. It may be, of course, that some of Paul's variant textual readings are *ad hoc* creations, either by the apostle himself or stemming in some manner from earlier Christian interpreters. Such an explanation was in vogue from the mid-fifties through the mid-sixties,[17] though continuing studies on the Dead Sea texts and the targumic traditions have tended to minimize this as an explanation.[18] It is probable that the combination of (1) Paul's Gentile interest, (2) his rabbinic training, (3) his wider knowledge of variant readings, and (4) his incorporation of early Christian pesher text-forms, accounts most adequately for this rather peculiar mixture of textual readings in the apostle's citations. But the present state of Old Testament textual criticism is in such a flux, due to newer evidence coming to the fore and the necessary reevaluation

[16] Cf. E. E. Ellis, *Paul's Use of the Old Testament*, pp. 11-16, 150-185.

[17] For more moderate positions, see K. Stendahl, *The School of St. Matthew* (1954), and E. E. Ellis, *Paul's Use of the Old Testament*; for more extensive developments, see B. Lindars, *New Testament Apologetic* (1961), and E. D. Freed, *Old Testament Quotations in the Gospel of John* (1965). Stendahl acknowledges in the preface to the second edition of his *School of St. Matthew* (1967), iv-vi, that recent textual evidence has tended to minimize the creative activity of his "school."

[18] Cf. W. H. Brownlee, *The Text of Habakkuk in the Ancient Commentary from Qumran* (1959); J. de Waard, *A Comparative Study of the Old Testament Text in the Dead Sea Scrolls and in the New Testament* (1965); M. McNamara, *The New Testament and the Palestinian Targum to the Pentateuch* (1966). Note also the articles by F. M. Cross, Jr., and P. W. Skehan cited on p. 64, n. 31.

of existing materials in light of this newer evidence, that it is perilous to posit any final solution for this variety of textual readings in the Pauline writings.

Introductory formulae are associated with the great majority of Paul's quotations. "As it is written" (*καθὼς γέγραπται*) and "it is written" (*γέγραπται*) appear most frequently, though references to "God," "Moses," "David," "Isaiah," "Hosea," "the Scriptures," and "the Law" as speaking are common. Variations of these basic formulae also appear; for example, "according to that which was said" (*κατὰ τὸ εἰρημένον*), "this is the word of promise" (*ἐπαγγελίας ὁ λόγος οὗτος*), and "the divine response said to him" (*λέγει αὐτῷ ὁ χρηματισμός*). The most varied of the introductory formulae is the one to Deut. 30:12-14 in Rom. 10:6-8: "the righteousness which is by faith speaks in this manner." And its variation is particularly noticeable since it occurs between the rather conventional formula of Rom. 10:5 and those of Rom. 10:11ff. It may be that by such an introduction Paul was endeavoring more to alert us to a proverbial employment of biblical language than to identify a biblical quotation. But with this one possible exception, the variations in the introductory formulae, other than exhibiting in various ways the apostle's high regard for Scripture and signalling that he is quoting from Scripture, seem to be principally stylistic and tell us little about his use of the Old Testament.

LITERALIST AND MIDRASHIC TREATMENTS

At the turn of the century, Henry St. J. Thackeray opened his discussion of Paul's use of the Old Testament with the comment: "There is perhaps no aspect of the Pauline theology in which the influence of the Apostle's Rabbinic training is so clearly marked as the use which is made of the Old Testament."[19] And that dictum is still valid today, after extensive testing in the crucible of comparative talmudic, hellenistic and sectarian studies.

There is in the apostle's employment of Scripture a great deal that is common to any reverential or respectful treat-

[19] H. St.J. Thackeray, *Relation of St. Paul to Contemporary Jewish Thought*, p. 180.

ment of the Bible, Jewish or Christian, and which would require comment only if it were absent or spoken against. He agrees, for example, with the psalmist that God is true, just and prevailing in his judgments.[20] He quotes the fifth through the tenth commandments as applying to various ethical situations,[21] and asserts that whatever has been left untouched in the sphere of human relations by these divine principles is covered by the precis of Lev. 19:18: "You shall love your neighbor as yourself."[22] He takes quite seriously the monogamous and indissoluble character of marriage as presented in Gen. 2:24, and employs the wording of that passage as a warning against immorality[23] and an illustration of the believer's relationship with Christ.[24] He cites the Jewish maxim of two or three witnesses establishing a matter, as based on Deut. 19:15, as having validity.[25] And he treats as highly significant in redemptive history—the prototype, in fact, of salvation history—God's covenantal promises to Abraham.[26]

A recurring feature in Paul's biblical quotations, and one that points up his midrashic heritage, is the Pharisaic practice of "pearl stringing"; that is, of bringing to bear on one point of an argument passages from various parts of the Bible in support of the argument and to demonstrate the unity of Scripture.[27] This is most obviously done in Rom.

[20] Rom 3:4 (Ps. 51:4).
[21] Rom. 7:7; 13:9; Eph. 6:2f. (Exod. 20:12-17; Deut. 5:16-21); cf. Mark 7:10 (par.); 10:19 (par.).
[22] Rom 13:9; Gal. 5:14; cf. Mark 12:31 (par.); Matt. 19:19; Jas. 2:8.
[23] I Cor. 6:16; cf. Mark 10:7f. (par.).
[24] Eph. 5:31.
[25] II Cor. 13:1; cf. Matt. 18:16.
[26] Rom. 4:17f.; 9:7-9; Gal. 3:8; 3:16.
[27] Rather typical of various types of "pearl stringing," and also illustrative of an analogous treatment of passages in which appears the same word or expression, are the following examples from the Babylonian Talmud:

Shab. 20a: "R. Judah b. Bathyra [early second-century Tannaim] said: The fire should take hold on both sides. And though there is no proof of the matter, there is a hint thereof: 'the fire hath devoured both the ends of it, and the midst of it is burned' [Ezek. 15:4], and 'there was a fire in the brazier burning before him' [Jer. 36:22]."

Ber. 18a: "R. Issi [third-century Amoraim] says: To him apply the texts: 'He that is gracious unto the poor lendeth unto the Lord' [Prov. 19:17], and 'he that is gracious unto the needy honors Him' [Prov. 14:31]."

3:10-18 (Ps. 14:1-3; 5:9; 140:3; 10:7; Isa. 59:7f.; Ps. 36:1); Rom. 9:12-29 (Gen. 25:23; Mal. 1:2f.; Exod. 33:19; 9:16; Hos. 2:23; 1:10; Isa. 10:22f.; 1:9); Rom. 10:18-21 (Ps. 19:4; Deut. 32:21; Isa. 65:1f.); Rom. 11:8-10 (Isa. 29:10; Deut. 29:4; Ps. 69:22f.); Rom. 15:9-12 (Ps. 18:49; Deut. 32:43; Ps. 117:1; Isa. 11:10) and Gal. 3:10-13 (Deut. 27:26; Hab. 2:4; Lev. 18:5; Deut. 21:23); but it appears as well in Rom. 4:1-8 (Gen. 15:6; Ps. 32:1f.); Rom. 9:33 (Isa. 8:14; 28:16); Rom. 12:19f. (Deut. 32:35; Prov. 25:21f.); I Cor. 3:19f. (Job 5:13; Ps. 94:11);[28] I Cor. 15:54f. (Isa. 25:8; Hos. 13:14) and II Cor. 6:16-18 (Lev. 26:11f.; Isa. 52:11f. and possibly II Sam. 7:14).[29] Involved in "pearl stringing," of course, is the highlighting of analogous words or expressions in the various passages, which serves as the basis for their union. And this feature of midrashic exposition is also apparent in the Pauline quotations: *οὐ λαός μου* (Rom. 9:25f.), *λίθος* (Rom. 9:33), *ὀφθαλμοὺς τοῦ μὴ*

Mak. 16a: "The All-Merciful ordained, 'thou shalt not oppress thy neighbor nor rob him' [Lev. 19:13], and then directs that, 'he shall restore that which he took by robbery' [Lev. 5:23]; then again . . . the All-Merciful ordained, 'thou shalt not go into his house to fetch his pledge' [Deut. 24:10-13], and then, 'thou shalt stand without . . . thou shalt surely restore to him the pledge when the sun goes down' [Deut. 24:19-21]."

Sanh. 38b: "R. Johanan [first-century Tannaim] said: In all the passages which the heretics have taken for their heresy, their refutation is found near at hand. Thus: 'Let us make man in our image' [Gen. 1:26]; 'And God created man in His own image' [Gen. 1:27], 'Come, let us go down and there confound their language' [Gen. 11:7]; 'And the Lord came down to see the city and the tower' [Gen. 11:5]; 'Because there was revealed to him God' [Gen. 35:7]; 'Unto God who answers me in the day of my distress' [Gen. 35:3]; 'For what great nation is there that hath God so nigh unto it, as the Lord our God is nigh unto us whensoever we call upon Him' [Deut. 4:7]; 'And what one nation in the earth is like thy people, Israel, whom God went to redeem for a people unto Himself' [II Sam. 7:23]; 'Till thrones were placed and one that was ancient did sit' [Dan. 7:9]."

In Mak. 24a, four contrasts with the Mosaic teaching are strung together and introduced with the formulae: "Moses said . . . Amos came and revoked that, as it is said . . . Jeremiah came and said . . . Ezekiel came and declared . . . Isaiah came and said."

[28] Note how by a midrashic combination of Job 5:13 with Ps. 94:11 the words of Eliphaz the Temanite become Scripture and authoritative, whereas the context of Job would seem to suggest otherwise.

[29] Cf. O. Michel, *Paulus und seine Bibel*, p. 83; E. E. Ellis, *Paul's Use of the Old Testament*, pp. 49-51; J. Jeremias, "Paulus als Hillelit," *Neotestamentica et Semitica*, p. 88.

βλέπειν (Rom. 11:8-10), *ἔθνη* (Rom. 15:9-12), *σοφοί* (I Cor. 3:19f.), *θάνατος* (I Cor. 15:54f.), *ἐπικατάρατος* (Gal. 3:10, 13), and *ζήσεται* (Gal. 3:11f).

The seven hermeneutical *middoth* attributed by tradition to Hillel, and evidently practiced to some extent by first-century rabbis,[30] appear to underlie the manner of Paul's presentation at a number of places in his letters. Rule one, *qal waḥomer* (light to heavy), is expressed, for example, in the argument of Rom. 5:15-21 that, if death is universal through one man's disobedience and sin has reigned as a result of Adam's act, much more (*πολλῷ μᾶλλον*) shall God's grace and the gift of grace supremely abound (*[ὑπερ]επερίσσευσεν*) and reign to life eternal by Jesus Christ.[31] It also undergirds his contrasts between the fall and the fulness of Israel in Rom. 11:12 and between the "ministry of death/condemnation" and the "ministry of the Spirit/righteousness" in II Cor. 3:7-18. The apostle can even reverse the procedure and, in demonstration of his thorough familiarity with this first logical and exegetical principle, argue *a maiori ad minus* in such passages as Rom. 5:6-9; 5:10; 8:32; 11:24 and I Cor. 6:2f.[32]

Rule two of Hillel, *gezerah shawah* (analogy), has been illustrated above in Paul's joining of various passages on the basis of a particular *Stichwort* or phrase. A further instance is to be found in Rom. 4:1-12, where Gen. 15:6 and Ps. 32:1f. are brought together on the basis of a contrast which possesses analogous features: God's imputation of righteousness to Abraham (*ἐλογίσθη αὐτῷ εἰς δικαιοσύνην*) and God's nonimputation of sin to the "blessed man" (*οὐ μὴ λογίσηται ἁμαρτίαν*). Rule five, *kelal upherat* (general and particular), can be seen in the apostle's discussion of love in action, in Rom. 13:8-10. After itemizing the last five Mosaic commandments, he goes on to say that "if there is any other commandment, it is summed up in this word: You shall love your neighbor as yourself."[33] Rule six, *kayoze bo*

[30] Cf. *supra*, pp. 33-35.

[31] Cf. particularly J. Jeremias, "Paulus als Hillelit," pp. 92-94, on Hillel's *middoth* in Paul's letters.

[32] Likewise Jesus is represented in Matt. 10:25 as reversing the *qal waḥomer*; see *supra*, p. 68.

[33] Rom. 13:9 (Lev. 19:18); cf. Gal. 5:14.

bemaqom 'aḥer (as found in another place), expresses itself in Paul's argument of Gal. 3:8ff. regarding the nature of God's promise to Abraham. Quoting Gen. 12:3, he speaks of Abraham as the immediate recipient and "all nations" as the ultimate beneficiaries. But by bringing Gen. 22:18 into the discussion, a passage generally similar to the first, he is enabled to speak of Abraham and his "seed" as the ones immediately in view, which allows him (as we'll note below) then to focus his attention on the meaning of "seed" (σπέρμα). Rule seven, *dabar halamed me'inyano* (context), is probably most aptly illustrated by Paul's observations in Rom. 4:10f. that Abraham was accounted righteous *before* he was circumcised and in Gal. 3:17 that the promise was confirmed by God four hundred and thirty years *before* the giving of the Mosaic law.

Paul also reflects his rabbinic training in certain of the themes he employs. I Cor. 10:1-4 is particularly significant here, with its reference to the Red Sea experience as a baptism and its explication of the rock that followed the Israelites in the wilderness. That Judaism understood the exodus as involving a baptism is implied in some of the discussions on proselyte baptism. Proselytes were required to be circumcised, baptized and offer their first sacrifice—and in that order, according to the Beth Hillel (whose ruling became dominant)—for "as your forefathers entered into the Covenant only by circumcision, immersion and the sprinkling of the blood, so shall they enter the Covenant only by circumcision, immersion and the sprinkling of the blood."[34] To the query, "But whence do we know the immersion?," the answer is given: "It is written, 'And Moses took the blood, and sprinkled it on the people' [Exod. 24:8], and there can be no sprinkling without immersion."[35] Probably, therefore, judging as well by the apostle's rather abrupt introduction of this episode into the argument as though it were self-evident, Paul is simply developing in a Christian fashion what he learned in catechism at the feet of Gamaliel; that is, that the legitimacy of

[34] B. Ker. 9a; cf. b. Yeb. 46a.
[35] B. Ker. 9a; b. Yeb. 46a reads: "and there is a tradition that there is no sprinkling without immersion."

proselyte baptism is defensible in terms of understanding the exodus as involving a baptism.[36] His statement that they were "all baptized unto Moses" (*πάντες εἰς τὸν Μωυσῆν ἐβαπτίσαντο*), that is, incorporated into that fellowship which God established with Moses as its chosen leader, is in keeping with Exod. 14:31: "and they believed in the Lord and in his servant Moses."[37]

Likewise, Paul's allusion to "the rock" (*ἡ πέτρα*) that followed the Israelites in the wilderness may have the rabbinic legend of a following rock, based on Num. 21:17 ("Rise up, O well; sing unto it!"), in mind.[38] In its developed form, the legend had the rock rolling along after the wanderers in the wilderness, providing all sorts of nourishment and services for the people.[39] Yet, as Ellis rightly points out, "it is quite difficult to determine the precise character of the fable in the first century; . . . the story grew erratically with each writer so as to preclude any definite classification at a given date, but it is probable that the first century version spoke only of a following stream of water."[40] A. J. Bandstra cogently argues that I Cor. 10:3f. rests not upon Num. 21:17 and the legend built upon that passage, but upon Deut. 32:1ff. with its references to the Lord being "the Rock," the Lord providing for his people in the wilderness by means of a "flinty rock," and "the Rock of his [God's] salvation."[41] Probably, Bandstra is right. Or, perhaps, some conflation of Num. 21:17 and Deut. 32:1ff. had already occurred in early Pharisaic circles, and was in the apostle's mind when writing his Corinthian converts.

[36] Cf. F. Gavin, *The Jewish Antecedents of the Christian Sacraments* (1969 repr.), pp. 26-58; J. Daniélou, *The Bible and the Liturgy* (1956), pp. 88ff.; J. Jeremias, "Paulus als Hillelit," pp. 90f.

[37] Cf. A. J. Bandstra, "Interpretation in I Corinthians 10:1-11," *CTJ*, VI (1971), p. 7.

[38] Cf. H. St.J. Thackeray, *Relation of St. Paul to Contemporary Jewish Thought*, pp. 205-212 (citing Targ. Onkelos on Num. 21); E. E. Ellis, *Paul's Use of the Old Testament*, pp. 66-70 (giving a synthetic reconstruction of the full legend based on a number of talmudic references); J. W. Doeve, *Jewish Hermeneutics in the Synoptic Gospels and Acts*, pp. 110f.

[39] Cf. E. E. Ellis, *Paul's Use of the Old Testament*, p. 67.

[40] *Ibid.*, p. 68.

[41] A. J. Bandstra, "Interpretation in I Corinthians 10:1-11," pp. 10-14.

But however the precise details are to be spelled out, it seems fairly certain that in speaking of Israel's baptism in the sea and of the rock that followed them in the wilderness, Paul was (1) recalling certain rabbinic treatments of the biblical narrative, and (2) reinterpreting them from the dual perspectives of corporate solidarity and messianic fulfilment in the person of Jesus of Nazareth. In so doing, he expressed the typically Christian conviction that "in the historical Christ-event the pattern of God's historical dealings with Israel in the exodus is brought to fulfillment and finds its focal point."[42]

In a few passages, Paul seems to be arguing *ad hominem* in typically rabbinic fashion from certain Jewish legends and developments on Old Testament personages and events. In Gal. 3:19f., for example, he picks up the widely disseminated notion that angels were instrumental in the giving of the Law at Sinai,[43] and insists that such a state of affairs really demonstrates the Law's basic inferiority rather than its superiority—for, as Judaism frankly confesses, the Law was mediated, whereas God's grace and promises are unilateral. In Gal. 4:29f. he employs the rabbinic theme of the persecution of Isaac by Ishmael,[44] turning it to his own purpose to argue that Christians, being persecuted, are evidently the spiritual descendants of Isaac, and should therefore "cast out" the Ishmaelian persecutors. In II Cor. 3:13-18 he points to the veil worn by Moses to cover the reflected radiance of his face, which covering Judaism took to be a symbol of the greatness of Moses and of the glory of the Mosaic legislation,[45] and rather ironically acknowledges that such a veil is still Israel's possession—sadly, serving now only as a blindfold of the eyes and the heart to God's greater glory in Jesus Christ. In each of these cases, however, the apostle seems to attach no necessary weight to the

[42] *Ibid.*, p. 7.
[43] Cf. the LXX translation of Deut. 33:2; Josephus, Antiq. XV. 5. 3 (136); Acts 7:53; Heb. 2:2.
[44] Stemming from Gen. R. 53:15, on Gen. 21:20. Cf. H. St.J. Thackeray, *Relation of St. Paul to Contemporary Jewish Thought*, pp. 212-15.
[45] Exod. 34:33: "When Moses was done speaking to them, he put a veil on his face."

particular notion involved, but rather employs them to his own advantage in *ad hominem* fashion.[46]

In the majority of his Old Testament citations, Paul adheres to the original sense of the passage. Or, if he extends it, it is possible to understand his rationale if we grant him the Jewish presuppositions of "corporate solidarity" and "historical correspondences" and the Christian presuppositions of "eschatological fulfilment" and "messianic presence."[47] In three instances, however, he appears to be quoting Scripture quite without regard to the original context; and many have classed these as examples of either his own personal ingenuity or rabbinic ingenuity, or both.

The first such passage is Rom. 10:6-8, where what was said by Moses regarding the nearness of the Law is used by Paul of the Gospel against the Law. The wording of Deut. 30:12-14 is either quoted or employed somewhat proverbially:

> The righteousness which is by faith speaks in this manner: *Do not say* in your heart, "*Who will ascend into heaven?*"—that is, to bring Christ down—or "*Who will descend into the abyss*?"—that is, to bring Christ up from the dead. But what does it say? *The word is near you, in your mouth and in your heart*—that is, the word of faith which we preach.[48]

In their almost classic commentary on the letter to the Romans, W. Sanday and A. C. Headlam have treated the passage as a proverbial allusion rather than a quotation, arguing that:

> (1) The context of the passage shows that there is no stress laid on the fact that the O.T. is being quoted. The object of the argument is to describe the characteristics of δικαιοσύνη ἐκ πίστεως, not to show how it can be proved from the O.T.
> (2) The Apostle carefully and pointedly avoids appealing to Scripture, altering his mode of citation from that employed in the previous verse. . . .

[46] Perhaps rabbinic legends are also involved to some extent in II Cor. 11:3, on Eve being beguiled by the subtlety of Satan (but not Adam [?]), and in II Tim. 3:8, on Jannes and Jambres; cf. H. St.J. Thackeray, *Relation of St. Paul to Contemporary Jewish Thought*, pp. 52-55, 215-221.
[47] Cf. *supra*, pp. 93-95.
[48] Italics indicate the biblical language.

(3) The quotation is singularly inexact. An ordinary reader fairly well acquainted with the O.T. would feel that the language had a familiar ring, but could not count it as a quotation.
(4) The words had certainly become proverbial, and many instances of them so used have been quoted [citing Philo, Quod Omnis Prob. Liber 10; IV Ezra 4:8; Baruch 3:29f.; Jubilees 24:32; Amos 9:2].
(5) St. Paul certainly elsewhere uses the words of Scripture in order to express his meaning in familiar language, cf. ver. 18; xi. 1.[49]

They therefore concluded: "For these reasons it seems probable that here the Apostle does not intend to base any argument on the quotation from the O.T., but only selects the language as being familiar, suitable, and proverbial, in order to express what he wishes to say."[50]

It is, of course, extremely difficult to determine the precise intent of any author at the time of his writing. Yet, probably, Sanday and Headlam are at least generally correct in viewing Paul's purpose here to be more a proverbial use of Scripture than an explicit quotation. We have already noted that his introductory formula evidences a greater degree of variation than one would expect for a Pauline quotation, focusing as it does upon "the righteousness which is by faith" as doing the speaking rather than the Scriptures, the Law or God.[51] The passage in Paul's day, as Sanday and Headlam have pointed out, was already somewhat proverbial and came to expression in a number of contexts.[52] And the fact that in I Cor. 15:32 Paul quotes Isa. 22:13 in quite a proverbial fashion, joining it to a Gentile proverb in I Cor. 15:33, lends some support to the suggestion that he may have done likewise with Deut. 30:12-14 here. The words, of course, even though possibly proverbial in Paul's day, are taken from Scripture and can therefore be considered something of a biblical quotation. And it is to these words that the apostle assigns a Christo-

[49] W. Sanday and A. C. Headlam, *The Epistle to the Romans*, 5th ed. (1902), p. 289.
[50] *Ibid.*; cf. also H. St.J. Thackeray, *Relation of St. Paul to Contemporary Jewish Thought*, pp. 187f.
[51] Cf. *supra*, p. 114.
[52] Cf. also Deut. R. 8.6, which may, however, be a rabbinic rebuttal to Paul. Thackeray also cites Targ. Jer. I on Deut. 30:12-14: "For the word is nigh you *in your schools*" (italics his).

logical significance, entering into a running commentary in the form of a short midrash (the phrase τοῦτ' ἔστιν being employed to introduce the three explications)[53] and selecting that form of the saying which best suited his purpose.[54] But rather than being engaged in biblical exegesis *per se*, he seems more here to be turning a proverbial maxim to his own use and setting it into what he believes to be a more appropriate setting.

A second place where Paul is often viewed as departing from the original meaning of a text and twisting it to his own design is in Gal. 3:16, where the promise of God to Abraham and to his "seed" (זרע, σπέρμα) is applied to Christ.[55] The term "seed" in the Abrahamic promise is a generic singular, and refers to the posterity of Abraham as an entity. Jews, of course, prided themselves on being descendants of Abraham, and therefore on being recipients of the promises made to Abraham. The Targums, in fact, take this corporate understanding of the promise so much for granted that they uniformly and unequivocally cast the expression into the plural: "and to your sons"—which plural may have had some significance for the specific form of Paul's polemic.[56] Paul, however, for whom physical descent was no guarantee of spiritual relationship,[57] and with a possible swipe at the targumic plural, argues that Christ is the "seed" in view in the Abrahamic covenant (ὅς ἐστιν Χριστός) and goes on to speak of Christ's own as sharing in the promises of that covenant as Abraham's legitimate

[53] The presence of τοῦτ'ἔστιν in Rom. 10:6-8 is sometimes cited as a pesher motif in Paul. In reality, however, it is just a common midrashic explication (cf., e.g., b. Ber. 6a; Sifre Num. 139; Rom. 9:8; Heb. 2:14; 7:5; 10:20).

[54] Neither the MT nor the LXX has, "Who will descend into the abyss?" Rather, they read, "Who will go over the sea for us?" Perhaps the apostle picked up the text-form he quotes from the early Church, for the term ἄβυσσος could mean (1) the depths of the sea, (2) the grave, or (3) the underworld—which would allow the employment of a κατάβασις-ἀνάβασις theme in the early Church (see my *Christology of Early Jewish Christianity*, p. 60).

[55] Cf. Gen. 12:7; 13:15; 15:18; 17:7f.; 22:17f.; 24:7.

[56] Cf. F. Pereira, "The Galatian Controversy in the Light of the Targums," *IJT*, XX (1971), p. 27.

[57] Cf. Rom. 9:6b-7a: "For they are not all Israel who are of Israel. Neither because they are the seed of Abraham are they all children [of Abraham]."

"seed."[58] The apostle is not just forcing a generic singular into a specific mold, though D. Daube has shown how such an artificial procedure could have been possible for one trained in rabbinic exegetical methods.[59] Rather, he is invoking a corporate solidarity understanding of the promise to Abraham wherein the Messiah, as the true descendant of Abraham and the true representative of his people, and the Messiah's elect ones, as sharers in his experiences and his benefits, are seen as the legitimate inheritors of God's promises.[60] The Judaizers at Galatia may have been proclaiming that the promises were made to Abraham and to his "seed" the nation (a generic singular), or, possibly, as Daube suggests, to Abraham and to his "seed" Isaac (a specific singular);[61] and some of Paul's converts may have been taken in by their exposition. But whatever the precise form of the heresy afflicting Christians at Galatia, Paul "deliberately furnishes them with a deeper application" of the promises of God made to Abraham and to his "seed."[62]

The third instance where Paul appears to depart from the meaning of a passage he cites is in Eph. 4:8, quoting Ps. 68:18. As Paul employs the verse, the reading is "he gave gifts to men" (*ἔδωκεν δόματα τοῖς ἀνθρώποις*), which alters both the MT and LXX text-forms by changing the second person singular to the third person singular and substituting for "take" or "receive" (MT לקחת, LXX *ἔλαβες*) the idea of "give" or "apportion" (*ἔδωκεν*). The change of person might not be very significant, but the substitution of "gave" for "received" entirely reverses the idea of the passage in the Hebrew and Greek Bibles. That this is neither an incidental nor an accidental variation is evidenced in that the apostle builds on this idea of Christ giving gifts to men in v. 11, and without this reading his argument would have been considerably truncated—if not impossible altogether.

One can, of course, argue that Paul is here creating a

[58] Gal. 3:29.
[59] D. Daube, *The New Testament and Rabbinic Judaism*, pp. 440-44.
[60] Cf. C. A. A. Scott, *Christianity According to St. Paul* (1927), pp. 154f., on the application of the concept of solidarity at this point.
[61] D. Daube, *The New Testament and Rabbinic Judaism*, p. 440.
[62] *Ibid.*, p. 441.

text-form to support his conclusions. Knowing the proper meaning of the Old Testament as both a man "in Christ" and an apostle, he may have felt free to bring specific readings of the Old Testament into line with what he knew to be true as Christ's apostle. But recourse to such an explanation seems hardly necessary, since a targumic rendering of this passage has the verb חלק ("to give") rather than לקח ("to take"), and the Peshitta later carried this on in its translation.[63] In all likelihood, therefore, Paul is employing in Eph. 4:8 a variant reading then extant of the text of Ps. 68:18 at his disposal—one which we know from the targumic traditions, and which presumably antedated the apostle's ministry. Such a variant reading may well have been somewhat traditional in Paul's day, either in Palestinian Judaism or in the early Church. And upon this text he employs a Jewish type of argument based on inference—rabbinic, indeed, but not specifically rabbinic[64] —in support of the incarnation and ascension of Christ. But both the citation and the almost parenthetical comments that follow it are given in such a manner as to suggest that they were commonly assumed, lending some support to the idea that both were widely accepted as being traditional within at least early Christianity, and should not therefore be considered strictly Pauline creations. In picking up these (possibly) traditional elements, the apostle was able to bridge the gap in his argument between "the gift of Christ" in v. 7 and the "gifts" of Christ elaborated in vv. 11ff.

We have dealt very briefly with the content of Paul's biblical citations. All we have really attempted to do was to illustrate his literalist and midrashic treatments of Scripture. But enough has been given to suggest that midrashic exegetical methods are prominent in the Pauline letters. In fact, it

[63] On a targumic basis for the text of Eph. 4:8, see H. St.J. Thackeray, *Relation of St. Paul to Contemporary Jewish Thought*, p. 182; G. B. Caird, "The Descent of Christ in Ephesians 4, 7-11," *Studia Evangelica*, II, ed. F. L. Cross (1964), pp. 540f.; M. Wilcox, *The Semitisms of Acts*, p. 25 (citing W. C. van Unnik). Conversely, crediting the form of the text to *ad hoc* Christian theologizing, see particularly B. Lindars, *New Testament Apologetic*, pp. 52-56.

[64] G. B. Caird speaks of Paul "Christianizing the Rabbinic exegesis of the Pentecostal psalm" ("The Descent of Christ in Ephesians 4, 7-11," p. 543, see also pp. 541-45).

is midrashic exegesis more than pesher or allegorical exegesis that characterizes the apostle's hermeneutical procedures. Where he speaks to a Judaizing problem in the Church or to issues having Jewish nuances, he sometimes employs midrashic exegesis in an *ad hominem* fashion. But even apart from the catalyst of Jewish polemics, Paul's basic thought patterns and interpretive procedures were those of first-century Pharisaism. The dictum of Jeremias regarding the apostle's biblical interpretation seems fully justified: "Paulus Hillelit war."[65]

ALLEGORICAL INTERPRETATIONS

In two passages Paul goes beyond the limits of midrashic exegesis and interprets the Old Testament allegorically,[66] subordinating the literal sense and elaborating an additional meaning which spoke to the situation addressed. In I Cor. 9:9f. he seems to leave the primary meaning of the injunction in Deut. 25:4, "You shall not muzzle the ox that threshes" (οὐ κημώσεις βοῦν ἀλοῶντα), to insist that these words were written for a reason not obvious in the passage itself. And in Gal. 4:21-31 he goes beyond the Genesis account of the relations between Hagar and Sarah to stress a hidden and symbolic meaning.

I Cor. 9:9f. is certainly allegorical. But the degree of allegorical interpretation involved largely depends upon the meaning assigned to πάντως. If, as Thackeray long ago pointed out, we translate it as "altogether" or "entirely," the literal meaning of the passage in Paul's usage is apparently given up. But if we take it to mean something like "undoubtedly," as its usage elsewhere in the writings of Paul and Luke supports,[67] then the passage reads: "Did he

[65] J. Jeremias, "Paulus als Hillelit," p. 89.

[66] Rejecting H. St.J. Thackeray's inclusion of I Cor. 10:1-11 among the Pauline allegorical treatments, though he speaks only of the apostle's "typical" use of the Old Testament (*Relation of St. Paul to Contemporary Jewish Thought*, p. 195), and K. J. Woollcombe's inclusion of I Cor. 5:6-8 ("Biblical Origins and Patristic Development of Typology," *Essays on Typology* [1957], p. 55).

[67] Cf. Luke 4:23; Acts 18:21; 21:22; 28:4; Rom. 3:9; I Cor. 5:10; 9:22; 16:12. Thackeray's comment on these verses is pertinent: "There is no support here for the meaning 'altogether', i.e. for our sakes, 'to the exclusion of all others' " (*op. cit.*, p. 194n).

say it, as doubtless he did, for our sake? For our sake it was written!" Interpreting it thus, "the literal sense will be subordinated but not rejected."[68] The argument then becomes a form of the rabbinic *qal waḥomer* (light to heavy), though in that it so pointedly subordinates the literal meaning of the injunction it passes over into the area of the allegorical.

O. Michel insists, echoing sentiments of the Antiochian fathers in their reactions to Alexandrian allegorical extremes, that in Gal. 4:24 Paul has misrepresented himself in saying "these things are allegorical utterances," for here "Paulus denkt mehr typologisch als allegorisch im eigentlichen Sinne."[69] But accepting the definition of typology as "linkages between events, persons, or things *within the historical framework of revelation*," and of allegorical interpretation as "the search for a secondary and hidden meaning underlying the primary and obvious meaning of a narrative,"[70] we must reject the view that Hagar and Sarah are here treated merely typologically. Allegorical interpretation has entered in. In fact, Gal. 4:21-31 is a highly allegorical representation of Old Testament history. While it is true that the apostle begins with the historical situation, he definitely goes beyond the literal and primary sense of the narrative to insist upon hidden and symbolic meanings in the words.

We noted earlier that allegorical exegesis played a part in all the known branches of first-century Judaism—dominantly in the writings of Philo, more mildly in Pharisaic and sectarian exegetical practice.[71] And in his two allegorical treatments, Paul reflects this general Jewish background. But what needs to be noted as well, particularly in regard to the Hagar-Sarah treatment, is the seemingly circumstantial factor in the apostle's employment of the method. E. D. Burton pointed out that Paul's argument in Gal. 4:21-31 is "a supplementary argument" which was invoked "appar-

[68] *Ibid.*, p. 194; see also E. E. Ellis, *Paul's Use of the Old Testament*, p. 47.
[69] O. Michel, *Paulus und seine Bibel*, p. 110.
[70] K. J. Woollcombe, "The Biblical Origins and Patristic Development of Typology," *Essays on Typology*, p. 40 (italics his).
[71] Cf. *supra*, pp. 45-48.

ently as an after-thought" to buttress his more experiential, biblical and personal appeals of 3:1–4:20.[72] And H. St.J. Thackeray has observed that "the arguments by which he tried to convince his opponents of the true meaning of the O.T. as pointing forward to Christ, are those which they would themselves have employed for another purpose; and to some extent we need not doubt that they were selected for that very reason."[73]

It would not be difficult to postulate that throughout the letter to the Galatians, Paul is interacting with a typically rabbinic view that truth presents itself in two guises, the first an elemental form and the second a developed,[74] and that he is counteracting in particular the Judaizers' application of this Jewish motif which argued in effect that Paul's teaching is the elemental while theirs is the developed. The Judaizers' argumentation could very well have run along the following lines: (1) while Paul directed the Galatians to Gen. 15:6, they must realize that the developed form of God's covenant with Abraham appears in Gen. 17:4-14, with its requirement of circumcision emphatically expressed in vv. 10-14; (2) while Paul spoke of Abraham, the full development of Israel's religious laws are spelled out by Moses; (3) while Paul spoke of the promises of the Gospel, the promises were in actuality made to Abraham and to his "seed," which means the nation; and (4) while Paul assured his converts that by accepting the Gospel they became identified with the son of Abraham, the question must be raised as to which son they represented, for Abraham had two sons—the first was Ishmael, and only later was Isaac born. To this line of argumentation, as we have seen, Paul responds by asserting that Christ and Christ's own are Abraham's true "seed."[75] He goes on to insist that the covenant with Abraham was confirmed by God (*προκεκυρωμένην ὑπὸ τοῦ θεοῦ*) four hundred and thirty years before the giving of the Mosaic law, and having been con-

[72] E. D. Burton, *The Epistle to the Galatians* (1921), pp. 251f.
[73] H. St.J. Thackeray, *Relation of St. Paul to Contemporary Jewish Thought*, p. 203.
[74] Cf. D. Daube, "Public Retort and Private Explanation," *The New Testament and Rabbinic Judaism*, pp. 141-150.
[75] Cf. *supra*, pp. 123f. on Gal. 3:16, 29.

firmed it can neither be annulled nor added to by later developments.[76] And in regard to the claim that his Gospel represents an Ishmaelian form of truth, he "indeed" (note the two uses of μέν in vv. 23f.) can allegorize as well: it is Hagar, who has contacts with Mt. Sinai (from whence came the Law that the Judaizers so extol), that should be associated with (συνστοιχεῖ, "it belongs to the same row or column with") the present Jerusalem, which explains the bondage of Jerusalem and her emissaries; while it is Sarah, Isaac and spiritual Jerusalem who are involved in the promises of God, and we are children of promise in association with them.[77] Such a reconstruction of Paul's argument is admittedly somewhat conjectural. Yet it is highly plausible. And it serves to point up the suggestion that, while I Cor. 9:9f. portrays a mild allegorical exegesis such as was undoubtedly part-and-parcel of the apostle's exegetical equipment, Gal. 4:21-31 may very well represent an extreme form of Palestinian allegorical interpretation that was triggered by polemic debate and is strongly circumstantial and *ad hominem*.

PESHER INTERPRETATIONS

But is there any evidence of a pesher treatment of the Old Testament by Paul? Three matters warrant comment here: (1) textual deviations, (2) the "this is that" fulfilment motif, and (3) a *rāz-pesher* understanding of the prophetic message.

Earle Ellis has argued that about twenty of the Pauline quotations evidence a pesher type molding of the biblical text in which "the variation seems to be a deliberate adaptation to the NT context; in some cases the alteration has a definite bearing on the interpretation of the passage."[78] The problem, of course, is to what extent these deviations are (1) explainable on the basis of contemporary variants now extinct and not *ad hoc* creations, and (2) distinctive to pesher exegesis and not also true of rabbinic midrashic treatments.

[76] Gal. 3:15-18.
[77] Gal. 4:22-28.
[78] E. E. Ellis, *Paul's Use of the Old Testament*, p. 144.

In the present state of our knowledge regarding early textual traditions, definiteness on the first issue is manifestly impossible. And opinions regarding the second are a matter of judgment. Ellis, following Stendahl's handling of similar phenomena in Matthew's Gospel, tends to view many of these as *ad hoc* creations of Paul in the explication of his pesher approach to Scripture. Yet, significantly I believe, Ellis points out as well that what he calls "the pesher method" is "not used extensively in Paul's quotations," and that where it does occur "it often appears to go behind the Greek to reflect an interpretation of the Hebrew ur-text"; moreover, "some of the most significant instances appear to point back to a pre-Pauline usage in the early Church."[79]

Whether it be judged a process of selection among variants or the creation of interpretive readings—and after deducting the maximum of renderings that could stem from a tradition within the early Church—the conclusion is nevertheless inevitable that Paul felt somewhat free in his handling of the Old Testament text as we know it. T. W. Manson has rightly characterized the apostle at this point, as well as the Jerusalem apostles, in saying:

> The meaning of the text was of primary importance; and they seem to have had greater confidence than we moderns in their ability to find it. Once found it became a clear duty to express it; and accurate reproduction of the traditional wording of the Divine oracles took second place to publication of what was held to be their essential meaning and immediate application.[80]

But the question must be asked, Is this true of pesher exegesis only, or does it also find parallels in rabbinic midrash as well? I would suggest that pesher interpretation is somewhat wrongly understood if it is defined only on the basis of deviations in text-form, for rabbinic midrash differs more quantitatively than qualitatively from pesher at this point.

In regard to the "this is that" fulfilment motif, Paul's letters indicate that he used it very sparingly. In Gal. 5:14

[79] *Ibid.*, p. 146. Probable pre-Pauline text-forms include Rom. 12:19; I Cor. 14:21; 15:45; II Cor. 6:16ff.; Eph. 4:8.
[80] T. W. Manson, "The Argument from Prophecy," *JTS*, LXVI (1945), pp. 135f.

he speaks of all the Law being fulfilled (πεπλήρωται) in the precis of Lev. 19:18: "You shall love your neighbor as yourself." But that is hardly an eschatological use of the expression, and therefore not of pertinence here.[81] In I Cor. 15:3-5 he twice employs the phrase "according to the scriptures." But the context and manner of citation suggest that Paul is here employing a formula of earlier Christians who themselves made use of the fulfilment theme. His inclusion of their words indicates his agreement, but the verbal expression itself probably did not originate with him. In II Cor. 6:2 he asserts that the "acceptable time" and "the day of salvation" spoken of in Isa. 49:8 are upon us "now," and in Gal. 4:4 he speaks of "the fulness of time" taking place in God's sending of his Son, both passages reflecting his consciousness of living in the days of eschatological consummation. But only in his address in the synagogue at Antioch of Pisidia, as recorded in Acts 13:16-41, is Paul represented as making explicit use of the fulfilment theme. And that, of course, is directed to a Jewish audience. It seems, therefore, that Paul's habit in his Gentile mission was not a demonstration of eschatological fulfilment in any explicit manner. Evidently such a procedure would carry little weight with those unaccustomed to thinking in terms of historical continuity and unschooled in the Old Testament.

In regard to the *rāz-pesher* understanding of the prophetic message, F. F. Bruce has pointed out that "in the Greek versions of the Septuagint and Theodotion, this term *rāz*, wherever it occurs in Daniel, is represented by *mystērion*." And he further suggests that "it is helpful to bear this in mind when we meet the word *mystērion* in the Greek New Testament."[82] Now Paul employs μυστήριον some twenty times, and in a number of ways. But in three instances in his use of the term he seems to be definitely involving himself in a *rāz-pesher* understanding of the unfolding of redemptive history:

1. In the doxology of Rom. 16:25-27, where he identifies "my gospel" as being "the preaching of Jesus Christ according to the revelation of the mystery which was kept secret for long ages (χρόνοις αἰωνίοις), but now is disclosed

[81] Note a similar use of τελειόω in Jas. 2:8; cf. *infra*, p. 191.
[82] F. F. Bruce, *Biblical Exegesis in the Qumran Texts*, p. 8.

and through the prophetic writings is made known to all nations."[83]

2. In Col. 1:26f., where he mentions "the mystery hidden for ages and generations but now made manifest to his saints."

3. In Eph. 3:1-11, where he speaks of "the mystery" which was "made known to me by revelation" and "which was not made known to the sons of men in other generations as it has now been revealed to his holy apostles and prophets by the Spirit"—"the mystery hidden for ages in God who created all things."

What is this "mystery"? From his reference to "my gospel" in Rom. 16:25 and his insistence in Gal. 1:11ff. that his gospel came to him by means of "a revelation of Jesus Christ," we may take it that it is something which he considered uniquely his. And this consciousness of distinction comes to expression again in Eph. 3:6-8, where he explicitly associates the mystery to which he had been given the interpretive key with his Gentile ministry and the equality of Gentile and Jew before God. Evidently, then, Paul's gospel, which had been given by revelation, was not a gospel that differed in kerygmatic content from that of the early Church, but a gospel that included a new understanding of the pattern of redemptive history in these final days involving the legitimacy of a direct approach to Gentiles and the recognition of the equality of Jew and Gentile before God.

Paul could not claim the usual apostolic qualifications, as expressed in John 15:27 and Acts 1:21f. His understanding of the Old Testament could not be directly related to the teaching and example of the historic Jesus. And he was dependent upon the early Church for much in the Christian tradition, as his letters frankly indicate. But he had been confronted by the exalted Lord, had been directly commissioned an apostle by Jesus himself, and considered that he had been given the key to the pattern of redemptive history in the present age. The Jerusalem apostles had the key to many of the prophetic mysteries, but he had been entrusted with a pesher that was uniquely his. Together, they combined to enhance the fulness of the Gospel.

[83] Understanding the *καί* of v. 25 to be explicative.

V: THE EVANGELISTS AND THE OLD TESTAMENT

No discussion need be undertaken regarding what should be included among the Evangelists' writings. The four Gospels are readily identifiable, and have been since at least the early second century. And while textual questions are legitimately raised in regard to the inclusion or exclusion of certain units within the Gospels, none of these affects the discussion with which we are here concerned. Nor would it be profitable at this point to enter into the complex set of questions regarding the nature of the Gospel materials generally or of the individual Gospels in particular. An understanding of the Evangelists' own use of Scripture has a greater influence on conclusions regarding such larger questions than any general observations concerning the nature of the Gospels have upon the issues at hand.

It is the thesis of this chapter that the treatment of the Old Testament by the Evangelists themselves (as distinguished from that of Jesus and their common narrative)—particularly by Matthew and John—represents a distinctive employment of biblical material. While there are definite lines of continuity with both Jewish and Christian exegetical presuppositions and practices, the Gospels of Matthew and of John exhibit a particular strand of exegesis within early Christian proclamation and evidence a development in that strand over what we have seen so far in the apostolic period. It is to these exegetical presuppositions and practices, together with their developments, that we now turn.

THE PHENOMENA OF THE QUOTATIONS

The Evangelists' own use of the Old Testament is reflected to some extent in their arrangement of their narratives (where they parallel certain Old Testament features), in their emphases (where they highlight certain Old Testament themes), and in their employment of biblical language. But it is most aptly seen in their editorial comments where they employ, at times and to varying degrees, biblical material. Some arbitrariness of classification is, of course, inevitable in any listing of biblical quotations apart from allusions. Nevertheless, the following twenty-two citations form the basis for the present investigation.[1]

I. Quotations occurring in Mark's editorial comments:

1. Mark 1:2f. (Mal. 3:1; Isa. 40:3)—I.F.: "as it is written (*καθὼς γέγραπται*) in Isaiah the prophet."

II. Quotations occurring in Matthew's editorial comments:

2. Matt. 1:23 (Isa. 7:14)—I.F.: "that the word of the Lord by the prophet might be fulfilled (*ἵνα πληρωθῇ*), saying."
3. Matt. 2:15 (Hos. 11:1)—I.F.: "that the word of the Lord by the prophet might be fulfilled (*ἵνα πληρωθῇ*), saying."
4. Matt. 2:18 (Jer. 31:15 [LXX=38:15])—I.F.: "then was fulfilled (*τότε ἐπληρώθη*) the word by Jeremiah the prophet, saying."
5. Matt. 2:23 (probably Judg. 13:5-7; 16:17)—I.F.: "that the word by the prophets might be fulfilled (*ὅπως πληρωθῇ*), that."
6. Matt. 3:3 (Isa. 40:3)—I.F.: "for this is the one spoken of by Isaiah the prophet, saying."
7. Matt. 4:15f. (Isa. 9:1f. [MT & LXX=8:23–9:1])—I.F.: "that the word by Isaiah the prophet might be fulfilled (*ἵνα πληρωθῇ*), saying."
8. Matt. 8:17 (Isa. 53:4)—I.F.: "that the word by Isaiah the prophet might be fulfilled (*ὅπως πληρωθῇ*), saying."
9. Matt. 12:18-21 (Isa. 42:1-4)—I.F.: "that the word by Isaiah the prophet might be fulfilled (*ἵνα πληρωθῇ*), saying."
10. Matt. 13:35 (Ps. 78:2 [LXX=77:2])—I.F.: "that the word by the prophet might be fulfilled (*ὅπως πληρωθῇ*), saying."

[1] Only the major source or sources are listed, without the inclusion of possible parallels.

11. Matt. 21:5 (Isa. 62:11; Zech. 9:9)—I.F.: "that the word by the prophet might be fulfilled (ἵνα πληρωθῇ), saying."
12. Matt. 27:9f. (Zech. 11:12f.; Jer. 18:1f.; 32:6-9)—I.F.: "then was fulfilled (τότε ἐπληρώθη) the word by Jeremiah the prophet, saying."

III. Quotations occurring in Luke's editorial comments:

13. Luke 2:23 (Exod. 13:2, 12)—I.F.: "as it is written (καθὼς γέγραπται) in the law of the Lord."
14. Luke 2:24 (Lev. 12:8)—I.F.: "according to what is said (κατὰ τὸ εἰρημένον) in the law of the Lord."
15. Luke 3:4-6 (Isa. 40:3-5)—I.F.: "as it is written (ὡς γέγραπται) in the book of the words of Isaiah the prophet."

IV. Quotations occurring in John's editorial comments:

16. John 2:17 (Ps. 69:9 [MT=69:10; LXX=68:10])—I.F.: "it is written" (γεγραμμένον ἐστίν).
17. John 12:15 (Zech. 9:9, possibly Isa. 40:9)—I.F.: "as it is written" (καθώς ἐστιν γεγραμμένον).
18. John 12:38 (Isa. 53:1)—I.F.: "that the word of Isaiah the prophet might be fulfilled (ἵνα πληρωθῇ), which said."
19. John 12:40 (Isa. 6:9f.)—I.F.: "again Isaiah said."
20. John 19:24 (Ps. 22:18 [MT=22:19; LXX=21:19])—I.F.: "that the scripture might be fulfilled (ἵνα πληρωθῇ), which says."[2]
21. John 19:36 (probably Ps. 34:20, perhaps also Exod. 12:46; Num. 9:12)—I.F.: "that the scripture might be fulfilled" (ἵνα πληρωθῇ).
22. John 19:37 (Zech. 12:10)—I.F.: "again another scripture says."

What strikes one immediately in surveying the phenomena of the quotations in the editorial comments of the Evangelists is the repeated employment by Matthew and John of an introductory formula stressing fulfilment. Mark and Luke introduce their few citations by the standard "it is written" or "according to what is said." But in ten of Matthew's eleven quotations and four of John's seven (considering 12:40 as covered by the formula to 12:38), a

[2] The citation of Ps. 22:18 is included only here, and not also at the end of Matt. 27:35 where it has weak textual support.

"fulfilment formula" introduces the biblical wording: usually ἵνα πληρωθῇ, three times ὅπως πληρωθῇ, and twice τότε ἐπληρώθη. Also noteworthy is that in Matthew's Gospel and John's Gospel biblical quotations have an important place in the presentation of the argument, whereas Mark and Luke employ biblical citations in their editorial comments hardly at all, and then only in a rather obvious fashion. These two features of (1) stress on eschatological fulfilment and (2) greater frequency of biblical citations in the First and Fourth Gospels can be compared to the pattern we've seen in the preaching of the earliest Christians and in the letters of Paul.[3] And they lend some support to the claim that Matthew and John among the four Gospels were written to Jewish Christians and/or Jews, for whom their approach would be understandable and pertinent.[4]

Also of significance in regard to the rather formal features of the Evangelists' citations is that the text of Matthew's own eleven quotations generally reflects a semitic influence. Whereas the septuagintal nature of the biblical materials in Mark, Luke and the common narrative in Matthew comes across quite clearly, the "fulfilment formulae" quotations of Matthew deviate from the LXX throughout. About half of Matthew's citations, in fact, vary in text-form from all known versions, whether Greek, Hebrew or Aramaic; though, at the same time, they reflect influences from one or more of these traditions.[5] Four of the quotations

[3] Cf. *supra*, pp. 96, 112.

[4] W. C. van Unnik has suggested that the reason for John's less frequent use of the Old Testament in his argument, as compared to the frequency found in Matthew (also Hebrews), may be because John wrote to the unconverted, for whom an overabundance of biblical citations would possibly fail to carry conviction: "Helpful though that proved in some cases, especially for those already convinced, the man who used these testimonies in debate with the unbelievers was met by completely different explanations of the same texts from the side of his opponents and could hear the reproach: 'All the words of the prophecy which, Sir, you adduce, are ambiguous and contain nothing decisive in proof of your argument' (Dial. 51. 1)" ("The Purpose of St. John's Gospel," *Studia Evangelica*, I, ed. K. Aland [1959], p. 399). The possibility of diametrically opposed treatments of the prophets on the part of believers and unbelievers is acknowledged in John 7:41-43.

[5] For a detailed treatment of the textual variations in the formula quotations of Matthew, see K. Stendahl, *School of St. Matthew*, pp. 97-126.

would have made no sense had the LXX text been employed (2:15; 4:15f.; 8:17; 27:9); and in six of the other cases, the LXX reading would have served satisfactorily but it was not used (1:23; 2:18; 3:3; 12:18-21; 13:35; 21:5). The inability to locate readily the passage in mind in Matt. 2:23, "he shall be called a Ναζωραῖος," only emphasizes the extent of textual variation in Matthew's usage. The texts of John's quotations evidence less deviation from known versions than do those of Matthew. The citations of 12:38 and 19:24 are exact reproductions of the LXX, and that of 2:17 differs only in the tense of the verb—probably an inevitable alteration in recasting a historical type into prophecy. The readings of 12:15; 12:40 and 19:36 are apparently paraphrastic variations of the LXX which have been influenced by the MT. And J. de Waard has shown that the text of 12:40 closely parallels the Qumran reading in 1QIs[a].[6] Only in 19:37 is there deviation of such a type as to preclude an explanation along the lines of paraphrase or extant variant. This may be an *ad hoc* creation, or it may reflect a textual tradition presently unknown. As with the similar phenomena found in the quotations of the Dead Sea texts, of Jesus, of the early Christian preaching, and of Paul,[7] our evidence, however, is insufficient to make any final determination on this point.

THE QUOTATIONS OF MARK AND LUKE

The use of the Old Testament in Mark's Gospel has proven difficult to isolate and characterize. On the one hand, Austin Farrer has interpreted the Gospel as built upon biblical typology throughout[8] and Ulrich Mauser finds the wilderness theme undergirding Mark's entire presentation,[9] while on the other hand, Alfred Suhl, explicating the position of Willi Marxsen, has denied altogether any promise-fulfilment

[6] J. de Waard, *Comparative Study of the Old Testament Text in the Dead Sea Scrolls and in the New Testament*, pp. 6-8, 82f. Cf. K. Stendahl, *School of St. Matthew*, p. 131, n. 2. This is also true for the quotation attributed to Jesus in John 13:18.
[7] Cf. *supra*, pp. 40, 74f., 88f., 113f.
[8] A. Farrer, *A Study in St. Mark* (1951).
[9] U. Mauser, *Christ in the Wilderness: The Wilderness Theme in the Second Gospel and its Basis in the Biblical Tradition* (ET 1963).

schema or interest in building upon Old Testament themes in the Second Gospel.[10] But both the attempt to make Mark something of a Jewish Christian midrash and the denial to Mark of any interest in the same are extreme positions, and have been rightly recognized so of late.[11] Yet it is true that in his editorial comments, as distinguished from his common narrative, Mark is very reserved in his explicit use of the Old Testament, citing only Mal. 3:1 and Isa. 40:3 in Mark 1:2f.

The Gospel opens on a fulfilment theme, declaring that "the beginning of the gospel of Jesus Christ" (ἀρχὴ τοῦ εὐαγγελίου Ἰησοῦ Χριστοῦ) has to do with the fulfilment of the prophecies of Mal. 3:1 and Isa. 40:3 in the ministry of John the Baptist. The two passages are brought together in a midrashic fashion on the basis of their common expression "prepare the way" (κατασκευάσει/ἑτοιμάσατε τὴν ὁδόν),[12] with both passages accepted widely within Judaism and Christianity as being messianically relevant. The ascription of both passages to Isaiah alone (καθὼς γέγραπται ἐν τῷ Ἠσαίᾳ τῷ προφήτῃ) probably stems from a testimonia collection, existing either within Judaism generally or in the early Church in particular, wherein composite citations or multiple passages were credited to the more prominent prophet in the listing.[13]

What we have in Mark's one conflated quotation are two passages of obvious messianic relevance which seem to have

[10] A. Suhl, *Die Funktion der alttestamentlichen Zitate und Anspielungen im Markus-evangelium* (1965); cf. W. Marxsen's stress on the dominance in Mark's thought of parousia imminence over a promise-fulfilment scheme, in *Mark the Evangelist* (ET 1969).

[11] On the first, see E. Best, *The Temptation and the Passion: The Marcan Soteriology* (1965), pp. 25ff.; on the second, H. Anderson, "The Old Testament in Mark's Gospel," *The Use of the Old Testament in the New and Other Essays*, ed. J. M. Efird (1972), pp. 280-306.

[12] The two texts both read פנה־דרך in the MT. The LXX translates the verb of Mal. 3:1 as a qal (επιβλέψεται) while the New Testament takes it as a piel, which suggests something of a semitic milieu for the joining of these two verses, whether Jewish or Jewish Christian.

[13] Cf. A. M. Hunter, *Paul and his Predecessors*, p. 61; K. Stendahl, *School of St. Matthew*, p. 51; J. A. Fitzmyer, "4Q Testimonia and the New Testament," *TS*, XVIII (1957), pp. 515f. On the relation of testimonia collections to larger blocks of selected Old Testament material, see *supra*, pp. 89-92.

been so closely connected with the proclamation of the gospel in the early Church that, though the Evangelist did not employ any other explicit citations in his editorial comments, he could hardly have introduced the good news of God's activity in Christ without employing them. Matt. 11:10 and Luke 7:27, of course, attribute Mal. 3:1 to Jesus' teaching, but Mark employs both Mal. 3:1 and Isa. 40:3 as the opening of his narrative—probably in continuity with more traditional practice within the Church. Beyond this one conflated citation, however, there are no further quotations in the editorial material of Mark's Gospel. We may suspect that there should be other places where a midrashic treatment would underlie his presentation, but, as E. E. Ellis observes, "in the absence of a clear allusion or an explicit quotation it is, in the nature of the case, difficult to establish a midrashic background for a New Testament passage."[14]

A number of features in Luke's Gospel deserve mention in regard to the Evangelist's use of the Old Testament. In the first place, the Lucan birth narratives of chapters 1 and 2 clearly (1) "anchor the birth of Jesus the Christ in the faith and piety of Israel, in the Hebrew Scriptures, and thus in the plan and purpose of God,"[15] and (2) "are built around the renewal of prophecy at the dawn of the messianic era."[16] While there are no fulfilment citations in his editorial comments, the biblical allusions and prophetic tone of these chapters certainly indicate the author's concept of the gospel's continuity with and fulfilment of the prophetic message to Israel of old. And the emphasis upon the activity of the Spirit both in the conception of Jesus and in the prophetic responses of Mary, Zachariah, Simeon and Anna, seems to be Luke's way of saying to a Gentile audience that the time of fulfilment was inaugurated with the Incarnation.

Within these opening chapters, secondly, there are two

[14] E. E. Ellis, "Midrash, Targum and New Testament Quotations," *Neotestamentica et Semitica*, ed. E. E. Ellis and M. Wilcox (1969), p. 69.

[15] D. M. Smith, Jr., "The Use of the Old Testament in the New," *The Use of the Old Testament in the New and Other Essays*, ed. J. M. Efird (1972), p. 51.

[16] E. E. Ellis, *The Gospel of Luke* (1966), p. 29.

quotations from the Pentateuch: Exod. 13:2, 12 and Lev. 12:8 in Luke 2:23f. But these are only by way of explaining certain features of Jewish ritual law to a non-Jewish audience. Thirdly, in chapter 3, where the common narrative begins, Luke does much like Mark in quoting Isa. 40:3-5 as having been fulfilled in the ministry of John the Baptist. Unlike Mark, however, he quotes three verses from Isaiah and reserves Mal. 3:1 for the lips of Jesus. But beyond these evidences of his consciousness of redemptive continuity and eschatological fulfilment, and beyond his straightforward treatment of two ritualistic portions and a traditional messianic prophecy, there is a decided lack of explicit biblical material in the editorial comments of Luke's Gospel. Some have drawn up a list of impressive parallels between the Lucan "travel narrative" (9:51–18:14) and Deuteronomy (chs. 1–26), and feel justified in calling this special material in the Third Gospel "A Christian Deuteronomy."[17] But the evidence for such a view, while imposing, is highly inferential and cannot be considered on a par with that drawn from Luke's more explicit usage, with which we are here concerned.

THE QUOTATIONS OF MATTHEW

While Mark and Luke are quite reserved in their explicit employment of biblical material, Matthew's use of Scripture is extensive and goes much beyond what has been called historico-grammatical exegesis or even what we have seen of earlier Christian interpretation. Who would have suspected, for example—apart from a knowledge of Matthew's Gospel—that anything of messianic significance could be derived from (1) God's calling Israel's children out of Egypt, (2) Jeremiah's reference to Rachel weeping for her children in Rama, (3) a statement regarding the lands of Zebulun and Naphtali, or (4) the payment to Zechariah of thirty pieces of silver and his subsequent action of giving them to the

[17] Cf. C. F. Evans, "The Central Section of St. Luke's Gospel," *Studies in the Gospels*, ed. D. E. Nineham (1955), pp. 37-53. On a more devotional level, see J. Bligh, *Christian Deuteronomy (Luke 9-18)* (1970).

potter. All of these might sound like familiar themes to those reared on the New Testament, but they would never have been guessed apart from Matthew's treatment. And any similar development of Old Testament themes today would be considered by most Christians to be quite shocking. The quotations within the Evangelist's editorial comments, therefore, are distinctive not only in their introductory formulae and their textual variations, but also in their oft-times surprising applications.

In seeking to understand Matthew's use of the Old Testament, it is well to remind ourselves of a phenomenon in the First Gospel that has been frequently noted and variously explained: that many parallels between the life of Jesus and the early experiences of the nation Israel seem to lie inherent within the narrative of Matthew's Gospel, particularly in its earlier chapters. As even a cursory glance at a "synopsis" of the Gospels reveals, Matthew's presentation in the first half (approximately) of his work varies noticeably from the order in Mark and Luke. The First Evangelist seems to be following a thematic arrangement of his material in the structuring of his Gospel. And in this first half of his Gospel, modern commentators believe they can detect echoes and reminiscences of Israel's earlier experiences. Thus in his portrayal of the life and ministry of Christ, there have been found particularly suggestive parallels between Jesus and the nation: (1) a child of promise (1:18ff.), (2) delivered from Herod's slaughter (2:1ff.), (3) coming out of Egypt (2:15, 19ff.), (4) passing through the waters (3:13ff.), (5) entering the wilderness for testing (4:18ff.), (6) calling out the "twelve sons of Israel" (4:18ff.), (7) giving the Law from the mount (chs. 5–7), (8) performing ten miracles (chs. 8–9), (9) sending out the Twelve to "conquer" the land (10:1ff.), (10) feeding the multitudes with "manna" from heaven (14:15ff.; 15:32ff.) and (11) being transfigured before his disciples (17:1ff.). Not all these features, of course, are equally evident. Nor are they equally significant. But the general parallelism cannot be easily set aside.

It may be questioned whether these parallels, together with such other inferences as may be drawn from the

Gospel, can be subsumed under a particular "Pentateuchal" or "New Moses-New Exodus" interpretation of the First Gospel.[18] The parallels are not so clearly explicated as to warrant a confident assertion that these particular themes dominated the Evangelist's presentation. As W. D. Davies concludes, "while these motifs have influenced Matthew's Gospel, it is not clear that they have entirely fashioned or moulded it."[19] But what can be claimed with confidence, without seeking to procrusteanize the Gospel, is (1) that behind the Evangelist's presentation stand the Jewish concepts of corporate solidarity and typological correspondences in history, (2) that the phenomenon of historical parallelism seen in the First Gospel is a reflection of such conceptualization, and (3) that this background is important in understanding Matthew's treatment of specific Old Testament statements and events. By the employment of such concepts, Jesus is portrayed in Matthew's Gospel as the embodiment of ancient Israel and the antitype of earlier divine redemption.

To this conceptual background for the First Gospel should be coupled a pesher handling of the biblical text and application of its meaning. As has been frequently pointed out, particularly since Stendahl's 1954 monograph, there is a striking similarity between Matthew's own formula quotations and the exegesis of the Habakkuk commentary from Qumran. There are decided differences, of course. In addition to the obvious fact that the introductory formulae vary, there is a difference of degree in the liberty taken with the text itself. Matthew's readings can be supported more adequately, though not entirely, by known variants than can those of 1QpHab. And there is a definite difference in the application of prophecy. Whereas both employ a "this is that" theme in their treatment, Matthew, following more a prophetic pattern, does not necessarily preempt prophecy so as to make it meaningless in its earlier context, while 1QpHab treated the prophecies as pertinent exclusively to the present situation.[20] But inasmuch as Matthew's own

[18] For a survey and evaluation of various "Pentateuchal" and "New Moses-New Exodus" hypotheses, see W. D. Davies, *Setting of the Sermon on the Mount*, pp. 14-93.

[19] *Ibid.*, p. 93.

[20] Cf. F. F. Bruce, *Biblical Exegesis in the Qumran Texts*, pp. 16f.

formula quotations (1) have their point of departure in certain events of the present rather than first of all in the ancient text itself, (2) are used to demonstrate fulfilment rather than to elucidate inherent principles, and (3) are affected in their textual form by the application made, it is proper to speak of them as pesher treatments. It may be, as Stendahl suggests, that the fulfilment formula itself is "something of a technical term which Matthew uses to distinguish the *pesher* type of quotation,"[21] though this need not be insisted upon.

The eleven Matthean quotations, I would suggest, should be understood as pesher treatments of the Old Testament. And in dealing with them, the following factors should be continually kept in mind: (1) the Jewish concepts of corporate solidarity and typological correspondences in history; (2) the Christian convictions of eschatological fulfilment and messianic presence;[22] (3) the treatment of certain prophecies and biblical events in the analogous eschatological and charismatic community at Qumran; and (4) the realization that prior to the standardization of the consonantal text at Jamnia there probably existed more versions and recensions of the Old Testament than are now extant, as the discoveries at Qumran seem to indicate.[23] It is to these eleven biblical citations found in the editorial comments of the Evangelist that we must now turn, considering them individually and surveying their features.

1. Matt. 1:23, quoting Isa. 7:14 ("Virgin-Immanuel" passage), parallels and perhaps is founded upon the textual tradition found in the larger Isaiah scroll at Qumran. As J. de Waard has shown, Matthew's impersonal use of the third person plural, "they shall call (καλέσουσιν) his name Immanuel," and his understanding of "Immanuel" as a title are not to be considered necessarily *ad hoc* creations, but find

[21] K. Stendahl, *School of St. Matthew*, p. 203.
[22] Cf. *supra*, pp. 93-95.
[23] J. T. Milik points out that the determination of the text at Jamnia was arrived at in a somewhat mechanical manner by selecting only the majority reading in each case, that after this standardization of the text took place all diverging recensions were eliminated, and that the situation is illustrated by the variety of readings found at Qumran that are prior to Jamnia but the identity of the texts in the fragments from the Murabbaat caves (so far as the evidence goes) with the MT after Jamnia (*Ten Years of Discovery in the Wilderness of Judaea*, pp. 28f.).

support in 1QIs^{a}.[24] Yet Matthew's text also evidences influence from the LXX in its rendering of עלמה by παρθένος. The application of Isa. 7:14 to Jesus was probably considered by Matthew to be (employing our more refined distinctions) a case of a literal fulfilment of an explicit messianic prophecy. The Greek παρθένος was commonly equated with the Hebrew עלמה in the synagogues of Judaism through the influence of the LXX.[25] And whether it be judged legitimate or not, the association of the two words for two centuries or so must certainly have counted for something theologically. Furthermore, Isa. 7:14 may well have been one of those passages identified by Jesus as being significant for his own person and ministry,[26] thereby clarifying the enigmatic in an Immanuel passage and explicating the intended *sensus plenior* for his followers. On the other hand, it may be that Matthew considered Isa. 7:14 more a typological statement finding its antitype in the Messiah Jesus than a direct messianic prophecy, as we would understand direct messianic prophecy. Distinctions of this sort, however, were probably not consciously present in the Evangelist's mind. His purpose was to stress fulfilment of God's redemptive activity in the person of Jesus Christ, whether that fulfilment be later analyzed as "direct" or "typological," and in so doing he employed a pesher treatment of the passage in both its text-form and its application.

2. Matt. 2:15, quoting Hos. 11:1 ("Out of Egypt I called my son"), differs from the LXX in reading "my son" (*τὸν υἱόν μου*) for "his [Israel's] children" (*τὰ τέκνα αὐτοῦ*), and from the Targums in its use of the singular. But it translates the MT exactly, with *υἱός μου* equalling בני. The context of the expression "out of Egypt I called my son" in Hos. 11 clearly indicates that the prophet was employing "my son" as a collective synonym for the nation Israel, which as a "child" was dearly loved by God but as time went on

[24] Cf. J. de Waard, *Comparative Study of the Old Testament Text*, pp. 9f., 82 (correcting Stendahl).

[25] Aquila's version reads *ἡ νεανίς* (young woman) rather than *ἡ παρθένος*, but this is later than Matthew's Gospel and may be in reaction to Christian usage. Likewise, also Symmachus' translation.

[26] Cf. *supra*, pp. 72, 91f.

drifted away from God into idolatry. In applying the passage to Jesus, Matthew seems to be thinking along the lines of corporate solidarity and rereading his Old Testament from an eschatologically realized and messianic perspective. He has no desire to spell out all the features of the nation's history, for many would be entirely inappropriate for his purpose. But he is making the point that that which was vital in Israel's corporate and redemptive experience finds its ultimate and intended focus in the person of Jesus the Messiah. "This is that" which was prefigured in Israel's history is his emphasis. And in both his selection of a proper text-form and his application, he evidences a pesher handling of the passage.

3. Matt. 2:18, quoting Jer. 31:15 (Rachel weeping for her children), is an abbreviated translation of the MT, and evidently rests only upon the Hebrew text. The passage in Jeremiah is a poetic allusion to a calamitous event in Israel's history, with no obvious messianic significance. For Matthew, however, who thought as a Jew in terms of corporate solidarity and typological correspondences in history—and was convinced as a Christian concerning eschatological fulfilment and messianic presence in the person and work of Jesus Christ—the lament of God for his people of old finds its fullest expression and can be legitimately applied to Herod's murder of the infant boys in Bethlehem at the time of Jesus' birth. And by means of a pesher treatment of the passage he can say, "then was fulfilled the word by Jeremiah the prophet."

4. The Old Testament portion in view in Matt. 2:23 (a Nazirite from Nazareth) has been extensively investigated by a vast number of scholars, and cannot be easily determined. Many are of the opinion that the Evangelist is making a "punning allusion" to the "branch" (נצר) of Isa. 11:1.[27] Probably, however, he has in mind the statements of Judg. 13:5-7 and 16:17 regarding the Nazirite Samson. G. F. Moore and W. F. Albright have shown that, despite repeated assertions to the contrary, Matthew's

[27] E.g., M. Black, *Aramaic Approach to the Gospels and Acts*, pp. 143f.; K. Stendahl, *School of St. Matthew*, pp. 103f.; F. V. Filson, *Gospel according to St. Matthew*, p. 25.

Ναζωραῖος does mean "an inhabitant of Nazareth,"[28] thereby demolishing a vital philological argument in support of deriving the term from נצר of Isa. 11:1. And E. Schweizer has cogently argued that there is in the reference to Jesus as a Ναζωραῖος in Matt. 2:23 both a typological correspondence to the Nazirite Samson, who is portrayed in Judg. 16:17 as a נזר—which LXX^B translates as ἅγιος, but LXX^A as ναζιραῖος—and a wordplay on the village named Nazareth; and that the understanding of Jesus in light of the Nazirite Samson probably was original, to which was added the factor of Nazareth as Jesus' home village—thereby making him doubly a Ναζι[ω]ραῖος.[29] And Matthew's seemingly vague reference to "the prophets" (τῶν προφητῶν) in his introductory formula fits nicely into this theory that the Evangelist is alluding to Samson in Judges and not to the "branch" of Isaiah, and may very well have been intended to be more precise in its identification than has been usually supposed. As the book of Judges is anonymous and belongs to the Hebrew category of the "Former Prophets," a reference to it by the seemingly vague phrase "the prophets" could be viewed as entirely appropriate. It may even be, in fact, that the Evangelist attempted by means of his reference to "the prophets" to reflect this anonymity and to distinguish his source from the writings of the named "Latter Prophets."[30] Assuming, then, the essential validity of such a view as Schweizer proposes, Matthew's quotation seems to be invoking something of a double correspondence. In the first place, it is setting up a typological relationship between Samson and Jesus. In the second place, it brings in the fact that Nazareth was Jesus' home village and sees in that a heightened significance. If the Evangelist had treated only the typological relationships in history, there would be little difficulty in classifying his method. We have seen other such historical correspondences

[28] G. F. Moore, "Nazarene and Nazareth," *The Beginnings of Christianity*, ed. F. J. Foakes Jackson and K. Lake, I (1920), pp. 426-432; W. F. Albright, "The Names 'Nazareth' and 'Nazoraean'," *JBL*, LXV (1946), pp. 397-401.

[29] E. Schweizer, " 'Er wird Nazöraer heissen' (zu Mc 1.24, Mt. 2.23)," *Judentum, Urchristentum, Kirche*, ed. W. Eltester (1960), pp. 90-93.

[30] Cf. J. A. Sanders, "*NAZŌRAIOS* in Matt. 2.23," *JBL*, LXXXIV (1965), p. 170.

so emphasized. But in that the quotation treats the text allusively and involves also a contemporary correspondence, it stretches our ideas regarding corporate solidarity, historical correspondence and pesher interpretation. Nonetheless, it seems to fit these categories better than any others known to date.

5. Matt. 3:3, quoting Isa. 40:3 ("the voice of one crying in the wilderness"), is the one biblical citation of Matthew's own eleven quotations that is not introduced by a "fulfilment formula." It is also the one whose text-form is identical to the text of the LXX, except for its simplification of "the paths of our God" (*τὰς τρίβους τοῦ θεοῦ ἡμῶν*) to "his paths" (*τὰς τρίβους αὐτοῦ*). The Evangelist is evidently taking a widely employed text which was commonly considered to have messianic relevance,[31] and, in Christian fashion, applying it to the ministry of John the Baptist. And in his assertion that "this is the one spoken of by Isaiah the prophet," he is employing a pesher type of interpretation.

6. Matt. 4:15f., quoting Isa. 9:1f. (Zebulun and Napthali), deviates from both the MT and LXX in its replacement of the future tenses by past tenses and in its stress on the people "dwelling" (*ὁ καθήμενος*) in "darkness" and in "the land and shadow of death." The change of tenses, of course, reflects the new eschatological perspective of Christians, and the emphasis upon the people "dwelling" in darkness is undoubtedly also theologically motivated. But apart from these alterations, the text-form of the citation is heavily dependent upon the MT. In its application, the quotation evidences a corporate solidarity and typological correspondences in history background of thought which has been triggered by the fact of Jesus' ministry in these regions, producing a typically pesher insistence that Christ's residence in Capernaum (the 'this' of the motif) was a fulfilment of God's promise to the lands of Zebulun and Naphtali that "in the days to come he will confer glory on the Way of the Sea on the far side of Jordan, Galilee of the Gentiles" (the 'that' of the motif).

7. Matt. 8:17, quoting Isa. 53:4 ("he took our sicknesses and bore our diseases"), departs from the LXX and tar-

[31] Note this same simplification in Mark 1:3 and Luke 3:4.

gumic traditions, which give a spiritualized translation of "sins" for "sicknesses," and translates the MT exactly, reading *τὰς ἀσθενείας ἡμῶν* for חלינו. In determining Matthew's use of the passage, much depends upon the difficult and controversial issue of how the Isaian Servant Songs were understood within the early Church. The use of Isa. 53 with reference to Jesus, as we have seen, appears to have become fixed quite early in Christian thought, stemming, perhaps, from Jesus' own reinterpretation of the passage.[32] If this be true, Matthew could have considered Isa. 53:4 to be fulfilled in Jesus' ministry either as a direct messianic prophecy or on a corporate solidarity basis. In either case, however, the Evangelist's textual selection and his fulfilment application signal the use of a pesher approach to Scripture.

8. Matt. 12:18-21, quoting Isa. 42:1-4 (Jesus' mighty works and his withdrawal from conflict were prophesied by Isaiah), deviates from all known variants in its designations of Jesus as *ὁ παῖς μου* and *ὁ ἀγαπητός μου*, in its altered order of the three negatives, and in its abbreviated form. Precise determination of Matthew's use depends, again, upon the view taken toward the understanding of the Servant Songs in the early Church. But at least a pesher treatment is involved in the variations within the text and the stress on fulfilment, whether Isa. 42:1-4 was taken as having individual messianic significance or understood more along the lines of corporate solidarity.

9. Matt. 13:35, quoting Ps. 78:2 (Asaph's words regarding dark sayings applied to Jesus' teaching in parables), agrees with the LXX for the first half of the quotation and the MT for the rest. Here the concept of typological correspondence seems to come to the fore. It is not that history is repeating itself, or that Asaph necessarily spoke of Jesus' teaching ministry, but that an earlier meaningful statement is now seen to have been a God-ordained prefigurement of a more meaningful antitype in the days of eschatological fulfilment. And Asaph's words are treated in pesher fashion throughout.

10. Matt. 21:5 is a composite quotation of Isa. 62:11 and Zech. 9:9 (Israel's king comes riding upon an ass). The

[32] Cf. *supra*, pp. 72, 91f., 101f.

Zechariah passage is *prima facie* messianic, and its connection with the "new Jerusalem" passage of Isa. 62 may be presumed to have been traditional in at least some quarters. But the text of Matt. 21:5 deviates from all extant versions in its abbreviation of Zech. 9:9. And it distinguishes itself from its parallel in John 12:15 chiefly in its literal rendering of the parallelism in the MT and LXX texts, thereby resulting in a reference to two asses. The abbreviation might not be very significant, for, as K. Stendahl points out, it is clear from Gen. R. 98:9 that rabbinic tradition stressed only "poor and riding on an ass" in the prophecy—and "it is to a Jewish tradition that Matthew wants to relate his argument for the prophecy as fulfilled by Jesus' entry."[33] And in regard to Matthew's reading of Zech. 9:9 as two asses, whereas John mentions only a donkey's colt, B. Lindars has pertinently observed:

> The point is that Jesus was riding on a colt never put to this use before. This can be expressed by reducing the parallel phrases to the simple πῶλον ὄνου [as in John 12:15]. . . . But the chief motive in Matthew's version is again to draw attention to the freshness of the colt. This time it is done, not by abbreviating, but by a fuller and more literal rendering of the Hebrew. This is also the reason why Matthew's narrative mentions the ass in addition to the colt (Matt. 21.2, 7). It is a refinement of exegesis, whereby the two members of the parallel have been used to say virtually the same thing as Mark 11.2. For it goes without saying that a colt "whereon no man ever yet sat" has not yet been parted from its mother. This is not a case of ignorantly misunderstanding the nature of Hebraic parallelism, but a way of correlating the text more closely to the facts for the sake of greater cogency.[34]

Further, it is possible that the argument of Gen. R. 98:9 against interpreting the parallelism of Zech. 9:9 by the expression "his foal and his ass's colt" of Gen. 49:11 reflects an earlier tradition of reading Zech. 9:9 as two asses. However that may be, Matthew's use of a "this is that" fulfilment motif and his "correlating the text more closely to the facts for the sake of greater cogency" evidence a distinctly pesher treatment of the biblical materials.

[33] K. Stendahl, *School of St. Matthew*, p. 119. B. Lindars notes that "it can be presupposed that the King, when he comes, will be 'just and having salvation' " (*New Testament Apologetic*, p. 113).
[34] B. Lindars, *ibid.*, pp. 113f.

11. Matt. 27:9f. quotes Zech. 11:12f. and alludes to Jer. 18:1f. and 32:6-9 (Judas' thirty pieces of silver given for the potter's field). The introductory formula ascribes the quotation to Jeremiah, though it is actually derived from Zech. 11:12f. Such a phenomenon, as with the ascription of both Mal. 3:1 and Isa. 40:3 to Isaiah alone in Mark 1:2, probably is best explained on the hypothesis of a testimonia collection being employed wherein composite citations or multiple listings were assigned to the more prominent prophet.[35] The text of the quotation deviates from both the MT and LXX, though its hebraic dependence is most evident. The expression *βαλεῖν αὐτὰ εἰς τὸν κορβανᾶν* of Matt. 27:6 is important in understanding the Evangelist's interpretation of 27:9, for it suggests that in Matthew's view Judas returned the money to the temple treasury and therefore that he quoted Zech. 11:13 as though יוצר ("potter") could also be read or understood as אוצר ("treasury"). Or at least, to quote Lindars, "the Aramaic *κορβανᾶν* is a sign that the writer was aware of the interpretation of יוצר in Zech. 11:13 as אוצר, if indeed it was not actually so written in the Hebrew text which he was using."[36] In so doing, whether expressly from some existing Hebrew variant or (more likely) inferentially from some current usage within Judaism,[37] the reading of the prophecy was "brought into line with what actually happened when the high priest received the money from Judas. It is thus a matter of making the words fit the facts, rather than making the facts fit the words, as has so often been assumed."[38]

In Matthew's own use of the Old Testament, therefore, as seen in the thematic structuring of his Gospel (particularly

[35] Cf. *supra*, p. 139.
[36] *New Testament Apologetic*, p. 118. Lindars comments in a footnote that "the possibility that such a text existed is indicated by the OT Peshitta (*bēth gazzā*), but is denied by C. C. Torrey, *Documents of the Primitive Church*, 1941, pp. 87f."
[37] The rationale for understanding "treasury" while reading "potter," or actually reading "treasury" instead of "potter," may have been similar to that of W. C. Allen, citing J. Wellhausen: "It is probable that in Zec. 11:13 אוצר is original. It alone gives a good sense, and a reason for בית יהוה. Why should the potter be in Jehovah's house? The treasury was naturally there" (*A Critical and Exegetical Commentary on the Gospel according to St. Matthew* [1912], p. 288).
[38] B. Lindars, *New Testament Apologetic*, p. 25.

the first half) and in the eleven quotations in his editorial material, the Jewish concepts of corporate solidarity and typological correspondences in history coupled with the Christian convictions of eschatological fulfilment and messianic presence come to expression in a distinctly Christocentric fashion. A pesher handling of Old Testament history and of certain Old Testament passages is dominant in his treatment, and, in the main, such a Christocentric pesher approach is in continuity with the hermeneutics of Jesus and early Christian preaching. Yet the degree to which the Evangelist employs the pesher mode of interpretation, and the development of pesher interpretation to include a number of features not previously explicated, go beyond what we have seen of Christian exegesis to date. One gets the decided impression in surveying his treatment of the Old Testament that the Evangelist believed himself to be working from a revelational insight into the Scriptures as given by Jesus himself, following out common apostolic hermeneutical procedures, and explicating further the theme of eschatological fulfilment under the guidance of the Holy Spirit. The question as to whether Matthew acted legitimately in this or not, of course, is more than a strictly historical issue, involving faith commitments regarding the distinctiveness of Jesus, the reality and activity of the Spirit, the authority of an apostle or of 'apostolic men', and the relation of the First Gospel to the early apostolate. Of such matters we must speak later.[39] Suffice it here to note that it is Matthew's Gospel, and not Mark's or Luke's, that develops the pesher approach to Scripture in such a distinctive fashion and that bears the name of one of Jesus' chosen disciples.

The further question as to whether Matthew's text-forms in his own biblical citations are to be explained as (1) variant readings drawn from existing texts, (2) independent corrections of existing texts, or (3) *ad hoc* creations, must remain for the present unresolved. The readings of at least 1:23; 2:15; 2:18; 8:17 and 13:35 appear to be the result of selection among existing variants, while those of 3:3; 21:5 and 27:9f. may have resulted in large measure from wide

[39] *Infra*, pp. 207ff.

and diverse employment within Judaism. Some of the textual features of the quotations in 4:15f.; 12:18-21 and 21:5, for example, quite obviously reflect distinctive Christian emphases, and cannot be supported by extant versions. But until more is known regarding the state of the Hebrew text prior to Jamnia, and of septuagintal and targumic traditions during the first Christian century, we are able to do little more than speculate as to possible relationships.

THE QUOTATIONS OF JOHN

Whereas Matthew's portrayal of Jesus seems to have been developed generally along the lines of the Messiah as the embodiment of the nation of Israel and the fulfilment of its typological history, John appears to have thought of Jesus more as central in the life of the nation and the fulfilment of its festal observances. A number of features in support of such a hypothesis are readily apparent in the Fourth Gospel, though they may be variously explained as to their details.

Most obvious in this regard is the prominence given to the festivals of Judaism (particularly Passover), and the way in which the Evangelist shows that Jesus fulfils the symbolism of these festal occasions. Seventeen times the word *ἑορτή* ("feast") occurs in John's Gospel, whereas it is found in Matthew and Mark only twice, in Luke three times, and in Paul's writings once; and ten times the Evangelist specifically names the Passover, once the festival of Tabernacles, and once Dedication (Hanukkah),[40] whereas the only feast the synoptists mention by name is the Passover.[41] A number of times Jesus' activity is dated in relation to a festival: usually the Passover (2:13; 6:4; 11:55; 12:1; 13:1; 19:14), though once Tabernacles (7:2), once Dedication (10:22), and once just "a feast of the Jews" (5:1). And inherent to certain units of the Evangelist's festal structure is the repre-

[40] Τὸ *πάσχα*: 2:13, 23; 6:4; 11:55 (twice); 12:1; 13:1; 18:28, 39; 19:14; *ἡ σκηνοπηγία*: 7:2 (also referred to by *ἡ ἑορτή* seven times in ch. 7, and perhaps in 5:1); *τὰ ἐγκαίνια*: 10:22.

[41] Matthew four times, Mark five, Luke seven; also Acts once and Paul once.

sentation of Jesus as the fulfilment of that which was symbolized by the feast. Thus, for example, in chapter 6, prior to the Passover, Jesus speaks of himself as the living bread that came down from heaven, of which the manna in the wilderness was a type; in chapter 7, at the festival of Tabernacles, he proclaims himself to be the giver of living water, as symbolized in the water-pouring ceremony; and in chapter 8, probably also at the festival of Tabernacles,[42] he announces himself as the light of the world, as symbolized in the lighting of the candelabra. All of this suggests that the Fourth Evangelist had a great interest in the relation of Jesus to the Jewish festivals. Such an observation, of course, can be exaggerated, as is undoubtedly the case with those theses which view the Fourth Gospel as exclusively following the Jewish liturgical calendar for its 'chronological' framework and the synagogue's lectionary cycle of readings for its biblical quotations and allusions.[43] Nonetheless, the emphasis upon the festal observances—particularly upon Passover[44] —is an important feature in the Evangelist's portrayal of Jesus as the fulfilment of Israel's messianic hope and the substance of Israel's ritual symbolism.[45]

The interests of the Evangelist are also to be seen in his typological emphases and the arrangement of his material. Interwoven into his festal pattern is the presentation of Jesus as the true Temple,[46] the antitype of the brazen serpent,[47] the true manna,[48] the true water-giving rock,[49]

[42] Considering chs. 7 and 8 to be joined, apart from the *pericope adulterae* of 7:53–8:11.

[43] E.g., A. Guilding, *The Fourth Gospel and Jewish Worship* (1960). For a pertinent interaction with such theses, dealing particularly with Guilding's views, see L. Morris, *The New Testament and the Jewish Lectionaries* (1964).

[44] On the importance of the Passover in John's Gospel, and Jesus' fulfilment of its symbolism, see Morris, *ibid.*, pp. 67-72.

[45] J. J. von Allmen correctly observes that "this determination of Jesus to be present [at Passover and Tabernacles] is, as it were, a declaration that He Himself is the 'substance' of these festivals and that He is come to fulfil them, as He also comes to fulfil the whole law (cf. Matt. 5:17)" (*The Vocabulary of the Bible* [1958], p. 123).

[46] John 2:18-22.

[47] John 3:14f.

[48] John 6:30-58.

[49] John 7:37-39.

the true fiery pillar,[50] the eschatological Moses,[51] the new Torah,[52] and the true Paschal Sacrifice.[53] As L. Morris observes: "The use of types is not a complete explanation of John's method. But it is certainly part of the explanation."[54] In addition, the Evangelist builds his narrative around Jesus' visits to Jerusalem. At the Passover Jesus purifies the temple,[55] at "a feast of the Jews" he comes simply as a pilgrim,[56] at Tabernacles he presents himself as the substance of the festival's symbolism,[57] and at another Passover he comes to finalize his redemptive mission.[58] In the Fourth Gospel, therefore, Jesus is presented as the fulfilment of Israel's hope (whether explicit or implied) and central in the life of the nation. The imagery varies, of course, from that of Matthew, but the presuppositions are the same as those inherent to the First Gospel and the stress on fulfilment is strikingly similar.

Likewise, the seven biblical quotations in John's editorial material are closely parallel in many respects, if not essentially identical, to Matthew's eleven. The text-forms, as we have noted, evidence less deviation from known versions and are more septuagintal than Matthew's.[59] But in application and purpose, the citations in the editorial comments of the First and Fourth Gospels are comparable. The Jewish

[50] John 8:12.
[51] Jesus' feeding of the multitude in John 6, together with such passages as John 1:17; 5:39-47 and 14:6, explicitly makes this point. T. F. Glasson, while somewhat extreme in pressing the parallels between Moses and Jesus, is nonetheless generally correct in insisting that "there can be little doubt that the way in which Christ is presented in the Fourth Gospel is intended to indicate that he is the fulfilment of Deut. 18. 15-19" (*Moses in the Fourth Gospel* [1963], p. 30).
[52] The prologue of John's Gospel, together with such passages as John 5:39-47 and 14:6, also carries this theme. Cf. further C. H. Dodd, *The Interpretation of the Fourth Gospel* (1963), pp. 82-86; T. F. Glasson, *Moses in the Fourth Gospel*, pp. 45-64, 86-94 and *passim*.
[53] The Baptist's acclaim of Jesus as the "Lamb of God" (John 1:29, 36) and, particularly, the passion narrative highlight this feature; cf. L. Morris, *The New Testament and the Jewish Lectionaries*, pp. 71f.
[54] *Ibid.*, p. 71.
[55] John 2:13ff.
[56] John 5:1ff.
[57] John 7:2ff.
[58] John 12:1ff.
[59] *Supra*, p. 137.

presuppositions of corporate solidarity and typological correspondences in history and the Christian convictions of eschatological fulfilment and messianic presence underlie John's employment of the Old Testament as well, and a pesher treatment is involved in his demonstration of prophetic fulfilment. Considering them individually and surveying their features, the Evangelist's seven biblical quotations are probably to be understood as follows:

1. John 2:17 quotes Ps. 69:9 ("the zeal of your house has eaten me up"), applying a Davidic lament to Jesus' action of cleansing the temple. In so doing, the corporate relationship of king to people and of David to the Messiah comes to the fore. Also involved is a typological correspondence between the responses of king David and of the Messiah Jesus. And under a pesher treatment, the fulfilment theme is invoked.

2. John 12:15 quotes Zech. 9:9, with a possible allusion to the "fear not" of Isa. 40:9 (Israel's king comes riding upon an ass). Here the Evangelist quotes a *prima facie* messianic passage, which probably existed traditionally in certain quarters in abbreviated form and may have been associated with Isa. 40:9 in midrashic fashion on the basis of their common appeal to "Zion" and "Jerusalem" to proclaim good tidings of God's intervention. Both passages had direct messianic relevance in pre-Christian Judaism, and John's purpose is to demonstrate that in Jesus' "triumphal" entry into Jerusalem they were literally fulfilled.[60]

3. John 12:38 quotes Isa. 53:1 ("Lord, who has believed our report?"). If the Evangelist understood Isa. 53 as having individual messianic significance (perhaps stemming from Jesus' own reinterpretation of the passage), his treatment here should be classed as a literal fulfilment; if corporately of Israel, then the fulfilment theme is explicated on a corporate solidarity basis.[61] In either case, however, his emphasis upon fulfilment signals a pesher approach to Scripture.

[60] On Matthew's use of Zech. 9:9 and its association with Isa. 62:11, see *supra*, pp. 148f.
[61] On the employment of Isa. 53 by Jesus, Philip and Matthew, with the same issue of whether literal or corporate fulfilment is involved, see *supra*, pp. 72, 101f., 148.

4. John 12:40 quotes Isa. 6:9f. (blinded eyes and hardened hearts). On the basis of typological correspondences in redemptive history, the Evangelist views the unbelieving reception of Jesus by the people of Jerusalem as the greater fulfilment of God's words to the prophet Isaiah. And by means of a pesher treatment of the passage, he makes the point that the prophetic type has been fulfilled in Jesus' experience.

5. John 19:24 quotes Ps. 22:18 ("they parted my garments among them and cast lots"). Probably this should be classed as fulfilment of Scripture based on typological correspondence; though the fact that Ps. 22 is quoted five times in 1QH—without, however, the same verses employed in the Gospels being used—may suggest that this passage could have been considered to be directly messianic by John. At any rate, whether thought of as typological or direct prophecy, a pesher treatment is involved in the fulfilment theme.

6. John 19:36 probably quotes Ps. 34:20[62] and may have Exod. 12:46 and Num. 9:12 also in mind ("a bone of him shall not be broken"). The exegetical rule *qal waḥomer* (light to heavy) is here employed, arguing that what applies generally to the righteous man applies specifically to God's Righteous One. If Exod. 12:46 and Num. 9:12 are in view as well, the Evangelist is also making the point that what applies to the sacrifices in general applies specifically to Christ's final sacrifice for all men. But in that John takes pains to demonstrate fulfilment, a pesher flavor comes to the fore in his treatment.

7. John 19:37 quotes Zech. 12:10 ("they shall look on him whom they pierced"). From the perspective of the completed work of Christ, as interpreted by the Spirit after and on the basis of Christ's resurrection, the Evangelist understands an enigmatic passage set in a context that is *prima facie* messianic as being fulfilled in the experience of Jesus. Such a demonstration that the ambiguous has been clarified by its fulfilment is, as we have seen, a distinctive pesher motif.

In John's own use of the Old Testament, therefore, as

[62] The agreement between John 19:36 and Ps. 34:20 in the form of the verb *συντριβήσεται* seems to support this identification.

seen in his relating Jesus to certain of the Jewish festivals (particularly Passover), his emphasis upon certain biblical types, his focusing attention upon Jesus' activity in and around Jerusalem, and, especially, his seven biblical quotations in the editorial material of his Gospel, a pesher type of interpretation is dominant. From the perspective of the completed ministry of Jesus, as validated by his resurrection and interpreted by the Spirit, the Evangelist was able to move back into the Old Testament and to explicate a Christocentric fulfilment theme involving both direct messianic prophecies and corporate-typological relationships. In so doing, he treated the Scriptures in continuity with the practices of Jesus and the earliest Christian preaching; though, like Matthew, the degree to which he employed such a pesher interpretation and the development of the corporate-typological relationships went somewhat beyond what seems to have been common in early Christian exegesis—perhaps not as extensively developed as in the First Gospel, but a development in pesher interpretation nonetheless. And as was observed in regard to Matthew's Gospel, it is pertinent to note here that it is John's Gospel as well, and not Mark's or Luke's, that develops the pesher approach to Scripture in such a distinctive fashion and that bears the name of one of Jesus' chosen disciples.

VI: HEBREWS AND THE OLD TESTAMENT

The Letter to the Hebrews represents in many ways something of a hybrid blending of Jewish Christian themes and expressions, Pauline theological perspectives, and the author's own highly individualized treatment. Historically, while it is Jewish Christian in character, its author takes his stance outside of the Jewish Christian mission and urges his readers to be prepared to depart from their former allegiances if need be.[1] Theologically, while its thought is compatible with the Pauline proclamation, its argument is framed according to the interests of its Jewish Christian audience. And exegetically, while employing a number of distinctly Jewish methods and expressing distinctly Christian presuppositions, it is, as Barnabas Lindars rightly observes, "a highly individual biblical study in its own right, so that its scriptural interpretation witnesses more to the outlook of the author than to a previous apologetic tradition."[2] While exegetically it exhibits continuity with certain Jewish practices and with typical Christian presuppositions, in some ways its employment of the Old Testament is so unique as to prohibit fitting it into any particular type or any identifiable pattern of development in Christian exegesis. Yet while the letter cannot be classed as a typical representative of biblical exegesis in the apostolic period, in both its similarities to and its differences from those more standard treatments of the Old Testament it deserves to be considered as expressing another facet of early Christian interpretation.

[1] Cf. Heb. 13:12-14.
[2] B. Lindars, *New Testament Apologetic*, p. 29.

THE PROVENANCE OF THE LETTER

The problem of identifying the proper historical setting for the Letter to the Hebrews—and, thereby, of coming to a determination regarding its canonical status—has been a perennial one, existing at least as early as the second century. While I Clement 9–13 and 36 closely parallel the thought and wording of Hebrews, the so-called Muratorian Canon, representing the views of the Western Church at the end of the second century, does not even allude to the letter in its enumeration of writings that were either accepted as being canonical or disputed—nor, for that matter, among its listing of heretics and their writings.[3] William Barclay has aptly and interestingly characterized the situation of Hebrews among the early Church Fathers:

> Its problem was this. No one knew who wrote it; it arrived on the scene like Melchizedek, without father or mother. At that time in the very earliest days the ultimate test of any book was whether or not it was the work of an apostle or at least of an apostolic man. If therefore a book was not the work of an apostle, it was not regarded as Scripture. So the position of the Letter to the Hebrews was that no one denied its spiritual greatness; no one denied that it was a book on which a man might feed his soul and enrich his mind and confirm his heart; no one denied that there were Churches in which for long it had been read and valued. But at the same time no one knew who the author was; and therefore it was not easy for it to become a part of the canon of the New Testament.[4]

Alexandrian Christians early attributed its content to Paul in some manner, though they often explained its form by reference to either a translator or a Pauline disciple.[5] Elsewhere, however, Christians seem to have been generally unconvinced, and only through the efforts of Jerome and Augustine was the letter widely accepted as Pauline and canonical. Since the fifth century, the canonicity of He-

[3] Likewise, of course, Marcion (c. A.D. 145) did not acknowledge Hebrews to be by Paul, though this could be explained on theological grounds. The Muratorian Canon is admittedly defective at both its beginning and its close. But Hebrews would hardly have been referred to before "the third book of the Gospel, Luke," and it is difficult to believe it would have been listed among the heretics at the close.

[4] W. Barclay, *Epistle to the Hebrews* (1965), p. 11.

[5] E.g., Clement of Alexandria (c. A.D. 190-202) and Origen (c. A.D. 202-230); note also Chester Beatty P^{46} (c. A.D. 225), which places Hebrews after Romans in its collection of Pauline letters.

brews has been commonly accepted within Christendom, though its Pauline authorship has been frequently debated. John Calvin, for example, had his doubts about Paul's authorship; and Martin Luther took it as a composition of Apollos, which suggestion has been widely accepted today.

Probably the most crucial question historically, however, and that which affects interpretation the most, has to do with the identification of the recipients of the letter. Critical opinion during the last century has vacillated between viewing Hebrews as written to Jewish Christians living in or near Jerusalem[6] and to Gentile Christians living somewhere in the Empire outside of Palestine[7]—though it seemed in the fifties to have finally found direction in William Manson's carefully developed thesis that its addressees were Jewish Christians residing in Rome.[8] The main problem in identifying the nature of the addressees has been the very strange combination of beliefs which the readers are urged not to return to or exhorted to move away from. What Jewish group would have held to a theology that combined the veneration of angels, a Mosaic prophetology, the supremacy of the Aaronic priesthood, the exaltation of Melchizedek, the portrayal of the cultus in terms of the wilderness tabernacle, and the vital importance of the sacrificial system—and in this approximate order of ascending significance? The Sadducees centered their attention upon the priesthood and the sacrificial system, but were not interested in angels and would hardly have spoken of the temple in terms of the tabernacle. Pharisees were oriented around the Law and the prophets, but would hardly have considered the apex of Judaism to be the priesthood and the cultus. And what Jewish Christian group would have been enticed to apostatize by such a combination of features or prevented from going ahead in their Christian faith by such a complex of commitments? Evidently, so many concluded, the letter is

[6] E.g., B. F. Westcott, *The Epistle to the Hebrews* (1889); A. B. Bruce, *The Epistle to the Hebrews* (1899).

[7] E.g., J. Moffatt, *A Critical and Exegetical Commentary on the Epistle to the Hebrews* (1924); E. F. Scott, *The Epistle to the Hebrews* (1922); H. Windisch, *Der Hebräerbrief* (1931); G. Vos, *The Teaching of the Epistle to the Hebrews* (1956).

[8] W. Manson, *The Epistle to the Hebrews* (1951); cf. the earlier treatment along these same lines of G. Milligan, *The Theology of the Epistle to the Hebrews* (1899), pp. 34-52.

presenting a highly idealized portrayal of Judaism and one that never really existed in fact, which suggests that the author and his audience were ideologically, geographically, and perhaps also chronologically somewhat removed from affairs as they actually existed within Palestinian Judaism.

But with the publication of the texts from the first few caves at Qumran, a new approach toward the interpretation of the Letter to the Hebrews set in. Yigael Yadin inaugurated this new understanding of the provenance of the letter in his 1958 article, in which he spelled out certain important emphases in the Dead Sea materials that are parallel to the type of Judaism presupposed in Hebrews, and asserted that therefore the addressees were probably Jewish Christians with some type of an Essene background as represented in the Dead Sea Scrolls.[9] The change that his presentation effected in critical thought is most clearly seen in the writings of Ceslas Spicq, who, after publishing his excellent introductory volume on the epistle in 1952, found that in 1959 he had to modify extensively his earlier views to bring them into line with Yadin's evidence and conclusions.[10] And in 1965, with the publication of the Melchizedek scroll from Cave 11 of Qumran, Yadin was able to support his hypothesis further in regard to the very significant point of the prominence of Melchizedek in Hebrews.[11] Today, the Jewish Christian character of the recipients of the Letter to the Hebrews has widespread acceptance—whether on the basis of William Manson's views (which are still highly respectable and respected)[12] or some form of Yadin's thesis (which I personally favor).[13]

[9] Y. Yadin, "The Dead Sea Scrolls and the Epistle to the Hebrews," *Aspects of the Dead Sea Scrolls* (Scripta Hierosolymitana IV), ed. C. Rabin and Y. Yadin (1958), pp. 36-55.

[10] Cf. C. Spicq's "L'Epître aux Hébreux, Apollos, Jean-Baptiste, les Helleniste et Qumran," *RQ*, I (1959), pp. 365-390, with his earlier *L'Epître aux Hébreux*, I (1952), esp. pp. 39-91.

[11] Y. Yadin, "A Note on Melchizedek and Qumran," *IEJ*, XV (1965), pp. 152-54. On Melchizedek in Jewish thought, see my *Christology of Early Jewish Christianity*, pp. 113-19.

[12] Cf. F. F. Bruce, " 'To the Hebrews' or 'To the Essenes'?" *NTS*, IX (1963), pp. 217-232; *idem, The Epistle to the Hebrews* (1964), pp. xxxi-xxxv. Bruce's review of the question in light of 11QMelch is more moderate, and contains a good summation of the current state of scholarly opinion: "Recent Contributions to the Understanding of Hebrews," *ExpT*, LXXX (1969), pp. 260-64.

[13] Cf. D. Flusser, "The Dead Sea Sect and Pre-Pauline Christianity,"

Regarding the date and purpose of the letter, over half a century ago Alexander Nairne cogently and convincingly argued that it was written in that tense period before A.D. 70 when Jewish Christians in Palestine and throughout the Diaspora were facing the supreme test of loyalty either to their nation or to their Messiah, and that the letter was written to urge them not to revert back to Judaism but to go on with Christ.[14] And contemporary criticism, after extensive debate and in light of newer evidence, finds itself in substantial agreement. While many arguments have been marshalled for a date of composition in the sixties—some even arguing for the late fifties—the most telling seems to be that which concerns the polemic of the epistle itself in relation to then existing circumstances. Only on the supposition that the sacrificial worship of the Jerusalem temple still existed as the heart of the nation's life and an intact Judaism continued to offer a live option for the author's readers does the letter become historically intelligible. After the temple was destroyed and its cultus snuffed out, "such an argument," as Hugh Montefiore reminds us, "becomes a mere academic irrelevancy. The best argument for the supersession of the old covenant would have been the destruction of the Temple."[15]

On the issue of the letter's author, modern study has progressed little beyond Origen's judgment:

> But as for myself, if I were to state my own opinion, I should say that the thoughts are the apostle's, but that the style and composi-

Aspects of the Dead Sea Scrolls (Scripta Hierosolymitana IV), ed. C. Rabin and Y. Yadin (1958), pp. 215-266; J. Daniélou, *The Theology of Jewish Christianity* (ET 1964), pp. 353f.; J. W. Bowman, *Hebrews, James, I & II Peter* (1962), pp. 9-16. H. Kosmala provides a wealth of material on the parallels between the Dead Sea Scrolls and Hebrews in his *Hebräer-Essener-Christen* (1959), but has taken Yadin's thesis to an unwarranted extreme in claiming the recipients of Hebrews to have been non-Christian Essenes—as J. Daniélou did at first in his *The Dead Sea Scrolls and Primitive Christianity* (ET 1958), pp. 111-13. For criticisms of the theses of Yadin and Kosmala (unfortunately, usually lumping them together in refutation), see J. Coppens, "Les Affinites qumranienes de l'Epitre aux Hebreux," *NRT*, LXXXIV (1962), pp. 128-141, 257-282; F. F. Bruce, " 'To the Hebrews' or 'To the Essenes'?" *NTS*, IX (1963), pp. 217-232; H. Montefiore, *The Epistle to the Hebrews* (1964), pp. 17f.

14 A. Nairne, *The Epistle to the Hebrews* (1921), pp. lxxv-lxxvi.

15 H. Montefiore, *Hebrews*, p. 3.

> tion belong to one who called to mind the apostle's teachings and, as it were, made short notes of what his master said. If any church, therefore, holds this epistle as Paul's, let it be commended for this also. For not without reason have the men of old handed it down as Paul's. But who wrote the epistle, in truth only God knows for sure.[16]

Apollos, or a man like Apollos, is usually seen as the most likely candidate on the basis of the letter's style and treatment of the Old Testament—and such an ascription is probably as good as any. But though it is usual to assign the work to a hellenistic Christian author who comes from a non-Palestinian background because of its "Alexandrian-type" exegesis, important considerations have been brought forward to question such a position. Ronald Williamson, after a detailed examination of the linguistic, conceptual and hermeneutical similarities between Philo and the author of Hebrews, has pertinently concluded (1) that the letter and its addressees are basically Jewish Christian in character, (2) that the letter itself ought to be considered "as in the centre of the mainstream of primitive Christian theology, not as somehow off-centre, deflected from the central stream of Early Christian thinking by extraneous philosophical doctrines (doctrines that had reached the Writer from Plato *via* Philo)," and (3) that the writer of the letter should not be judged as in any essential manner dependent upon Philo simply because of "a set of similarities of language."[17] Significant as well are the oft-neglected demonstration by Jacob Lauterbach of two groups of tannaitic Jewish teachers who employed a mild allegorical hermeneutic;[18] the arguments of Joseph Bonsirven and David Daube that rabbinic exegesis had been influenced by hellenistic patterns of thought and expression prior to the first Christian century;[19] and the amanuensis thesis of Otto Roller.[20]

A great deal of work remains to be done on the prove-

[16] Eusebius, Eccl. Hist. VI. 25. 13f.
[17] R. Williamson, *Philo and the Epistle to the Hebrews* (1970), pp. 579f.
[18] J. Z. Lauterbach, "The Ancient Jewish Allegorists in Talmud and Midrash," *JQR*, I (1911), pp. 291-333, 503-531.
[19] See *supra*, p. 48, n. 109.
[20] O. Roller, *Das Formular der paulinischen Briefe* (1933).

nance of the Letter to the Hebrews, particularly in light of more recent evidence. But sufficient data have been brought to the fore of late to justify the contention that Hebrews should not automatically be classed an example of hellenistic Christian argumentation and hermeneutics, but is to be viewed in continuity with early Christian exegetical procedures and in conformity with common Jewish exegetical practices, even though it employs these in its own highly individualized fashion.

THE PHENOMENA OF THE QUOTATIONS

Nowhere in the New Testament is the listing of biblical quotations more difficult than in the Letter to the Hebrews. Not only are we faced with the usual problem of distinguishing between direct quotations, on the one hand, and what may be called allusions, employment of biblical phraseology, or references to Old Testament history, on the other, but we are also confronted in Hebrews with certain passages that are formally quoted again and again in the same discussion (e.g., Ps. 95:7-11; 110:1, 4) and other passages that are so elusively introduced as to frustrate any confident enumeration (e.g., Isa. 8:17f.; Jer. 31:33f.; Deut. 32:35f.). Commentators have differed as to the exact number of quotations in the letter,[21] and one does not have to work long on the text to understand why.

Despite such difficulties, however, some determination must be made if any further discussion is to be undertaken. This study, therefore, works from the following thirty-eight quotations in the Letter to the Hebrews, which are based on twenty-seven Old Testament passages:

1. Heb. 1:5a (Ps. 2:7)—I.F.: "to which of the angels did he [God] ever say" (εἶπεν).
2. Heb. 1:5b (II Sam. 7:14)—I.F.: "and again."

[21] Note, e.g., the various numbers given by B. F. Westcott, *Hebrews*, pp. 471ff.; W. Dittmar, *Vetus Testamentum in Novo* (1903), pp. 239ff.; J. Bonsirven, *Exégèse rabbinique et exégèse paulinienne* (1939), pp. 339ff.; C. Spicq, *L'Épître aux Hébreux*, I, pp. 331f. The search for allusions is considerably more complex, for the smaller the unit allowed the greater the number proposed.

3. Heb. 1:6 (Deut. 32:43 in LXX and 4QDt, though not in MT; or perhaps Ps. 97:7 [LXX=96:7])—I.F.: "he [God] says" (λέγει).
4. Heb. 1:7 (Ps. 104:4 [LXX=103:4])—I.F.: "he [God] says" (λέγει).
5. Heb. 1:8f. (Ps. 45:6f. [MT=45:7f.; LXX=44:6f.])—I.F.: "but about the Son."
6. Heb. 1:10-12 (Ps. 102:25-27 [MT=102:26-28; LXX=101:26-28])—I.F.: "and."
7. Heb. 1:13 (Ps. 110:1 [LXX=109:1])—I.F.: "to which of the angels has he [God] ever said" (εἰρηκέν).
8. Heb. 2:6-8 (Ps. 8:4-6 [MT=8:5-7])—I.F.: "somewhere someone testified, saying" (διεμαρτύρατο πού τις λέγων).
9. Heb. 2:12 (Ps. 22:22 [MT=22:23; LXX=21:22])—I.F.: "he [Jesus] says" (λέγων).
10. Heb. 2:13a (Isa. 8:17)—I.F.: "and again."
11. Heb. 2:13b (Isa. 8:18)—I.F.: "and again."
12. Heb. 3:7-11 (Ps. 95:7-11 [LXX=94:7-11])—I.F.: "the Holy Spirit says" (λέγει).
13. Heb. 3:15 (Ps. 95:7f. [LXX=94:7f.])—I.F.: "while it is said" (ἐν τῷ λέγεσθαι).
14. Heb. 4:3 (Ps. 95:11 [LXX=94:11])—I.F.: "he [God] has said" (εἴρηκεν).
15. Heb. 4:4 (Gen. 2:2)—I.F.: "somewhere he [God] has said" (εἴρηκεν που).
16. Heb. 4:5 (Ps. 95:11 [LXX=94:11])—I.F.: "again in this passage" (ἐν τούτῳ πάλιν).
17. Heb. 4:7 (Ps. 95:7f. [LXX=94:7f.])—I.F.: "again, he [God] set a certain day . . . as was said before" (προείρηται).
18. Heb. 5:5 (Ps. 2:7)—I.F.: "the one who spoke [i.e. God] said" (ὁ λαλήσας).
19. Heb. 5:6 (Ps. 110:4 [LXX=109:4])—I.F.: "in another passage he [God] says" (ἐν ἑτέρῳ λέγει).
20. Heb. 6:14 (Gen. 22:17)—I.F.: "God . . . swore by himself, saying" (θεός . . . ὤμοσεν καθ' ἑαυτοῦ λέγων).
21. Heb. 7:17 (Ps. 110:4 [LXX=109:4])—I.F.: "he [God] testifies" (μαρτυρεῖται/μαρτυρεῖ).

22. Heb. 7:21 (Ps. 110:4 [LXX=109:4])—I.F.: "by the one [i.e. God] saying to him" (διὰ τοῦ λέγοντες πρὸς αὐτόν).
23. Heb. 8:5 (Exod. 25:40)—I.F.: "he [God] said" (φησίν).
24. Heb. 8:8-12 (Jer. 31:31-34 [LXX=38:31-34])—I.F.: "he [God] says" (λέγει).
25. Heb. 9:20 (Exod. 24:8)—I.F.: "he [Moses] says" (λέγων).
26. Heb. 10:5-7 (Ps. 40:6-8 [MT=40:7-9; LXX=39:7-9])—I.F.: "he [the eschatological Messiah] says" (λέγει).
27. Heb. 10:16 (Jer. 31:33 [LXX=38:33])—I.F.: "the Holy Spirit also testifies (μαρτυρεῖ) to us, for he said" (τὸ εἰρηκέναι).
28. Heb. 10:17 (Jer. 31:34 [LXX=38:34])—I.F.: "and."
29. Heb. 10:30a (Deut. 32:35)—I.F.: "we know him [God] who said" (τὸν εἰπόντα).
30. Heb. 10:30b (Deut. 32:36)—I.F.: "and again."
31. Heb. 10:37f. (Hab. 2:3f.)—I.F.: "for."
32. Heb. 11:18 (Gen. 21:12)—I.F.: "concerning whom it was said" (ἐλαλήθη).
33. Heb. 12:5f. (Prov. 3:11f.)—I.F.: "the exhortation that addresses (διαλέγεται) you."
34. Heb. 12:20 (Exod. 19:13)—I.F.: "that which was commanded" (τὸ διαστελλόμενον).
35. Heb. 12:21 (Deut. 9:19)—I.F.: "Moses said" (εἶπεν).
36. Heb. 12:26 (Hag. 2:6)—I.F.: "he [God] has promised, saying" (ἐπήγγελται λέγων).
37. Heb. 13:5 (Deut. 31:6, 8)—I.F.: "he [God] has said" (αὐτὸς εἴρηκεν).
38. Heb. 13:6 (Ps. 118:6 [LXX=117:6])—I.F.: "we are bold to say" (λέγειν).

There are also a number of clear Old Testament allusions, reminiscences of septuagintal phraseology, and references to biblical history in the Letter to the Hebrews. At least fifty-five such cases can be identified, of which forty-one are from the Pentateuch, seven from Isaiah, two from the

Psalms, two from Zechariah, and one each from Daniel, Hosea and Proverbs.[22] There are no quotations drawn from the apocryphal books of the Greek Bible, though Heb. 11:35ff. refers to incidents depicted in II Macc. 6–7—and may have other such incidents from other writings then extant in mind as well.

Surveying the range of the biblical materials employed, it is obvious that the writer felt himself to be at home in his Old Testament. Particularly is this so in regard to the Pentateuch and the Psalms—"the fundamental Law and the Book of common devotion," as Westcott called them.[23] From the Pentateuch he drew the basic structure of his thought regarding redemptive history, quoting some eleven times from ten different passages and alluding to forty-one others; from the Psalms he derived primary support for his Christology, quoting some eighteen times from eleven different passages and alluding to two others. With the exceptions of II Sam. 7:14; Deut. 32:43 (LXX) and Isa. 8:17f., all of which are taken to be direct messianic prophecies, the biblical portions used to explicate the nature of the person of Christ are drawn entirely from the Psalms. On the other hand, with the single exception of the prophecy of II Sam. 7:14, no use is made by the writer of the historical books; and with the exception of Isaiah, only minimal use is made of the prophetical books.

Compared with other New Testament authors in their selection of Old Testament portions, the writer of Hebrews exhibits certain similarities and certain differences. Some of the passages he employs appear elsewhere in the New Testament, and are in those instances used rather uniquely; for example, Ps. 110:1 (Mark 12:36 par.; Acts 2:34f.); Hab. 2:4 (Rom. 1:17; Gal. 3:11); Ps. 2:7 (Acts 13:33); II Sam. 7:14 (II Cor. 6:18, possibly); Gen. 21:12 (Rom. 9:7) and Deut. 32:35 (Rom. 12:19). On the other hand, nineteen or twenty of the passages quoted in Hebrews are not cited elsewhere in the New Testament. In addition,

[22] Accepting Westcott's tabulation of allusions (*Hebrews*, pp. 473f.), and including items 25 (Heb. 7:1ff.) and 27 (3:1ff.) on p. 472, which I consider to be allusive references to biblical history rather than quotations *per se*.

[23] *Ibid.*, p. 475.

even where the writer agrees with other New Testament authors in his selection of texts, he varies at times from them in his application or in his wording of the passage; for example, most prominently, in his different application of Ps. 8:6b in Heb. 2:8 from Paul's in I Cor. 15:27 (cf. Eph. 1:22), and his variant wording of Hab. 2:4 in Heb. 10:38 from Paul's in Rom. 1:17 and Gal. 3:11.

Also significant is the distinctive manner in which the biblical portions are introduced in Hebrews. In the majority of cases, it is God himself who is the speaker (see numbers 1-7, 14-24, 29-30, 36-37 above). In four quotations drawn from three Old Testament passages the words are attributed to Christ (numbers 9-11, 26) and in three quotations drawn from two passages the Holy Spirit is credited (numbers 12, 27-28)—though it is noteworthy that these three citations credited to the Spirit appear elsewhere in the letter also credited to God (numbers 17, 24). In many cases the words quoted are introduced as being spoken in the present, whether cited as being the words of God (numbers 3-4, 19, 21, 24), of Christ (number 26), of the Spirit (numbers 12, 27), or attributed more generally to "the exhortation that addresses you" (number 33). The rationale for this phenomenon is that, as B. F. Westcott expressed it, "the record is the voice of God; and as a necessary consequence the record is itself living. It is not a book merely. It has a vital connexion with our circumstances and must be considered in connexion with them."[24] In only two instances are words credited to a human speaker, in both cases to Moses (numbers 25, 35).[25] And in two or three instances the material is introduced with a comment so general as to be unparalleled by any other introductory formula in the New Testament: to Ps. 8:4-6, "somewhere someone testified, saying" (number 8), and to Gen. 2:2, "somewhere he has said" (number 15)—which are echoed to some extent by the

[24] *Ibid.*, p. 477. M. Barth bases his "dialogical interpretation" of Hebrews in large part on this phenomenon ("The Old Testament in Hebrews," *Current Issues in New Testament Interpretation*, ed. W. Klassen and G. F. Snyder [1962], pp. 65-78).

[25] The expression "in David" of Heb. 4:7 is probably employed synonymously with "in the Psalms," connoting location rather than authorship, and therefore is probably not a third exception to the general pattern of ascription in Hebrews.

introduction to Ps. 110:4, "in another passage he says" (number 19).

As to the biblical text employed in Hebrews, it appears that the writer was most familiar with the Greek Bible as preserved for us in Codex Alexandrinus and that he had no immediate knowledge of any Hebrew version.[26] Eighteen of his quotations agree with the LXX where the LXX agrees with the MT (numbers 1-2, 4-5, 7-11, 18-19, 21-23, 30, 32, 35, 38), while fourteen agree with the LXX and differ from the MT (numbers 6, 12-17, 24, 26-28, 31, 33, 36). None agrees with the MT against the LXX, and only six cannot be accounted for by reference to either LXX^A or LXX^B (numbers 3, 20, 25, 29, 34, 37—interestingly, all from the Pentateuch). These latter six textual deviations from the LXX have been explained, in whole or in part, in various ways: (1) "free renderings" of biblical passages;[27] (2) the use of a liturgical formulation of passages;[28] (3) the use of a testimonia collection of passages;[29] (4) *ad hoc* creations by the author;[30] or (5) the use of a now extinct septuagintal recension that was based on Hebrew readings also now extinct. This last suggestion has been strengthened by the discovery that 4QDt 32.43 parallels in its Hebrew the Greek of the LXX.[31] And such a convergence of textual interests between the Dead Sea Scrolls and the Letter to the Hebrews must be considered highly probable when one takes into account such similar features as (1) the joining of Ps. 2 and

[26] Cf. B. F. Westcott, *Hebrews*, p. 481; P. Padva, *Les citations de l'Ancien Testament dans l'Epître aux Hébreux* (1904), p. 33; C. Spicq, *L'Epître aux Hébreux*, I, pp. 334-36.
[27] B. F. Westcott, *Hebrews*, p. 481.
[28] Cf. M. Barth, "Old Testament in Hebrews," *Current Issues in New Testament Interpretation*, p. 73.
[29] F. C. Synge, *Hebrews and the Scriptures* (1959), pp. 53f.
[30] Cf. S. Sowers, *Hermeneutics of Philo and Hebrews*, pp. 139f.
[31] Cf. P. W. Skehan, "A Fragment of the 'Song of Moses' (Deut. 32) from Qumran," *BASOR*, 136 (1954), pp. 12-15; M. Burrows, *More Light on the Dead Sea Scrolls* (1958), p. 138; J. de Waard, *Comparative Study of the Old Testament Text*, pp. 13-16. M. Barth observes: "Since the studies in a possible pre-Masoretic text of the Old Testament have been given a new turn and impetus by the material found in the Qumran caves, it has become probable that the LXX edition used by the author may occasionally be nearer the oldest Hebrew texts than a *Biblia Hebraica* based upon the Masoretic revision" ("Old Testament in Hebrews," *Current Issues in New Testament Interpretation*, p. 55).

II Sam. 7:14 into something of a catena of messianic testimonia in both Heb. 1:5 and 4QFlor, and (2) the interest in Melchizedek as an eschatological figure in both Heb. 5–7 and 11QMelch.

In matters pertaining to selection, introduction and text-form, therefore, the writer to the Hebrews expresses both a measure of commonality and a great deal of individuality when compared with the apostolic tradition that preceded him. But it is in his hermeneutical presuppositions, his exegetical practices and his biblical argument that the author's profile is most clearly seen, and it is to these that we must now turn.

EXEGETICAL PRESUPPOSITIONS AND PRACTICES

Almost axiomatic among New Testament commentators is the view that the Letter to the Hebrews reflects an Alexandrian school of Jewish Platonists in its presuppositions and has its closest parallels to Philo of Alexandria in its exegetical practices. In a former generation James Moffatt, for example, characterized the writer as follows: "The philosophical element in his view of the world and God is fundamentally Platonic. Like Philo and the author of Wisdom, he interprets the past and the present alike in terms of the old theory that the phenomenal is but an imperfect, shadowy transcript of what is eternal and real."[32] H. A. A. Kennedy, likewise, spoke of the writer as being "true to his training in his employment of the allegorical method of exegesis so characteristic of Philo";[33] and T. H. Robinson could say that, "assuming the correctness of the Alexandrian methods of exposition, the writer offers convincing proofs of his thesis that Jesus is at once the 'ideal' High Priest and the Supreme Sacrifice."[34] In our day, scholarly treatments continue to be written in support of such a view. In his 1952 introductory volume on Hebrews, C. Spicq argued that Philonic Judaism affords the most appropriate

[32] J. Moffatt, *A Critical and Exegetical Commentary on the Epistle to the Hebrews* (1924), p. xlvi.
[33] H. A. A. Kennedy, *The Theology of the Epistles* (1919), p. 193.
[34] T. H. Robinson, *The Epistle to the Hebrews* (1933), p. xviii.

background for the study of the epistle—though, significantly, seven years later he modified his position quite radically in light of Yadin's evidence.[35] And in 1965, Sidney Sowers published his full-scale defense of the thesis "that the writer of Heb. has come from the same school of Alexandrian Judaism as Philo, and that Philo's writings still offer us the best single body of *religionsgeschichtlich* material we have for this N.T. document."[36]

Yet critical opinion, though dominated in large measure by the view described above, has not been entirely of that persuasion. Alexander Nairne put his finger on a fundamental difference between Philo and Hebrews when he wrote: "Philo deals with allegories, the Epistle with symbols."[37] In so doing, Nairne brought to the fore a vital exegetical issue in the discussion; namely, the distinction between allegorical interpretation and typological symbolism. It is this issue

[35] C. Spicq, *L'Épître aux Hébreux*, I, pp. 39-91; cf. *idem*, *RQ*, I, pp. 365-390.

[36] S. Sowers, *Hermeneutics of Philo and Hebrews*, p. 66. In his conclusion, Sowers almost gives his thesis away in admitting: "This study has underscored the lack of allegory in Heb. as it was defined and used by the allegorists. The absence of this hermeneutical tool is particularly conspicuous because of the Alexandrian background of the epistle. Because allegory was the outstanding exegetical principle practiced in Alexandrian circles, its omission in Heb. also means that the writer has excluded Alexandrian hermeneutics *par excellence*" (p. 137). Yet Sowers goes on to confidently affirm: "Nevertheless the exegetical conclusions reached by the Alexandrian school of Jewish allegorists are firmly in the writer's mind, and the results of their work can frequently be seen behind his argument. At times, as in chap. 11, the writer merely says things in passing which betray his exposure to the school's tradition, notions frequently having been worked out through allegory but whose original arguments and bases have now been omitted" (p. 137).

Rather strangely, Sowers devotes only one sentence of five lines to Yadin and a sentence and footnote to Kosmala—discrediting Yadin's views by the excesses of Kosmala (p. 65)—and fails to note anywhere Spicq's reevaluation of the evidence and shifting of his position; and this despite his challenge and conclusion: "Until some source dating earlier than the letter is discovered representing many of the things discussed in this chapter plus other uniquenesses found in Heb. [which is exactly what Yadin's thesis asserts has taken place], it seems best to hold fast to the conclusion reached by many, that the writer of Heb. has come from the Alexandrian school which historically runs from the LXX through *Wisdom of Solomon*, Aristobulus, and the *Letter of Aristeas* to Philo" (pp. 72f.).

[37] A. Nairne, *The Epistle of Priesthood* (1913), p. 37.

that K. J. Woollcombe attempted to highlight in defining typology as "linkages between events, persons, or things *within the historical framework of revelation*," and allegorical interpretation as "the search for a secondary and hidden meaning underlying the primary and obvious meaning of a narrative."[38] And it is in this regard that Jean Daniélou has rightly insisted, "we must make a rigorous distinction between such a typology—which is historical symbolism—and the kind of allegorism practiced by Philo and adopted by certain Fathers of the Church. For the latter is really a reappearance of a cosmic symbolism without an historical basis."[39]

A number of studies specifically devoted to Hebrews have been published of late which have tended to undermine the earlier estimation of the Alexandrian nature of the letter's outlook and presentation. In 1954, C. K. Barrett argued that "certain features of Hebrews which have often been held to have been derived from Alexandrian Platonism were in fact derived from apocalyptic symbolism."[40] In 1958, and again in 1965, Y. Yadin (as referred to earlier) spelled out a number of striking parallels between the argument of Hebrews and the distinctive doctrines of the Qumran community.[41] In 1959, G. B. Caird asserted that the scriptural exegesis of Hebrews, rather than being "Alexandrian and fantastic," was in reality "one of the earliest and most successful attempts to define the relation between the Old and New Testaments, and that a large part of the value of the book is to be found in the method of exegesis which was formerly dismissed with contempt."[42] And in 1970, R. Williamson, in an extensive study of linguistic, conceptual and hermeneutical affinities between Philo and Hebrews, concluded that Hebrews "differs radically from the outlook

[38] K. J. Woollcombe, "The Biblical Origins and Patristic Development of Typology," *Essays on Typology*, p. 40 (italics his).
[39] J. Daniélou, "The New Testament and the Theology of History," *Studia Evangelica*, I, ed. K. Aland, *et al.* (1959), p. 30.
[40] C. K. Barrett, "The Eschatology of the Epistle to the Hebrews," *The Background of the New Testament and its Eschatology*, ed. W. D. Davies and D. Daube (1954), p. 393.
[41] See *supra*, p. 161, notes 9 and 11.
[42] G. B. Caird, "The Exegetical Method of the Epistle to the Hebrews," *CJT*, V (1959), p. 45.

and attitude of Philo. Neither in his basic judgment about the essential character of the O.T. nor in his chief method of scriptural exegesis does the Writer of Hebrews appear to owe anything to Philo."[43]

Superficially, of course, Hebrews bears some resemblance to the writings of Philo. Both employ an Alexandrian version of the Greek Bible in their expositions; both explicate a fuller or deeper meaning from the biblical text; and both express themselves at times in ways that parallel Platonism—though, it must be insisted, Philo much more than the author of Hebrews.[44] But while there are obvious similarities, it is necessary, in light of the evidence brought forward by such men as Barrett, Yadin, Caird and Williamson (though without suggesting their agreement throughout), to point out as well certain fundamental distinctions between Philo and the writer to the Hebrews:

1. Whereas Philo thought in terms of cosmology, seeking to explicate the nature of reality as it exists behind the misleading and deceptive phenomena of history and the senses, the writer to the Hebrews thought in terms of historical redemption, seeking to explicate the nature of God's redemptive activity during "these last days" of history.

2. Whereas Philo viewed the essential tension of life to involve the eternal prototypes and their present shadowy transcripts, the message of Hebrews is concerned with the tension between prophetic anticipation and fulfilment or consummation, which is the fundamental tension of all biblical revelation.

3. Whereas Philo considered history as the occasion for revelational insights and religious speculation, but not necessarily revelatory itself, Hebrews begins on the premise that history is divinely purposed and revelatory by design, pointing by its avowed incompleteness and imperfection to a promised consummation by God.

---

[43] R. Williamson, *Philo and the Epistle to the Hebrews*, p. 538.
[44] Note such expressions as "a shadow of heavenly things" (σκιὰ τῶν ἐπουρανίων) in Heb. 8:5; "a shadow of good things to come" (σκιὰ τῶν μελλόντων ἀγαθῶν) in 10:1; "a figure for the present time" (παραβολὴ εἰς τὸν καιρὸν τὸν ἐνεστηκότα) in 9:9; and "the pattern of things in the heavens" (τὰ ὑποδείγματα τῶν ἐν τοῖς οὐρανοῖς) in 9:23.

4. Whereas Philo treated biblical history allegorically, setting aside the obvious meaning of a narrative in search of a deeper spiritual significance signalled by the verbal symbols, the writer to the Hebrews spells out typological correspondences existing within the framework of redemptive history, as viewed from the standpoint of fulfilment in Christ.

5. Whereas Philo interpreted his Old Testament in conformity to the categories and by the methods of Platonic philosophy, Hebrews represents an interpretation of the Old Testament from a Christocentric perspective and in continuity with Christian exegetical tradition.

On the surface, Hebrews is in some respects comparable to the Philonic corpus. This may reflect something of the author's personal background—though probably very little beyond the faint suggestion of an Egyptian homeland and an indication of some ability to express himself in the religious idiom of the day.[45] But in matters having to do with basic commitments, controlling presuppositions and outlook, the Letter to the Hebrews evidences that its author marched to a different beat than did Philo—a beat that originated with Christ and was mediated through the apostolic tradition. When combined with certain traditional exegetical procedures and his own individual manner of treatment, such a Christian perspective produced a distinctive exegesis of the Old Testament.

THE BIBLICAL ARGUMENT

The theme of the Letter to the Hebrews is immediately set in the first two verses of chapter 1: "In the past God spoke to our fathers through the prophets at many times and in various ways, but in these last days he has spoken to us by his Son." While there is no employment of the word "fulfil-

[45] Not even the "allegorical-etymological" treatment in Heb. 7:1-10 really helps in settling the issue—though it has often been supposed to be conclusive—for, as we have seen, a mild allegorism was prevalent in at least certain circles of Palestinian Pharisaism during the first century (see *supra*, pp. 47f.). The apostle Paul, in fact, who was from both Tarsus and Jerusalem, employed an allegorical exegesis more often than we find in Hebrews.

ment," the idea of fulfilment—or, more aptly, of "consummation"— is clearly inherent in such a statement. The entire letter, in fact, is structured according to an "anticipation-consummation" motif. And at a number of points in the course of the presentation particular passages are ascribed to Jesus in ways that strike a definite note of fulfilment; for example, in the ascription of Ps. 40:7f. in Heb. 10:7: "Lo, I come—in the roll of the book it is written of me—to do your will, O God." From the perspective of the Messiah's presence among his people in "these last days," Israel's life and worship are viewed as preparatory for the coming of the Lord's Christ. A more profound significance is seen in the prophetic words and redemptive experiences recorded in Scripture, and these words and events are understood to be looking forward to the consummation of God's salvific program in the person and work of Jesus. For the author of Hebrews, as B. F. Westcott pointed out, "the O.T. does not simply contain prophecies, but . . . it is one vast prophecy, in the record of national fortunes, in the ordinances of a national Law, in the expression of a national hope. Israel in its history, in its ritual, in its ideal, is a unique enigma among the peoples of the world, of which the Christ is the complete solution."[46]

In spelling out this theme, the argument of the Letter is built around five biblical portions: (1) a catena of verses drawn from the Psalms, II Sam. 7 and Deut. 32 (LXX), upon which Heb. 1:3–2:4 is based; (2) Ps. 8:4-6, upon which Heb. 2:5-18 is based; (3) Ps. 95:7-11, upon which Heb. 3:1–4:13 is based; (4) Ps. 110:4, upon which Heb. 4:14–7:28 is based; and (5) Jer. 31:31-34, upon which Heb. 8:1–10:39 is based.[47] All the exhortations of Heb. 11–13 depend upon the exposition of these five biblical portions, and all other verses quoted in the letter are ancillary to these.

The first of our author's expositions brings together six passages, which are interpreted Christologically as referring

[46] B. F. Westcott, *Hebrews*, p. 493.

[47] Cf. G. B. Caird, "Exegetical Method of the Epistle to the Hebrews," *CJT*, V (1959), pp. 47-51, who has stressed this approach in regard to Hebrews' use of Pss. 8, 95, 110, and Jer. 31.

to Jesus: Ps. 2:7; II Sam. 7:14; Deut. 32:43 (LXX); Ps. 45:6f.; 102:25-27 and 110:1.[48] Surveying this catena of passages and noting the way in which they are employed, two questions inevitably come to the fore: On what basis were these passages considered messianic? and How were they brought together? Some commentators believe that some, if not all, of these verses were widely accepted within pre-Christian Judaism as having messianic relevance, even though our extant sources for a knowledge of Judaism supply little support for such a position. Paul Billerbeck, for example, suggested that Ps. 2 "probably" (*vermutlich*) was considered messianic in first-century Judaism, even though the Talmud does not treat it as such,[49] and that Ps. 110 was viewed by the rabbis as having messianic significance, even though clear evidence for such a view comes only from A.D. 260 onward and earlier talmudic discussions are decidedly nonmessianic.[50] Simon Kistemaker argues for a similar view in regard to a number of these portions, though he is able to cite in support only some rather tenuous data from the apocryphal and targumic writings and to point rather lamely to the obvious fact that these passages were "quite familiar to Jewish ears."[51] And David Hay concludes that since Ps. 110 appears so repeatedly in the New Testament as a messianic passage, and was so interpreted by the rabbis from A.D. 260 onward, and since "there is nothing in the psalm

[48] Ps. 104:4, of course, is also quoted in Heb. 1:7, but only by way of contrast to the Christological emphasis of the others.

[49] *Str.-Bil.*, III, p. 675.

[50] *Str.-Bil.*, IV, pp. 453-58.

[51] S. Kistemaker's argument for a pre-Christian messianic understanding of Ps. 2:7 is based on the ascription of "Son of David" in Pss. Sol. 17 and 18 (esp. 17:23ff.), which he believes supports an early messianic interpretation of "my son" in Ps. 2:7 (*The Psalm Citations in the Epistle to the Hebrews* [1961], p. 17); for Ps. 110:1, on references to "the Chosen One sitting on the throne of glory" in the Similitudes of Enoch (*ibid.*, p. 27); and for Ps. 45:6f., that Targum Jonathan Ps. 45:3 speaks of "O king Messiah" (*ibid.*, p. 24). But it is extremely tenuous to assert that anyone in pre-Christian Judaism actually identified the "son" of Ps. 2:7 with the "Son of David" of Pss. Sol. 17 and 18, or equated "sit at my right hand" of Ps. 110:1 with "sitting on the throne of glory" in the Similitudes of Enoch (even granting for the moment that I Enoch 37–71 was pre-Christian, which is itself a tenuous view), or transferred the ascription "king Messiah" of the targumic Ps. 45:3 to "God" of Ps. 45:6f.

which, to our knowledge, Jews could not have predicated of the messiah, . . . it seems fair to suppose that in the NT era a messianic interpretation of Ps. 110 was current in Judaism, although we cannot know how widely it was accepted."[52] All of this, of course, may very well be true. To date, however, our only explicit evidence that any of these verses was considered to have messianic connotations by any group within Judaism at a time approximating the first Christian century comes from the Dead Sea text 4QFlorilegium, which (1) identifies the "he" of "I will be to him a father, and he will be to me a son," in II Sam. 7:14, as "the Scion of David who will function in Zion in the Last Days," and (2) connects Ps. 2:1-2 with II Sam. 7:10-14 and Ps. 1:1 in its testimonia collection of passages having to do with "the Last Days."

While these verses may have carried some messianic nuances in certain quarters of pre-Christian Judaism, and despite the misuse that has sometimes been made of the suggestion, it nevertheless seems true to say that the author of Hebrews is primarily dependent upon an interpretive tradition within the Church and only secondarily relies upon his Jewish heritage for the identification of these six passages as being messianic—perhaps also for his grouping them in such a manner. The first two, Ps. 2:7 and II Sam. 7:14, are brought together on a *gezerah shawah* principle because of their reference to the "Son," and they are applied in a corporate solidarity fashion to Jesus as the True King of Israel (Ps. 2:1-12) and David's Greater Son (II Sam. 7:12-17). But though common Jewish hermeneutical devices are employed, the identification of these passages as pertaining to Jesus stems from a tradition within the early Church. Acts 4:24-30 represents the early believers as viewing Ps. 2:1f. as predictive of both their own circumstances under affliction and God's "holy child Jesus";[53] Acts 13:33

52 D. M. Hay, *Glory at the Right Hand*, p. 30; cf. pp. 21-33.

53 Contrary to B. Lindars, *New Testament Apologetic*, p. 143, and J. A. T. Robinson, "The Most Primitive Christology of All?" *JTS*, VII (1956), p. 179, such a prayer has every reason to be considered authentic. For a discussion of Robinson's view of the Christology of Acts 3—4, upon which view Lindars constructs his opposition, see my *Christology of Early Jewish Christianity*, pp. 77-79.

presents Paul in a synagogue at Pisidian Antioch as quoting Ps. 2:7 as a messianic testimonium with reference to Jesus; and allusions to Ps. 2 occur a number of times in the Apocalypse in a Christological context.[54] Luke 1:32f. represents the angel Gabriel as alluding to II Sam 7:12f., 16 in his message to Mary; and Paul perhaps had II Sam. 7:14 in mind in II Cor. 6:18, though, admittedly, not in application to Jesus but with reference to Christians in their relationship to God. It is true, of course, as we've just observed, that the Qumran sectarians thought of both Ps. 2:1f. and II Sam. 7:10-14 as having messianic import. But this parallel between Christianity and the Dead Sea community may be more analogical than genealogical in nature. On the principle of corporate solidarity, such passages regarding Israel's king and David's son would lend themselves to a fulfilment understanding by any group that believed itself to be culminating the hope of Israel. It may even be that a common messianic appreciation of these verses was one of "the elementary teachings about the Messiah" (*τὸν τῆς ἀρχῆς τοῦ Χριστοῦ λόγον*) which the author believed he held in common to some extent with his addressees, both as believers in Jesus and prior to their conversion.[55] And this could be why he began his argument on the basis of these two verses—in an endeavor to start from some point of common ground.

The last three verses in this initial catena of passages, Ps. 45:6f.; 102:25-27 and 110:1, are evidently brought together on the basis of their similarity in addressing God: "Your throne, O God (*ὁ θρόνος σου, ὁ θεός*), "You, Lord" (*σὺ κύριε*), and "The Lord said to my Lord" (*εἶπεν ὁ κύριος τῷ κυρίῳ μου*). The last of these three passages, Ps. 110:1, seems to provide the key to the writer's use of the other two. C. H. Dodd has pointed out that "this particular verse was one of the fundamental texts of the kerygma," being interpreted messianically by Jesus with reference to himself in Mark 12:36 par. and cited by Peter at Pentecost in Acts 2:34f.[56] Once the *κύριος* of Ps. 110:1 became ascribed to

[54] Rev. 2:26 (vv. 8f.); 6:15 (v. 2); 11:15 (v. 2), 18 (vv. 1, 5, 12); 12:5 (v. 9); 17:18 (v. 2); 19:15 (v. 9), 19 (v. 2).
[55] Heb. 6:1; cf. 5:12.
[56] Allusions to Ps. 110:1 are to be found in Mark 14:62; Acts 7:55; Rom. 8:34; Eph. 1:20; Col. 3:1 and I Pet. 3:22, as well as in Heb. 1:3;

Jesus (evidently under his own instigation), it would have been inevitable as Christological thought developed for other passages where deity is addressed to be also so ascribed—particularly in such a passage as Ps. 45:6f., where God is addressed (ὁ θεός, understood as a vocative) and yet distinguished from "God, your God" (ὁ θεός, ὁ θεός σου). And the fact that Ps. 110:1 is quoted without its address in Heb. 1:13, even though it was probably that address which originally brought the three passages together, suggests that this grouping of Christological testimonia was not original with the author of Hebrews but stemmed from an earlier Christian exegetical tradition.

The third of the verses in the catena, Deut. 32:43 (LXX), seems to stand alone. Yet not entirely alone, for in Judaism the Song of Moses (Deut. 32:1-43) was employed on an equal footing with the Psalms in such various places and situations as the temple of Jerusalem, the synagogues of Palestine and the Diaspora, the homes of pious Jews, and the writings of Philo.[57] There are indications of its widespread use among Christians as well: Paul quotes from it in Rom. 10:19; 12:19 and 15:10;[58] and its messianic relevance in Christian theology is explicitly set forth in Rev. 15:3, where the victorious ones in heaven sing "the Song of Moses, the servant of God, and the Song of the Lamb." All this suggests that Deut. 32:43 (LXX) had messianic relevance within the Church before Hebrews was written, for a tradition as reflected in Romans and the Apocalypse from which the writer to the Hebrews drew is easier to postulate than that either Paul or the Seer of the Apocalypse had drawn from Hebrews at this point.

In the first of his biblical expositions, then, our author sets forth a catena of six Christological passages, which

8:1; 10:12; 12:2. As D. M. Hay points out, even if the tradition of Mark 12:36 par. is wrong in attributing such a messianic employment to Jesus, "belief that he had spoken about the psalm's christological significance must have encouraged Christians to study and appropriate its verses" (*Glory at the Right Hand*, p. 159).

[57] Cf. S. Kistemaker, *Psalm Citations in the Epistle to the Hebrews*, who cites a number of rabbinic studies along with IV Macc. 18:18f. and Philo's Quod Det. Pot. Insid. 114; Leg. All. III. 105; De Plant. 59.

[58] Cf. also the allusions in Rom. 11:11; I Cor. 10:20, 22; Phil. 2:15; Luke 21:22; Rev. 6:10; 10:5; 18:20; 19:2.

passages can reasonably be argued to have been so understood within the Church prior to his writing. How were they originally identified as pertaining to Jesus? Mark 12:36 par. tells us that in the case of Ps. 110:1, it was Jesus himself who so interpreted; and, while we may be unable to trace back so directly the other five, it is probable that they are in some manner to be related to Jesus and apostolic exegesis as well.[59] How were they brought together into this particular form and order? We just don't know. It may be that a testimonia collection then current within a sector of the Church was employed,[60] or it may be that a particular liturgical order was followed.[61] Ps. 45:6f.; 102:25-27 and 110:1 seem to have been associated prior to the writer's use, which may suggest either or both possibilities. On the other hand, the author may be responding, either in whole or in part, to some particular collection of messianically relevant texts known to his readers, such as is represented by 4QFlor. Or, knowing of certain scattered messianic passages, it may have been his own contribution to have brought them together in this manner. Any or all of these suggestions may have something to do with the answer, though we really can do no more than speculate.

But while certain issues must be left unresolved, one thing in the exegetical procedure seems certain: that from a Christocentric perspective, the author of Hebrews was asking concerning what the Scriptures mean when they speak of God's son (Ps. 2:7; II Sam. 7:14), of one whom all the angels of God are to worship (Deut. 32:43, LXX), and of one who is addressed as God by God, yet distinguished from God (Ps. 45:6f.; 102:25-27; 110:1). From a purely historical perspective, such a question may yield various answers—or be found to some extent unanswerable. But from a Christocentric perspective and in line with the apostolic tradition, there was for our author only one possible answer: Jesus of Nazareth. This he took to be straightforward and clear. And believing that his addressees accepted the

[59] See *supra*, pp. 77f., 91f.
[60] Cf. F. C. Synge, *Hebrews and the Scriptures*, pp. 53f.
[61] Cf. M. Barth, "Old Testament in Hebrews," *Current Issues in New Testament Interpretation*, p. 73.

messianic nature of these passages as well, he expected them to appreciate his conclusion and act accordingly.

The second biblical exposition of the writer to the Hebrews is his treatment of Ps. 8:4-6 in Heb. 2:5-18. What does the psalmist mean, he asks, when he talks about man's creatureliness and subordination, and yet also of his destined glory, honor and universal authority? The promise of the passage concerns man's exaltation and rule over all God's creation. But this has obviously not taken place yet. What has taken place, however, according to the author of Hebrews, is that the process which will culminate in the fulfilment of this promise has been inaugurated in the person and work of Jesus. Jesus has taken upon himself man's full estate in order that by means of his own redemptive work he might bring the anticipation of the psalmist to full consummation. The Old Testament's teaching about man avowedly points forward into the future, and that future is inextricably bound up with Jesus—the pioneer of man's salvation, who has come to lead many sons to the full realization of their destined glory. From the dual perspectives of Jesus as God's promised Messiah and the inauguration of the last days in Jesus' redemptive ministry, our author has looked back to the unfulfilled promise of Ps. 8:4-6 and expounded the passage in quite a straightforward manner.[62]

Our author's third exposition, on Ps. 95:7-11 in Heb. 3:1–4:13, is quite similar in intent to the first two. His whole argument has to do with the question: What does the psalmist mean when he speaks about entering God's rest?[63] Is the rest to which he refers a matter having to do principally with the land of Canaan and Israelite nationhood, as was widely thought in popular Judaism of the day,[64] or had the psalmist something greater and still future in mind? On a *gezerah shawah* principle, the writer brings Gen. 2:2 into the argument, thereby demonstrating how important the

[62] Note, on the other hand, Paul's Christological employment of Ps. 8:6b in I Cor. 15:27 (quotation) and Eph. 1:22 (allusion).
[63] Cf. G. B. Caird, "Exegetical Method of the Epistle to the Hebrews," *CJT*, V (1959), p. 48.
[64] Cf. G. Schrenk, λεῖμμα, *TDNT*, IV, pp. 212f.

concept of rest is in biblical revelation. But his major hermeneutic principle is *dabar halamed me'inyano*, by which he is able to point out that the invitation to rest offered in Ps. 95 was given long after Israel had entered the land and attained national status.[65] Obviously, therefore, the invitation pertains to what was still future for the psalmist: commitment to "Jesus, the apostle and high priest whom we confess," who is the one greater than Moses and Joshua.[66] "For if Joshua had given them rest, God would not have spoken later about another day. There remains, then, a sabbath-rest for the people of God [τῷ λαῷ τοῦ θεοῦ here referring to God's chosen people, the Jews]; for anyone who enters God's rest also rests from his own work, just as God did from his."[67]

The exposition in Heb. 4:14–7:28 focuses on Ps. 110:4, with the verse explicitly quoted in Heb. 5:6; 7:17 and 21. G. B. Caird has somewhat overstated the case when he argues that "it is important to recognize that throughout his treatment of Melchizedek our author is concerned *solely* with the exegesis of Ps. 110,"[68] for the narrative of Gen. 14:18-20—both in what is said about Melchizedek and what is not—plays a significant role in the author's argument as well. But Caird is quite right to insist that "he carries us back to the story of Genesis 14 not to compose a fanciful and allegorical *midrash* on that chapter after the manner of Philo, but rather because he wishes to answer the very modern question: 'What did the words "priest for ever after the order of Melchizedek" mean to the psalmist who wrote them?' "[69] The writer accepted Ps. 110 as being messianic, in continuity with Jesus' sanction and apostolic tradition, and he sought to explicate verse 4 along these lines.[70] Further, he could very well have known that at least one group within first-century Judaism—perhaps the very group

[65] Cf. Paul's use of this exegetical rule in Rom. 4:10f. and Gal. 3:17 (*supra*, p. 118).
[66] Heb. 3:1-6.
[67] Heb. 4:8-10.
[68] G. B. Caird, "Exegetical Method of the Epistle to the Hebrews," *CJT*, V (1959), p. 48 (italics mine).
[69] *Ibid.*
[70] Cf. his connection of Ps. 110:1 and 4 in Heb. 8:1, and note as well how these verses are logically joined in Ps. 110.

to which his readers owed their earlier allegiance—held Melchizedek to be in some manner an eschatological and messianic figure.[71] On the basis, therefore, of his Christian theological perspectives and exegetical heritage, and possibly in view of his addressees' understanding of the enigmatic personage in Gen. 14, the writer asks: Who was this Melchizedek and what was the nature of his priesthood—particularly in view of the fact that the psalmist speaks of him in a messianic passage?

We need not become diverted into a psychoanalysis of the psalmist at this point, as though millennia later we could assemble the exact details of his consciousness when writing. Nor need we become carried away with the writer's allegorical-etymological treatment of "Melchizedek" and "Salem," for, as R. P. C. Hanson points out, his handling of these names is "so simple and obvious" that their employment hardly signals an Alexandrian hermeneutic *per se*, much less a specifically Philonic interpretation.[72] For the writer of Hebrews, the solution to the enigma of Gen. 14:18-20 is incorporated in Ps. 110:4—but it is only clearly seen when Ps. 110 is understood as being messianic. And from this Christian view of the psalm, the typological correspondences that lie inherent in redemptive history can be drawn out and a fuller sense in the narrative explicated. The author of Hebrews, it seems, did not consider himself to be inventing a new interpretation or employing a deviant exegetical procedure. He was simply extending the application of a psalm that had already been identified within the Church as being messianic, and he was doing so in light of the interests and concerns of his readers. In the process, of course, he got involved in a mild allegorical-etymological treatment of the narrative in Gen. 14. But given his presuppositions, precedents and audience, his explication is in the main quite straightforward and telling.

The fifth of our author's expositions, and the climax of his biblical argument in the letter, centers on Jeremiah's prophecy of a new covenant in Jer. 31:31-34. The passage is

[71] For a discussion of Melchizedek in Jewish speculations generally and at Qumran in particular, see my *Christology of Early Jewish Christianity*, pp. 116-18.
[72] R. P. C. Hanson, *Allegory and Event* (1959), p. 86.

the longest connected citation in the New Testament; and while it is cited explicitly only in Heb. 8:8-12 and 10:16f., it serves as the basis for the whole discussion in Heb. 8:1–10:39. The question the writer here poses is: What did the prophet Jeremiah mean by a new covenant? Did he think of the Mosaic covenant as the culmination and apex of God's redemptive program (as, evidently, the addressees of Hebrews were tempted to do), or did he look beyond that covenant to consummation in the future when a new covenant would be established? Obviously the latter, the writer asserts, "for if that first covenant had been faultless, there would have been no occasion sought for a second. But God found fault with them and said, 'The days will come, says the Lord, when I will establish a new covenant with the house of Israel and with the house of Judah.'"[73] In speaking of a new covenant, therefore, Jeremiah obviously recognized that there was a built-in obsolescence to the old covenant; "and what is obsolete and growing old is ready to vanish away."[74] G. B. Caird has rightly insisted:

> Here is a perfectly sound piece of exegesis. Jeremiah predicted the establishment of a new covenant because he believed the old one to be inadequate for the religious needs of sinful men. The sacrifices of the old covenant were a perpetual reminder of sin and of man's need for atonement, but what men needed was the effective removal of sin, so that it could no longer barricade the way into the inner presence of God.[75]

Our author takes an undisputed messianic prophecy, and, from the perspective of eschatological consummation in Christ, emphasizes its confession of inadequacy for the Mosaic covenant and its promise of a new covenant—which new covenant, he insists, has come in the person and work of Jesus. It is a straightforward piece of biblical exegesis—granted his basic Christian presupposition—and our author expects that it will have telling effect upon his readers.

The argument of the Letter to the Hebrews, then, is constructed around five biblical portions: a catena of pas-

[73] Heb. 8:7f. The reading αὐτοῖς of P^{46} and B allows v. 8 to be read: "But God found fault and said to them."
[74] Heb. 8:13.
[75] G. B. Caird, "Exegetical Method of the Epistle to the Hebrews," *CJT*, V (1959), p. 47.

sages and four individual passages. These five portions were selected, evidently, because (1) they spoke of the eschatological Messiah and/or of God's redemption in the Last Days, either as traditionally accepted or as understood within the Church, and (2) they set forth the incompleteness of the old economy under Moses and looked forward to a consummation that was to come. The writer employs a number of exegetical procedures that were common in his day, both to Jews and to Christians; for example, *gezerah shawah* and *dabar halamed me'inyano*, an allegorical-etymological treatment of names, and a concept of fulfilment that included corporate solidarity and typological correspondences in history. But at the heart of his exegetical endeavors is the quite straightforward query: What do the Scriptures mean when viewed from a Christocentric perspective? He is probably not originating a pesher interpretation of the passages himself, for in chapter 1 he seems to be only repeating certain apostolic pesher treatments; nor is he engaged in midrashic exegesis *per se*, though at points he makes use of rather common midrashic techniques; nor is he developing an allegorical understanding of the Old Testament, though in chapter 7 he treats two names in a mildly allegorical fashion. Rather, what he seems to be doing is basing himself upon an accepted exegetical tradition within the Church and straightforwardly explicating relationships within that tradition and implications for his addressees in light of their circumstances. As such, his use of the Old Testament is in continuity with what has preceded him in Christian hermeneutics, but unique in his own treatment of relationships and implications.

VII: JEWISH CHRISTIAN TRACTATES AND THE OLD TESTAMENT

The canonical epistles of James, I and II Peter, I, II and III John, and Jude, together with the canonical Apocalypse of John, comprise a group of writings having many features in common. Particularly is this the case with regard to the semitic cast of their expressions, their arguments and the form of their presentations. In the use of the Old Testament, however, while evidencing continuity with earlier Christian exegesis and a degree of correspondence among themselves, there are significant differences between them. I Peter, for example, is replete with direct quotations and clear biblical allusions, and James is fairly similar; while the Apocalypse is saturated with allusions but has no direct quotations, and the Johannine letters are devoid of either quotations or allusions. In addition, I Peter, as well as treating the Scriptures literally, builds upon pesher treatments of particular themes and passages employed within the early Church and develops them, whereas James, II Peter and Jude confine themselves to a more literalistic usage. It is this complex of continuity, correspondence and dissimilarity that needs to be identified, spelled out and related to the patterns of biblical exegesis found in the rest of the New Testament.

THE NATURE OF THE MATERIALS

It was Eusebius who first spoke of James, I and II Peter, I, II and III John, and Jude collectively as the "seven catholic epistles,"[1] though earlier I John and then I Peter had been

[1] Eusebius, Eccl. Hist. II. 23. 24f.; cf. Canon 59 of the Council of Laodicea (A.D. 363).

so designated. The adjective καθολικός was employed in the sense of "encyclical" or "universal" on the assumption that these letters were intended for Christians generally, in contrast to those of Paul which were addressed to individual congregations and persons. But it is becoming increasingly evident, as a result of their conceptual and expressional affinities to the Qumran texts,[2] that these letters, as well as the Apocalypse of John, are basically Jewish Christian tractates which probably first circulated within the Jewish mission of the Church. Just as Paul identified the "pillars" of the Jerusalem Church as being James, Cephas and John, so these three in particular were associated in the mind of early Christians as the principal leaders of the Jewish mission in Palestine and throughout the Diaspora.[3]

James. At the turn of the century, the Letter of James was variously evaluated. A few agreed with F. Spitta that it was a Jewish ethical tractate which had undergone Christian redaction.[4] Most English-speaking scholars, however, viewed it as in some way connected with a Palestinian-based Jewish Christianity, though they were divided between the view of F. J. A. Hort and J. B. Mayor that it was written by James, the Lord's brother, and therefore reflects the thought and circumstances of pre-destruction Jerusalem Christianity,[5] and the position popularized by J. H. Ropes that "it is probably the pseudonymous production of a Christian of Jewish origin, living in Palestine in the last quarter of the

[2] Cf. W. F. Albright: "Each of the Catholic Epistles contains many Essene reminiscences. . . . I must stress the fact that it is not necessary to suppose that these reminiscences were exclusively Essene. They may also go back to other earlier Jewish sects whose literatures have been lost. We do know, however, that little of this material appears in Rabbinic sources, which reflect later Pharisaism in its development from the time of Christ onward" ("Retrospect and Prospect in New Testament Archaeology," *The Teacher's Yoke*, ed. E. J. Vardeman and J. L. Garrett [1964], p. 41).

[3] Gal. 2:9. Interestingly, the only three occurrences of the word διασπορά in the New Testament occur in writings ascribed to these three: Jas. 1:1; I Pet. 1:1; John 7:35.

[4] F. Spitta, "Der Brief des Jakobus," *Zur Geschichte und Litteratur des Urchristentums*, II (1896), pp. 1-239; cf. also R. H. Fuller, *A Critical Introduction to the New Testament* (1966), p. 153.

[5] F. J. A. Hort, *The Epistle of St. James* (1909), pp. xi-xxii; J. B. Mayor, *The Epistle of St. James* (1910), pp. i-lxv.

first century or the first quarter of the second."[6] On the continent, meanwhile, German scholarship tended to place it in a hellenistic context entirely.

Between World War I and the publication of the Dead Sea Scrolls, critical opinion regarding James became fairly solidified along the lines of a hellenistic interpretation. The "developed" ethical stance of the letter, its reference to elders in the Church (5:14), its apparent reaction to Pauline teaching (2:14-26), its homily or diatribe form of argument, its employment of the LXX, and its excellent quality of Greek all seemed to point quite conclusively to an early second-century Gentile Christian addressing fellow Greek believers.[7] In light of the Qumran texts, however, some of these objections to an early Palestinian provenance have been found to lack relevance.

Critical opinion of late has returned more and more to the recognition that, as W. L. Knox expressed it, "it is only as the expression of the attitude of the primitive Church in Jerusalem that the Epistle of S. James becomes intelligible."[8] The quality of the letter's Greek (though claims for its excellence have at times been overdone) may be explained along the lines of F. J. A. Hort's insistence and J. N. Sevenster's full-scale defense of the widespread prevalence of Greek in first-century Palestine[9] or on Otto Roller's amanuensis thesis.[10] The rationale for the letter's use of the LXX in its biblical citations and allusions may be the same as that suggested for the basically similar phenomenon in the book of Acts: accommodation to the addressees' usage

[6] J. H. Ropes, *A Critical and Exegetical Commentary on the Epistle of St. James* (1916), p. 1.

[7] Cf. E. J. Goodspeed, *An Introduction to the New Testament* (1937), pp. 289-295; R. H. Fuller, *Critical Introduction to the New Testament*, pp. 152-54.

[8] W. L. Knox, *St. Paul and the Church of Jerusalem* (1925), p. 21, n. 44. Cf., e.g., J. W. Bowman, *Hebrews, James, I & II Peter*, pp. 93-96; R. M. Grant, *A Historical Introduction to the New Testament* (1963), pp. 219-222; G. R. Beasley-Murray, *The General Epistles* (1965), pp. 18-20; C. L. Mitton, *The Epistle of James* (1966), pp. 9, 235-37; E. M. Sidebottom, *James, Jude and 2 Peter* (1967), pp. 1-24.

[9] F. J. A. Hort, *Epistle of St. James*, pp. iii-iv; J. N. Sevenster, *Do You Know Greek?*

[10] O. Roller, *Das Formular der paulinischen Briefe.*

and/or the employment of Greek testimonia portions then circulating within the Church.[11]

Many have proposed that James was first a homily or a sermon—perhaps a number of extracts drawn from several sermons—and only later cast into the form of a letter and circulated widely. The nature of the letter itself supports such a view, for, as J. H. Ropes observed in the first sentence of his commentary, "the Epistle of James is a religious and moral tract having the form, but only the form, of a letter";[12] and the Jewish proclivity to gather together characteristic maxims of revered teachers, as are found in the various "Sayings" collections of talmudic literature, suggests that such compendiums could be expected in Jewish Christian circles as well. And while it may be sufficient for historical purposes to view the epistle as "a collection of fragments" drawn from "the Jewish Christian tradition of Jerusalem" and "ascribed to James because he was the ruler of the Jerusalem Church,"[13] a convincing case can be made for James, the brother of Jesus, as the source of the letter's content, and that that content, as perhaps reworked stylistically by an amanuensis, was sent out or distributed in some manner prior to A.D. 62 to Jewish Christians living in the Diaspora. With C. L. Mitton, therefore, and allowing for the possibility of an amanuensis, "we proceed . . . on the assumption that the epistle was written by James the brother of our Lord, and that it was written for the benefit of Jewish Christian visitors to Jerusalem who wished to have some record of James' characteristic teaching to take back with them for the benefit of the Christians in their home towns."[14]

I Peter. The epistle of I Peter has also been prominent in the discussions of critical scholars during the past century, particularly with regard to the identity of its author and the nature of its presentation.[15] Its style, syntax and vocabu-

[11] See *supra*, pp. 87-89.
[12] J. H. Ropes, *Epistle of St. James*, p. 1.
[13] R. M. Grant, *Historical Introduction to the New Testament*, p. 222.
[14] C. L. Mitton, *Epistle of James*, p. 9.
[15] For two almost classic commentaries of recent vintage expressing diametrically opposing views on most introductory issues, see E. G.

lary are those of a writer fluent and at ease in Greek. It is heavily dependent on the LXX for its biblical citations and allusions. It echoes the Pauline writings at many places in its outlook and expression. It seems to reflect a time when believers were officially persecuted by Rome for bearing the name "Christian" (cf. 4:12-16). And, as is sometimes claimed, it incorporates ideas and practices that may be paralleled to some extent by those of the Greek mystery religions. All of this seems hardly characteristic of Peter, the Galilean fisherman, whom Acts 4:13 describes as being "unlearned and ignorant," and many have therefore opted for pseudonymous authorship and a Gentile provenance.[16] On the other hand, the letter claims to be written by "Peter, an apostle of Jesus Christ" and "a witness of the sufferings of Christ,"[17] and it has been traditionally so accepted. Its use of the Old Testament is in continuity with early Christian interpretation and reflects a distinctly apostolic treatment. And there are a number of parallels between its teachings and those attributed to Peter in the book of Acts.[18]

The problem of I Peter's authorship is greatly relieved, however, if we assume that "Silvanus the faithful brother" of I Pet. 5:12, through whom the author tells us he wrote, was the Silas of Acts and served as Peter's amanuensis with a considerable measure of freedom. Silas is portrayed in Acts as a leading member within the early Church, a Roman citizen, and a man of some culture.[19] He also, of course, was Paul's companion on the second and third missionary journeys of Acts, and he evidently had some part in the drafting of the Pauline correspondence.[20] Assuming, therefore, such an identity for Silvanus and that he was given a considerable measure of literary freedom in the composition of the epistle, the excellent quality of Greek in I Peter and its numerous resemblances to the letters of Paul are readily

---

Selwyn, *The First Epistle of St. Peter* (1946), and F. W. Beare, *The First Epistle of Peter* (1945, 1958).

[16] Cf. W. G. Kümmel, *Introduction to the New Testament*, pp. 296-98, where this view is espoused and a bibliography given.

[17] I Pet. 1:1; 5:1.

[18] Cf. E. G. Selwyn, *First Epistle of St. Peter*, pp. 33-36.

[19] Acts 15:22-40; 16:37; 17:4.

[20] Cf. I Thess. 1:1; II Thess. 1:1.

explainable.[21] Likewise, we need not be overly staggered by the epistle's use of the LXX, for, as may be true with regard to this similar phenomenon elsewhere in the New Testament as well,[22] "this is merely what we should expect of one writing to churches in the Roman Empire whose Old Testament would ordinarily be the ancient Greek translation."[23] Nor need we understand I Pet. 4:12-16 as having persecutions under Domitian or Trajan in mind, for, while the "fiery trials" could refer to a constitutional sentence, they could just as easily have in view "the rough justice of unofficial action";[24] and while "reproach for the name of Christ" was a factor when Emperor worship became a policy of Rome, it was also part and parcel of the Christians' experience much earlier. C. E. B. Cranfield has rightly said:

> It is pressing the language of 4:16 much too far, to read into it the distinction between condemnation "for the Name" and condemnation "for crimes associated with the Name." To the Christians themselves it can hardly have seemed a particularly important distinction, whether they were actually condemned on a trumped-up charge of incendiarism or for not worshipping the Emperor or simply for being Christians; from their point of view, whatever the legal complications may have been, Christians suffered because they were Christians.[25]

As to the nature of I Peter, a great variety of hypotheses have been proposed. Everyone notes the break in the exhortations after the doxology of 4:11, and many have observed that 1:3–4:11 appears to speak of suffering as a possibility whereas 4:12–5:11 refers to suffering as a present condi-

[21] Cf. A. S. Peake, *A Critical Introduction to the New Testament* (1909), pp. 90-95; E. G. Selwyn, *First Epistle of St. Peter*, pp. 7-17; C. E. B. Cranfield, *The First Epistle of Peter* (1950), pp. 7f.; A. M. Stibbs, *The First Epistle General of Peter* (1959), pp. 25-45 (introduction by A. F. Walls); J. W. Bowman, *Hebrews, James, I & II Peter*, pp. 116-120; R. M. Grant, *Historical Introduction to the New Testament*, pp. 223-26. Conversely, see F. W. Beare, *First Epistle of Peter*, pp. 24-31. For a radical interpretation of I Peter as a late corrective to the "militancy" of the Apocalypse, see E. J. Goodspeed, *Introduction to the New Testament*, pp. 267-272.

[22] See *supra*, pp. 87-89.

[23] J. W. Bowman, *Hebrews, James, I & II Peter*, p. 117.

[24] C. F. D. Moule, *Birth of the New Testament*, p. 113.

[25] C. E. B. Cranfield, *First Epistle of Peter*, pp. 8f.

tion.[26] Most, likewise, believe that various sermonic, catechetical and/or liturgical materials have been incorporated into the structure of the epistle. But scholars have drawn very diverse conclusions regarding the significance of such data. Some treat the differences between the two sections as inconsequential and think of the writing as a baptismal sermon that has been set into an epistolary framework; others view the first section as a baptismal sermon to which has been added an epistolary opening and concluding exhortations; some see it as catechetical teaching given prior to baptism and further instruction given after baptism; some believe that at the basis of the writing lies a baptismal liturgy for the Passover season; and a few propose that what we have are really two separate letters, one to those not yet under persecution and another to those actually suffering persecution, which two letters have been joined in our canonical epistle.[27] I personally favor the view that I Pet. 1:3–4:11 is a compendium of Petrine sermonic and catechetical material, to which has been added the epistolary opening of 1:1-2, the exhortations of 4:12–5:11, and the closing exhortation and salutation in Peter's own hand of 5:12-14. And it is this hypothesis that underlies my treatment of the letter here. In the form sent out to Christians in the five provinces of northern Asia Minor and preserved for us, the work is genuinely epistolary. But in that it incorporates earlier material representative of Peter's preaching and teaching—perhaps even an early baptismal hymn (3:18-22), as incorporated by Peter into his sermons and liturgical practice—it has the character as well of a Jewish Christian tractate.

I, II, III John. Determination as to authorship of the Johannine epistles is largely dependent upon conclusions regarding the Fourth Gospel, for the Epistles and Gospel are intimately related stylistically, conceptually and theologically. For the Fourth Gospel, the traditional ascription of John the son of Zebedee and disciple of Jesus still commends itself under careful scrutiny as the most probable

[26] Cf. I Pet. 1:6; 2:20 and 3:14, 17 with 4:12, 14, 19 and 5:6, 8.
[27] For listings of proponents of these various positions, see W. G. Kümmel, *Introduction to the New Testament*, pp. 294-96.

hypothesis—at least for its essential content, if not also for its form.[28] The parallels between I John and the literature stemming from an Essene cycle of influence indicate that the Johannine epistles are deeply rooted in a Jewish Christian milieu.[29] And the prominence given to the confession of Jesus as the Messiah (ὁ Χριστός) favors identifying the recipients as being in some sense Jewish as well,[30] whether religiously so or converts to Jesus from such a background.[31] Even those embryonic gnostic features that have sometimes been found within the epistle are not contrary to such a provenance, for, as J. C. O'Neill rightly maintains, "the time is now past when gnosticism and Judaism, for example, can be regarded as mutually exclusive terms."[32] Contrary to James and I Peter, no statement appears in I John regarding the addressees' residence. It seems probable, however, that I John at first circulated widely within that part of the Jewish Christian mission associated with the apostle John as a compendium of the apostle's characteristic teaching, and perhaps II and III John served as covering letters in two specific instances. But all this is somewhat irrelevant for our purposes here, since the Johannine epistles are devoid of either quotations or allusions, and therefore do not enter into our consideration of early Christian exegesis.

II Peter, Jude. The difficulties of establishing provenance and destination for the epistles of II Peter and Jude are considerable. Few today consider them written before A.D. 80, and most prefer a date ranging from a decade or two later to a half century later. Yet the correspondence be-

[28] For a constructive evaluation of the Fourth Gospel's authorship, though without adhering to all the details in his five-stage development hypothesis, see R. E. Brown, *The Gospel according to John*, I, pp. lxxxvii-cii.

[29] Cf. J. C. O'Neill, *The Puzzle of I John* (1966). While O'Neill has pushed his thesis to unwarranted extremes, the data upon which it is based certainly support a Jewish Christian provenance for the epistle.

[30] Cf. I Jn. 2:22; 5:1.

[31] On the recipients as unconverted Jews, see J. A. T. Robinson, "The Destination and Purpose of the Johannine Epistles," *NTS*, VII (1960), pp. 56-65, and J. C. O'Neill, *Puzzle of I John*, pp. 5f., 65-67; as Jewish Christians, see R. Schnackenburg, *Die Johannesbriefe* (1963), pp. 16f., 156.

[32] J. C. O'Neill, *Puzzle of I John*, p. 6.

tween the ideology, terminology and outlook of these epistles and that expressed in the Qumran texts and Jewish nonconformist literature of the day—particularly in regard to apocalyptic orientation, angelology and ethical dualism—has brought about some readiness in the scholarly world to entertain earlier dates and to root these letters in a more Jewish-Christian milieu than heretofore.[33]

A case for the traditionally ascribed authorship of each of these letters is by no means impossible. The absence of any reference to an amanuensis in II Peter may be the key to its stylistic and conceptual differences from I Peter. Perhaps here is how Peter himself wrote when not aided by Silas (I Pet. 5:12), Mark (*a la* Papias on the composition of Mark's Gospel), or Luke (cf. Peter's preaching in Acts). And the departure from the LXX in its one Old Testament quotation in II Pet. 2:22, evidently translating directly from the Hebrew of Prov. 26:11, seems to suggest a hebraic background for II Peter. Likewise, a circumstantial case can be made for Jude. Paul's reference to "brothers of the Lord" carrying on an itinerant ministry[34] suggests that Jude's conversion and prominence in the early Church is no more impossible than that of James. "It is not inconceivable," as G. R. Beasley-Murray points out, "that after the death of James, Jude should have addressed a similar circle of readers as his brother to safeguard them from new perils."[35] The reference to Enoch in verse 14 and the allusion to the Assumption of Moses in verse 9 seem to relate the author and his readers to the category of believers with a Jewish background. And it is difficult to see why a pseudonymous writer would assume the name of Jude to commend his work when a more prominent figure would surely have served better.

The Apocalypse. That the Apocalypse of John stems from a Jewish Christian milieu and was addressed to Jewish Christians seems beyond all reasonable doubt. In form, it is comparable to the spate of Jewish apocalyptic writings associated with the names of Enoch, Abraham, Moses,

[33] Cf. J. W. Bowman, *Hebrews, James, I & II Peter*, pp. 156-160.
[34] I Cor. 9:5.
[35] G. R. Beasley-Murray, *General Epistles*, p. 73.

Baruch and Ezra. Its very first word, in fact, furnishes the name for this distinctive type of literary genre. In content, it is thoroughly saturated with the Old Testament. Though it contains no formal quotations, 278 verses of its total 404 contain allusions to the Scriptures.[36] In style, its language is "particularly stained by 'Semitisms'."[37] In fact, "no New Testament book has a better claim to be written in 'Jews' Greek' than the Apocalypse."[38]

A good case for the apostolicity of the Fourth Gospel, the Johannine epistles, and the Apocalypse can be made on the basis of an amanuensis thesis applied to the Gospel and Epistles.[39] Assuming the validity of the Patmos reference in Rev. 1:9, it may be supposed that secretarial assistance was more available within the metropolitan Christian community of Ephesus and more difficult to come by in exile on Patmos. But if distinction must be made, with R. M. Grant, "we should incline to say that if either book is to be ascribed to the son of Zebedee it is the book of Revelation."[40] Just why the work is directed to seven churches in Asia Minor, and not to others, is a continuing problem. Various theories regarding prominence, geographical relationships and symbolic representation have been proposed. But perhaps the answer is simply that these were churches especially under John's care back on the mainland of Asia Minor, and it is to them that he sent this tractate on Christian hope and perseverance.

THE PHENOMENA OF THE QUOTATIONS

In the writings we have called Jewish Christian tractates, there is a somewhat confusing mixture of (1) biblical citations, (2) biblical allusions, (3) noncanonical materials, and (4) unidentifiable proverbial maxims. The lines of demarca-

36 As calculated by H. B. Swete, *The Apocalypse of St. John* (1909), p. cxl.

37 M. Black, "Second Thoughts—X. The Semitic Element in the New Testament," *ExpT*, LXXVII (1965), p. 23.

38 *Ibid.*

39 Cf. E. Stauffer, *New Testament Theology* (ET 1955), pp. 40f. for a strong assertion of common apostolic authorship.

40 R. M. Grant, *Historical Introduction to the New Testament*, p. 235.

tion between biblical and nonbiblical materials is in some of these letters not as clearly drawn as elsewhere in the New Testament, and the interplay between explicit citation and more indirect allusion is in some cases heightened. All of this makes any listing of biblical quotations in this body of literature extremely difficult, though the following fifteen are more or less able to be identified.

I. Quotations occurring in James:

1. Jas. 2:8 (Lev. 19:18)—I.F.: "If you fulfil the royal law according to the scripture (εἰ μέντοι νόμον τελεῖτε βασιλικὸν κατὰ τὴν γραφήν), you do well."
2. Jas. 2:11a (Exod. 20:14; Deut. 5:18)—I.F.: "for he who said" (ὁ γὰρ εἰπών).
3. Jas. 2:11b (Exod. 20:13; Deut. 5:17)[41] —I.F.: "also said" (εἶπεν καί).
4. Jas. 2:23a (Gen. 15:6)—I.F.: "the scripture was fulfilled that said" (ἐπληρώθη ἡ γραφὴ ἡ λέγουσα).
5. Jas. 4:5 (probably a proverbial maxim drawn from such passages as Gen. 6:3-7; Exod. 20:5 and Deut. 32:11f., 16-22)[42] —I.F.: "do you think the scripture says in vain" (δοκεῖτε ὅτι κενῶς ἡ γραφὴ λέγει).
6. Jas. 4:6 (Prov. 3:34)—I.F.: "therefore he says" (διὸ λέγει).

[41] This order, in which the sixth commandment follows the seventh, is probably due to the order found in Exod. 20 of LXX^A (though not LXX^B); cf. also Luke 18:20; Rom 13:9 and Philo, De Decal. 12, 24, 32; De Spec. Leg. III. 2. For the usual order, see Deut. 5:17f.; Matt. 5:21, 27 and 19:18. The order in Mark 10:19 varies in different MSS.

[42] The difficulty in identifying the passage or passages in question is notorious. Some suggest a lost writing is here being quoted, as the Book of Eldad and Medad (cf. Num. 11:29) or a variant LXX reading; others that the words following "the scripture says" are really parenthetic, and that the only quotation involved is Prov. 3:34 in verse 6; a few that the "scripture" referred to is the Dead Sea Manual of Discipline (1QS); while most postulate that the general sense of several Old Testament passages is here being employed (cf. J. B. Mayor, *Epistle of St. James*, p. 131; E. M. Sidebottom, *James, Jude and 2 Peter*, pp. 52f.; C. L. Mitton, *Epistle of James*, pp. 153f.). Elaborating on this latter view, it is the conjunction of this quotation with a canonical proverb and the parallel of a similar phenomenon in II Pet. 2:22 that has led to my calling this statement a proverbial maxim drawn from such biblical materials as Gen. 6:3-7; Exod. 20:5 and Deut. 32:11f., 16-22 (the "Song of Moses").

II. Quotations occurring in I Peter:

7. I Pet. 1:16 (Lev. 11:44; 19:2; 20:7)—I.F.: "for it is written" (διότι γέγραπται).
8. I Pet. 1:24f. (Isa. 40:6-8)—I.F.: "for" (διότι).
9. I Pet. 2:6 (Isa. 28:16)—I.F.: "for it is contained in scripture" (διότι περιέχει ἐν γραφῇ).
10. I Pet. 2:7 (Ps. 118:22 [LXX=117:22])—I.F.: none.
11. I Pet. 2:8 (Isa. 8:14)—I.F.: "and."
12. I Pet. 3:10-12 (Ps. 34:12-16 [LXX=33:12-16])—I.F.: "for" (γάρ).
13. I Pet. 4:18 (Prov. 11:31)—I.F.: "and."
14. I Pet. 5:5 (Prov. 3:34)—I.F.: "because" (ὅτι).

III. Quotation occurring in II Peter:

15. II Pet. 2:22 (Prov. 26:11)—I.F.: "it has happened to them according to the true proverb" (συμβέβηκεν αὐτοῖς τὸ τῆς ἀληθοῦς παροιμίας).

In addition to these explicit biblical citations, attention should also be drawn to (1) the many biblical allusions in these Jewish Christian tractates, (2) the employment of nonbiblical materials in Jude,[43] and (3) the use of an unidentifiable proverbial maxim in conjunction with a canonical proverb in II Peter.[44] The letters of James, I Peter, II Peter and Jude have slightly more allusions to the Old Testament than they do quotations,[45] with a number of those in I Peter so prominent in the argument of the letter as to come close to being direct citations: particularly, 2:9 (Exod. 23:22 [LXX]; 19:5f.; Isa. 43:20f.); 2:10 (Hos. 1:6, 8f.; 2:1, 23) and 2:22-25 (Isa. 53:4-6, 9, 12).[46] And the Apocalypse, as noted above, contains allusions to the Scriptures in over three-fifths of its verses.[47] In Jude, I Enoch 1:9 is quoted in verses 14 and 15, being introduced by "Enoch, the seventh from Adam, prophesied, saying." Fur-

[43] On echoes of apocryphal terminology in I Peter, see E. G. Selwyn, *Epistle of St. Peter*, p. 25.
[44] Cf. also Jas. 4:5 above, though there the maxim seems to be drawn from biblical sources.
[45] Cf. Jas. 1:10f.; 2:21, 23b; 3:9; 5:4, 11; I Pet. 2:3, 4, 9, 10, 22-25; 3:6, 10-12, 14f.; 4:8, 14; 5:7; II Pet. 1:17; 3:8, 13; and (possibly) Jude 9.
[46] Cf. also I Pet. 3:14f. (Isa. 8:12f.) and 4:8 (Prov. 10:12).
[47] See *supra*, p. 195.

ther influence from I Enoch can be seen in verse 6, and possibly from the Assumption of Moses in verse 9. Also, in II Pet. 2:22 a proverbial maxim of uncertain origin is joined with the quotation of Prov. 26:11, with both of them introduced by the one introductory statement: "it has happened to them according to the true proverb."

Surveying the biblical quotations in the Jewish Christian tractates, two matters of a purely formal nature stand out. In the first place, it is obvious that the quotations occur almost exclusively in James and I Peter. II Peter and Jude each employ quoted material once: II Peter citing Prov. 26:11 in conjunction with a proverb of undetermined origin and Jude citing I Enoch 1:9 as a prophecy—both cases being rather strange when compared with the rest of the New Testament. The Apocalypse is replete with biblical expressions and allusions, but lacks any clear quotation; while the Johannine epistles are devoid of either quotations or allusions. A number of problems, of course, come to the fore here—particularly in regard to the usage of II Peter and Jude, as well as the lack of any biblical employment in the Johannine epistles—for which there are no ready answers. It may be that such phenomena are indicative of pseudonymity. On the other hand, this type of data in such short letters is hardly conclusive, and may only suggest certain personal idiosyncrasies or certain exegetical developments in the apostolic period.

A second item of note in the quotations has to do with the form of the text employed. The citations in James and I Peter are entirely septuagintal in form, with only minor variations; and even the allusions are heavily dependent upon the LXX, as can most easily be seen in the reliance of I Pet. 2:9 upon the septuagintal form of Exod. 23:22. On the other hand, though rather strangely employed in conjunction with a nonbiblical proverb, the text of Prov. 26:11 in II Pet. 2:22 is thoroughly hebraic and not reflective of the LXX at all. Here, again, such phenomena may imply pseudonymity; though they can also be used in support of an argument for authenticity.[48]

[48] See *supra*, p. 194.

LITERALIST TREATMENTS

Of more significance than these formal matters, however, is the manner in which the Old Testament is employed in the canonical Jewish Christian tractates. And most prominent in this regard are the literalist treatments of Scripture.

James, it is true, introduces Lev. 19:18 with the words "if you fulfil the royal law according to the scripture" and prefaces Gen. 15:6 with "the scripture was fulfilled that said," which appear at first glance to signal pesher treatments involving a fulfilment theme. But the word used for "fulfil" in Jas. 2:8 (Lev. 19:18) is *τελέω*, which means to "carry out" or "put into practice," and is a different word from *πληρόω*, used by Jesus to describe his own purpose and intention to "fulfil the law" in Matt. 5:17, and by the apostolic writers almost always in the passive to present the fulfilment of prophecy. And while *πληρόω* is employed in Jas. 2:23 (Gen. 15:6), the author's point is that the "sacrifice" of Isaac in Gen. 22:1-19 explicates more fully the meaning of the statement about Abraham's faith in Gen. 15:6, which use of the idea of fulfilment is entirely in accord with rabbinic treatments of Abraham's faith rather than an expression of a distinctively Christian fulfilment theme.[49]

The passages quoted in James are drawn entirely from either the Pentateuch or Proverbs, and all of them are treated in quite a literalist fashion. In 2:8 the "royal law according to the scripture" (*νόμον βασιλικὸν κατὰ τὴν γραφήν*) is identified as, "You shall love your neighbor as yourself" (Lev. 19:18), which, James says, "you do well" (*καλῶς ποιεῖτε*) to "put into practice" (*τελέω*). In 2:11 he reminds his readers that the same God who said, "You shall not commit adultery" (Exod. 20:14; Deut. 5:18) also said, "You shall not kill" (Exod. 20:13; Deut. 5:17). In 2:23 he

[49] On James' use of Gen. 15:6 and its rabbinic parallels, see J. B. Mayor, *Epistle of St. James*, p. 97; J. W. Doeve, *Jewish Hermeneutics in the Synoptic Gospels and Acts*, pp. 107f.; E. M. Sidebottom, *James, Jude and 2 Peter*, p. 45. For the view that James believed Gen. 15:6 was a prophecy fulfilled in Gen. 22:1-19, see J. H. Ropes, *Epistle of St. James*, p. 221.

argues that Abraham's faith (Gen. 15:6) was proven and more fully expressed by his act of obedience in the matter of sacrificing Isaac (Gen. 22:1-19). In 4:5 he recalls what was probably a proverbial maxim drawn from a number of Pentateuchal passages to the effect that, "The Spirit that God caused to dwell among us longs to the point of envying";[50] and in 4:6 he cites the canonical proverb regarding the divine character, "God resists the proud, but gives grace to the humble" (Prov. 3:34). The letter of James, of course, is by nature a series of ethical exhortations, and therefore could be expected to stress the halakic portions of Scripture and a literalist hermeneutic. Nevertheless, James is unique among the New Testament writers in selecting quotations from only the Pentateuch and Proverbs,[51] and his treatment of those biblical materials is consistently literal throughout.

I Peter bears a number of resemblances to James in its ethical exhortations, though it goes beyond James in expressing a distinctly pesher approach to Scripture as well. In 1:16 there is the reminder that "it is written, 'You shall be holy, for I [God] am holy' " (Lev. 11:44; 19:2; 20:7). In 3:10-12 the psalmist's words regarding "whoever would love life and see good days" (Ps. 34:12-16) are quoted, laying out a pattern of proper behavior and giving a God-oriented rationale for such conduct. In 4:18 a canonical proverb speaking of the righteous being judged in this life (Prov. 11:31) is cited in support of the exhortation to rejoice when one suffers for Christ; and in 5:5 humility is urged by reference to the canonical proverb, "God resists the proud, but gives grace to the humble" (Prov. 3:34).[52]

PESHER INTERPRETATIONS

But while there are many points of similarity between the letters of James and I Peter in their literalist treatments of

[50] The possible translations of this maxim are manifold; but none of them minimizes its literalist application, however the words are understood.

[51] Allusions to Isaiah and Ps. 103 appear as well, of course, in the epistle, though always with an ethical rather than a prophetic thrust; cf. 1:10f. (Isa. 40:6f.); 2:23b (Isa. 41:8); 5:4 (Isa. 5:9); 5:11 (Ps. 103:8).

[52] Cf. Jas. 4:6.

the Scriptures, the Petrine epistles and Jude—particularly I Peter, though also to an extent II Peter and Jude—stand apart from the letter of James and the Johannine epistles and apocalypse in their employment of a pesher type of approach to Scripture. Immediately after the salutation, a doxology, and the setting of the theme for the composition, I Pet. 1:10-12 enunciates a clear-cut pesher attitude toward the nature of biblical prophecy:

> The prophets who spoke of the grace that was to come to you searched intently and with the greatest care concerning this salvation, trying to find out the time and circumstances to which the Spirit of Christ in them was pointing when he predicted the sufferings of Christ and the glories that would follow. It was revealed to them that they were not serving themselves but you, when they spoke of the things that have now been told you by those who have preached the gospel to you by the Holy Spirit sent from heaven—things into which angels long to look.

Though the terms "mystery" and "interpretation" are not employed, the thought here is strikingly parallel to the *raz-pesher* motif found in the Qumran commentaries and is in continuity with the use of Scripture by Jesus, the early preachers of the gospel, Paul in explicating his Gentile ministry, the First Gospel, and the Fourth Gospel.[53] And it is this understanding that underlies at least three of Peter's treatments of the Old Testament in his letters.

In I Pet. 1:24f., just a few sentences after expressing his attitude toward what the prophets were really doing, Peter quotes Isa. 40:6-8:

> All men are like grass,
> and all their glory is like the wild flower;
> the grass withers and the flower falls,
> but the word of the Lord stands forever.

Then he says, in typical pesher fashion, "this is the word (*τοῦτο ἐστιν τὸ ῥῆμα*) that was preached to you." It is the same type of introduction that we have seen Peter use in Acts 2:16 (*τοῦτό ἐστιν τὸ εἰρημένον*), prefacing his quotation of Joel 2:28-32, and in Acts 4:11 (*οὗτός ἐστιν ὁ λίθος*), introducing Ps. 118:22. And it is the same type of treatment we've seen employed in the Qumran texts and by

[53] See *supra*, pp. 38-45, 70-75, 98-103, 129-132, 142-152, 155-57.

certain New Testament authors: an atomistic focusing upon a single feature (in this case, *τὸ ῥῆμα*) and the explication of a fuller meaning seen to lie inherent within that feature from the perspective of eschatological fulfilment. There is also a pesher treatment of two proverbs (Prov. 26:11 and another of undetermined origin) in II Pet. 2:22: "It has happened to them according to the true proverb: 'A dog returns to its vomit', and, 'A sow that is washed goes back to her wallowing in the mud'." Just like Peter's application of Ps. 69:25 and 109:8 to Judas in Acts 1:20, where what was said about the unrighteous man in general is applied to the betrayer of Christ, so here Hillel's principle of "light to heavy" (*qal waḥomer*) is coupled with a Christian eschatological perspective to declare, in good pesher fashion, that these proverbs have their fullest application to apostates from Christ.

Nowhere in the writings attributed to him, however, does Peter so distinctly express the confluence of (1) his Jewish exegetical heritage, (2) his Christian hermeneutical presuppositions, and (3) his own development of a pesher theme, than he does in I Pet. 2:4-8. In verse 4 he speaks of Jesus Christ as a "living stone" (*λίθον ζῶντα*), alluding in the process to the "rejected stone" theme of Ps. 118:22 and the "chosen stone" theme of Isa. 28:16—and suggesting by his use of the particle *μέν* that the "rejected stone" theme of Ps. 118:22 was in some sense traditional. In verse 5 he describes Christians as "living stones" (*λίθοι ζῶντες*) in a spiritual house. And in verse 6 he justifies this relationship of Christ and the Christian by quoting Isa. 28:16: "Behold, I lay a stone in Zion, a chosen and precious cornerstone, and he who believes on him will never be put to shame"; and then in verse 7 goes on to cite Ps. 118:22, "The stone the builders rejected has become the capstone," and Isa. 8:14, "A stone that causes men to stumble and a rock that makes them fall."

That members of a religious community in days of eschatological consummation could corporately be called "living stones" is not so strange. The Manual of Discipline employs such imagery in describing the leadership of the Qumran community as a "tested wall" and a "precious cornerstone,"[54] and the Psalms of Thanksgiving refer to the corporate structure of the community as built of "tested stone."[55] But the Christological use of this stone imagery is unique to the New Testament. Jesus is reported in Mark 12:10f. par. as applying to himself the words of Ps. 118:22: "The stone which the builders rejected has become the capstone"; and in Luke 20:17f. he is depicted as grouping Ps. 118:22 together with allusions to the "stone of stumbling" of Isa. 8:14 and the apocalyptic "crushing stone" of Dan. 2:34f. While it must always remain a hypothesis in explanation of the data, and not a fully demonstrable element of New Testament theology, it nevertheless remains true that it was probably Jesus himself who "set the Stone rolling"[56] —both in his identification of this theme as having Christological significance and in his joining of various passages having a similar relevance.[57] On the basis, therefore, of Jesus' usage, Peter is reported to have ascribed Ps. 118:22 directly to Jesus before the Sanhedrin at Jerusalem.[58] And in continuity with Jesus' allusion to Isa. 8:14, Paul spoke of Jesus as the "foundation" and "cornerstone" of believers and their faith;[59] and he conflated this text with Isa. 28:16—which may have been drawn from some Jewish exegetical heritage (as witness 1QS 8.7f. and 1QH 6.26), though reinterpreted from a Christian perspective—to speak of Jesus as "a stone that causes men to stumble and a rock that makes them fall," yet one on whom, if a man believes, "he will never be put to shame."[60]

In I Pet. 2:4-8, therefore, Peter combines (1) a Jewish understanding of the stone imagery of the Old Testament as having relevance to the corporate community (cf. 1QS 8.7f.; 1QH 6.26); (2) a Christian identification of the same imagery as having Christological significance, which interpretation—at least for Ps. 118:22—seems to have been common

[54] 1QS 8.7f., alluding to Isa. 28:16.
[55] 1QH 6.26.
[56] J. R. Harris, *Testimonies*, II, p. 96; cf. K. Stendahl, *School of St. Matthew*, pp. 69, 212.
[57] See *supra*, pp. 70f., 77f., 91f.
[58] Acts 4:11.
[59] I Cor. 3:11; Eph. 2:20.
[60] Rom. 9:33.

within the early Church (cf. Acts 4:11 and the *μέν* of I Pet. 2:4) and to have originated with Jesus (cf. Mark 12:10f. par.); and (3) his own midrashic grouping of Ps. 118:22 (cf. I Pet. 2:4b, 7); Isa. 28:16 (cf. I Pet. 2:4c, 6) and Isa. 8:14 (cf. I Pet. 2:8)—possibly under Pauline influence (cf. I Pet. 5:12)—and his own pesher application of the passages to the situation at hand.[61] In such a treatment, Peter is fairly unique among the writers of the canonical Jewish Christian tractates. Only Jude contains anything similar in his application of I Enoch 1:9 to apostate teachers in verses 14 and 15, which words of warning he introduces by saying: "Enoch, the seventh from Adam, prophesied about these men, saying" (*ἐπροφήτευσεν . . . τούτοις . . . λέγων*). Whether I Enoch 1:9 is here quoted by Jude with the full authority of Scripture, or employed like the second proverb of II Pet. 2:22 as "true" whether or not it was canonical Scripture, Jude's introduction and use of the passage are certainly in line with what we have learned to call a pesher interpretation. But aside from these two instances in I Peter, one in II Peter, and one in Jude, the rest of the Jewish Christian tractates do not employ a pesher treatment of the Old Testament. James uses the Old Testament in quite a literalist fashion throughout; John's letters are devoid of either biblical quotations or allusions; and the Apocalypse, while permeated with biblical expressions and allusions, neither directly quotes the Scriptures nor enters into a pesher type of interpretation. Some of these differences, of course, may be due to differing circumstances and a different literary genre. Nonetheless, they are interesting, and to some extent suggestive.

[61] For further discussion of the stone imagery in the New Testament, see my *Christology of Early Jewish Christianity*, pp. 50-53. Also see M. Black, "The Christological Use of the Old Testament in the New Testament," *NTS*, XVIII (1971), pp. 11-14, for Jewish background and New Testament usage.

VIII: THE NATURE OF NEW TESTAMENT EXEGESIS

It has become all too common in theological circles today to hear assertions as to what God must have done or what must have been the case during the apostolic period of the Church—and to find that such assertions are based principally upon deductions from a given system of theology or supported by contemporary analogy alone. The temptation is always with us to mistake hypothesis for evidence, and to judge our theological and historical formulations by their coherence and widespread acceptance rather than first of all by their correspondence to historical and exegetical data. History is replete with examples of this sorry condition and its sorry results, and hindsight permits us to recognize it in the past for what it was: a perversion of truth. But we are "sons of our fathers," composed of the same stuff and subject to the same pressures and temptations. And nowhere do we need to guard against our own inclinations and various pressures more carefully than in our understanding of the New Testament writers' use of the Old Testament. Neither piety nor speculation—both of which are excellent in their own ways when properly controlled—can here substitute for careful historical and exegetical investigation. Nor can traditional views of either the right or the left be allowed to stand unscrutinized in light of recent discoveries.

The Jewish roots of Christianity make it *a priori* likely that the exegetical procedures of the New Testament would resemble to some extent those of then contemporary Judaism. This has long been established with regard to the hermeneutics of Paul and the Talmud, and it is becoming increasingly evident with respect to the Qumran texts as well. In view of these materials and the light they throw on early Christian presuppositions and practices, we must abandon the mistaken idea that the New Testament writers' treatment of the Old Testament was either (1) an essentially mechanical process, whereby explicit "proof-texts" and exact "fulfilments" were brought together, or (2) an illegitimate twisting and distortion of the ancient text. It is true, of course, that literal fulfilment of a direct sort occurs as one factor in the New Testament. The Christian claim to continuity with the prophets could hardly have been supported were there no such cases. And it is also true that the exegesis of the early Christians often appears forced and artificial, particularly when judged by modern criteria. But neither approach does justice to the essential nature of New Testament hermeneutics, for both ignore the basic patterns of thought and common exegetical methods employed in the Jewish milieu in which the Christian faith came to birth.

There is little indication in the New Testament that the authors themselves were conscious of varieties of exegetical genre or of following particular modes of interpretation. At least they seem to make no sharp distinctions between what we would call historico-grammatical exegesis, illustration by way of analogy, midrash exegesis, pesher interpretation, allegorical treatment, and interpretation based on a "corporate solidarity" understanding of people and events in redemptive history. All of these are employed in their writings in something of a blended and interwoven fashion, even though there are certain discernible patterns and individual emphases in their usage. What the New Testament writers are conscious of, however, is interpreting the Old Testament (1) from a Christocentric perspective, (2) in conformity with a Christian tradition, and (3) along Christological lines. And in their exegesis there is the interplay of Jewish presuppositions and practices, on the one hand, with Christian commitments and perspectives on the other, which joined to produce a distinctive interpretation of the Old Testament.

CHRISTOCENTRIC INTERPRETATION

From the evidence that has been brought together in the preceding chapters, three main points regarding the nature of New Testament exegesis can be made. In the first place, it is obvious that the earliest Christians employed many of the exegetical presuppositions and practices that were common within various branches of Judaism in their day, and that they did so quite unconsciously. Secondly, they looked to Jesus' own use of the Old Testament as the source and paradigm for their own employment of Scripture. And thirdly, they believed that they were guided by the exalted Christ, through the immediate direction of the Holy Spirit, in their continued understanding and application of the Old Testament.[1]

It is hardly surprising to find that the exegesis of the New Testament is heavily dependent upon Jewish procedural precedents, for, theoretically, one would expect a divine redemption that is worked out in the categories of a particular history—which is exactly what the Christian gospel claims to be—to express itself in all its various manifestations in terms of the concepts and methods of that particular people and day. And this is, as we have tried to show, what was in fact done—the appreciation of which throws a great deal of light upon the exegetical methodology of the New Testament. But the Jewish context in which the New Testament came to birth, significant though it was, is not what was distinctive or formative in the exegesis of the earliest believers. At the heart of their biblical interpretation is a Christology and a Christocentric perspective. C. F. D. Moule is certainly right when he insists:

> The Christians began from Jesus—from his known character and mighty deeds and sayings, and his death and resurrection; and with these they went to the scriptures, and found that God's dealings with his People and his intentions for them there reflected did, in fact, leap into new significance in the light of these recent happenings. Sooner or later this was to lead, through a definition of what God had done, to something like a definition of who Jesus was.[2]

Where Jesus had put his finger on certain messianically relevant passages and explicitly "transformed the premessianic Torah into the messianic Torah,"[3] his identifica-

[1] Cf. C. F. D. Moule, *Birth of the New Testament*, p. 58; note also pp. 53-85.
[2] *Ibid.*, pp. 57f.
[3] B. Gerhardsson, *Memory and Manuscript*, p. 327.

tions and interpretations were preserved. Thus it was that Jesus became the direct historical source for much of the early Church's understanding of the Old Testament. But in addition, the early Christians continued to explicate Scripture along the lines laid out by him and under the direction of the Spirit. And thus it was that because of the paradigm he had set and his exalted Lordship expressed through the Spirit, Jesus was also the continuing source of the Church's ongoing biblical exposition.[4]

But the Christocentric perspective of the earliest Christians not only caused them to take Jesus' own employment of Scripture as normative and to look to him for guidance in their ongoing exegetical tasks, it also gave them a new understanding of the course of redemptive history and of their own place in it. As Jews, they well knew that redemptive history was building toward a climax under God's direction. But the focal point of history was still to come, and only from that point in the redemptive program would all previous history and all future time fit into place. As Christians, convinced by the resurrection of their Lord from the dead, they were prepared to stake their lives on the fact that in Jesus of Nazareth the focal point of God's redemption had been reached.[5] From such a perspective, therefore, and employing concepts of corporate solidarity and correspondences in history, all the Old Testament became part-and-parcel of God's preparation for the Messiah. The Old Testament contained certain specific messianic predictions, but more than that it was "messianic prophecy" and "messianic doctrine" throughout when viewed from its intended and culminating focal point.[6] And from this Christocentric

[4] Cf. *supra*, pp. 70-78, 91f.

[5] Cf. O. Cullmann, *Christ and Time* (ET 1950), pp. 81ff.; G. Vos, *The Pauline Eschatology* (1930, 1952), pp. 38ff.; G. E. Ladd, *The Gospel of the Kingdom* (1959), pp. 24ff.

[6] At the turn of the century, W. J. Beecher pertinently observed: "We have been taught that the prophets uttered predictions of a coming Deliverer; that these were fulfilled in the events of the life and mission of Jesus; and that this proves, first, that the prophets were divinely inspired, and second, that the mission of Jesus was divine. All this is true if rightly understood, but full of difficulty if we stop here. It is correct procedure, when correctly carried out, to select passages from the Old Testament in which specific facts are foretold concerning the Messiah, and then show, from history, that these marks characterized

perspective, the mission and future of God's "true Israel" was laid out. For the earliest believers, "upon Jesus converged the whole history of Israel in the past, and from him deployed the whole future of the People of God."[7]

COMMON, DIVERSE AND DEVELOPED EXEGETICAL PATTERNS

There is a great deal that was held in common by the earliest Christian preachers and the New Testament writers in their use of Scripture. All shared in the Jewish presuppositions of corporate solidarity and redemptive correspondences in history, and all employed such widespread Hillelian exegetical principles as *qal waḥomer* and *gezerah shawah*.[8] All treated the biblical text with some degree of freedom, believing that from among the various textual traditions then current they could do something of textual

---

Jesus, that he is therefore the Christ, and that prediction, thus made and fulfilled, is a mark of supernatural knowledge, authenticating revealed religion. But if we go at it in this way we are liable to misconceive the terms we use in our reasoning. And we mislead ourselves if we imagine this to be an exhaustive study of messianic prophecy, or even of the much narrower subject, messianic prediction" (*The Prophets and the Promise* [1905], pp. 175f.).

Beecher went on to insist: "Messianic prophecy is doctrine rather than prediction. The prophets were preachers. If there was some one messianic prediction which they repeated and unfolded from age to age, we should expect that they would present it in the form of a religious doctrine, for the practical benefit of the men of their times. . . . As the biography of Jesus is really doctrine rather than biography, and is the heart of the apostolic Christian doctrine, so the prophetic forecast of the Messiah is doctrine rather than prediction, and is the heart of the religious teachings of the prophets.

"Certainly we should treat their utterances as predictive; but this by itself is inadequate. They teach a doctrine concerning God's purpose with Israel, intelligible in each stage of Israel's history, so as to be the basis of religious and moral appeal for that age, but growing in fulness from age to age until it becomes the complete doctrine of the Messiah" (*ibid.*, p. 177).

[7] C. F. D. Moule, *Birth of the New Testament*, pp. 69f.

[8] Exceptions could be cited where biblical quotations are either sparse or nonexistent (e.g., the editorial comments of Mark and Luke, or the letters of John); but we are here speaking of those who do employ the Scriptures, not of those who don't. Luke as a Gentile writer may not have thought in these terms himself, but he records in his Gospel and Acts numerous examples of those who did.

criticism on a theological basis since they knew the conclusion to which that biblical testimony was pointing. All seem prepared to employ not only biblical citations but also, to a limited extent, statements of truth found outside the canon, whether of Jewish, pagan or uncertain origin.[9] And all, most importantly, worked from the same two fixed points: (1) the Messiahship and Lordship of Jesus, as validated by the resurrection and witnessed to by the Spirit; and (2) the revelation of God in the Old Testament as pointing forward to him. Thus their perspective was avowedly Christocentric and their treatment thoroughly Christological.

On the other hand, there can be seen in the New Testament's formal use of the Old Testament certain diverse patterns of exegetical procedure and development. In the first place, there is a distinctive pattern that emerges in the purely external matter of the distribution of biblical quotations in the New Testament writings. The Acts of the Apostles suggests that while the earliest believers based their thinking in large measure upon the Old Testament, they quoted Scripture principally—if not exclusively—within their mission to Jews.[10] This same phenomenon of biblical citations within a Jewish context appears as well in the editorial comments of both the First and Fourth Gospels and in the epistles of Hebrews, James, I and II Peter and Jude—all of which were originally addressed to Jewish or Jewish Christian audiences.[11] The Johannine epistles are the only exception to this pattern, and pose a definite problem in this regard;[12] though there may be circumstantial factors to take into account here as well. Nonetheless, apart from this Johannine exception, the pattern of biblical quotations in material originally stemming from or circulating within the Jewish mission of the Church is firmly fixed in the New Testament. Even Paul's pastoral correspondence reflects something of this pattern, for it is only in letters addressed to churches or individuals having some Jewish

[9] E.g., Jesus (Luke 11:49), Paul (Acts 17:28; I Cor. 15:33; Titus 1:12), Peter (II Pet. 2:22), Jude (Jude 14f.).
[10] See *supra*, p. 96.
[11] See *supra*, chs. V-VII, *passim*.
[12] I have not counted the Apocalypse here as an exception, since, though devoid of quotations, it is replete with biblical allusions.

background or affected by some type of Jewish polemic that the explicit citation of Scripture comes to the fore.[13] Yet where the addressees may be presumed to have been mainly, if not entirely, Gentile Christians and relatively unaffected by Jewish propaganda, there is a striking lack of biblical quotations. The Gospels of Mark and Luke report Jesus' extensive use of Scripture in their common narrative, but are markedly devoid in their editorial comments—significantly so when compared with Matthew and John—of biblical material.[14] And in his letters to believers at Thessalonica, Colosse (including Philemon) and Philippi, Paul seems to have felt no qualms about not buttressing his words with quotations from the Old Testament.[15] The Scriptures were certainly important to all the early Christian preachers and writers, but their explicit employment of biblical material seems to have been reserved for a Jewish context—for, evidently, it was only among Jews and Jewish Christians that such a direct appeal to the Old Testament would be appreciated and could be understood.

Of greater importance than the distribution of biblical quotations, however, are the patterns that emerge within the New Testament as to the use and development of a pesher type of exegesis. Interestingly and significantly, the evidence we have cited indicates that such an approach was distinctive of only Jesus and his immediate disciples, and not of those who merely associated with them or followed after them.[16] Only Paul's explication of his Gentile mission and Jude's employment of I Enoch 1:9 are exceptions—but Paul considered his apostleship on a par with that of the Twelve and avowed direct revelation from the exalted Jesus as the basis for his Gentile mission,[17] leaving only the one instance in Jude as the exception to this New Testament pattern.[18] What we have in the preaching and writings of the early apostolic band indicates that the apostles were not so much interested in commentaries on the biblical texts or

[13] See *supra*, p. 112.
[14] See *supra*, pp. 138-140.
[15] See *supra*, p. 112.
[16] See *supra*, pp. 70-75, 98-103, 140-157.
[17] See *supra*, pp. 129-132.
[18] See *supra*, p. 204.

the application of principles to issues of the day as they were in demonstrating redemptive fulfilment in Jesus of Nazareth. Accepting the Messiahship and Lordship of Jesus, and believing that in his teaching and person was expressed the fulness of revelation, they took a prophetic stance upon a revelatory basis and treated the Old Testament more charismatically than scholastically. Our Lord having opened their eyes so that they could understand the Old Testament Christologically, they continued both to repeat his expositions and to explicate more fully previously ignored significances in the nation's history and the enigmatic in the prophets' message. Their major task, as they saw it, was to demonstrate that "this" which was manifest in the person and work of Jesus "is that" which was recorded in the Old Testament. And in that they were convinced that they possessed a more adequate knowledge of the real intent of Scripture than elsewhere available, they were not afraid to select among the variants then current that reading of the text which best conveyed the Scripture's true meaning—possibly, at times, even to create a wording to express that meaning—and to treat the passage in a truly creative fashion.

The pesher interpretations in the apostolic preaching of Acts and the early confessional portions incorporated in the epistles are fairly true to type and closely similar to those recorded of Jesus in the Gospels;[19] while the pesher exegesis appearing in the editorial comments of Matthew and John and in Peter's treatment of the "stone" motif, though in continuity with Jesus and earlier practice, shows definite signs of development—particularly Matthew's.[20] This is not to deny that the earliest apostolic preaching and writing attributed to these three disciples also treated the Scriptures in literalist and midrashic fashion. But it is to assert that what was distinctive in the exegesis of the apostolic witness to Christ was a pesher approach to Scripture which felt both compelled to reproduce Jesus' own understanding of the Old Testament and at liberty to develop it further along the lines he laid out.

On the other hand, such a pesher approach is not charac-

[19] See *supra*, pp. 98-103.
[20] See *supra*, pp. 140-157, 202-204.

teristic of those sermons and writings ascribed to men outside the circle of the Twelve. While Paul spoke of his Gentile mission in pesher fashion, his usual treatment of the Old Testament was not just the same as that ascribed to Peter, Matthew and John. He shared with them a common Christocentric perspective, a common body of testimonia biblical material and a common attitude toward the relationship of meaning and wording in the biblical text. But he differed from them in his historical relation to Jesus, his revelational understanding of the course of the redemptive program and his closer affinity to rabbinic exegetical norms. A different training, a different spiritual experience and a different audience all played their part in the apostle's life to produce a difference in exegesis from that credited to representatives of the Twelve. And this seems to have been true in varying degrees as well for the preaching of Stephen,[21] the teaching of James,[22] the exhortations of the writer to the Hebrews[23] and the omissions in the editorial comments of Mark and Luke.[24] Only the letters of John and Jude, as we have noted, do not conform to this pattern—the one because of its omissions and the other because of its use, which cause a number of problems. Nevertheless, apart from these two exceptions, the pattern of usage and development in the New Testament is fairly clear.

Again, this is not to value one approach or one methodology above the other.[25] Both the Twelve and those who followed after them viewed the revelation of God in the Old Testament and the revelation of God in Jesus of Nazareth as complementary as well as supplementary. And both seem to acknowledge the legitimacy of each other's exegetical procedures at those points where they overlap. It is only to recognize that such men as Paul, Stephen, James, the writer to the Hebrews, Mark and Luke could not claim the usual apostolic qualifications as expressed in John 15:27 and Acts 1:21f. Their understanding of the Old Testament could not

[21] See *supra*, pp. 96f., 101.
[22] See *supra*, pp. 199f.
[23] See *supra*, pp. 174-185.
[24] See *supra*, pp. 137-140.
[25] Cf. *supra*, pp. 105, 132.

be directly related to the teaching and example of the historic Jesus, and they were frankly dependent on early Christian tradition for much in their Christological expositions. But Paul had been entrusted with a pesher understanding of the course of redemptive history that was uniquely his. And they had a redemptive purpose to fulfil as well. The Jerusalem apostles, therefore, had the key to many of the prophetic mysteries, Paul had the key to the "redemptive logistics" for this age, and the rest were legitimately involved in propagating this glad message. Together, they combined to enhance the fulness of the gospel.

THE DESCRIPTIVE AND THE NORMATIVE IN EXEGESIS

Involved in any consideration of biblical exegesis in the New Testament are the dual issues of the descriptive (i.e., What actually took place?) and the normative (i.e., How relevant or obligatory are such exegetical procedures today? On what basis? How can they be employed?). Having given attention to the procedures and patterns of exegesis within the New Testament in light of Jewish practices then roughly contemporary, we must now deal with the issue of their normative character today. Or to state the matter more rhetorically, the question is: "Can we reproduce the exegesis of the New Testament?"—being concerned particularly with pesher, midrash and allegorical modes, and understanding "can we" in the sense of both "Are we able?" and "Ought we try?"

The question is of renewed and vital interest today, and various answers are currently being given to it. Answering negatively are those representing what may be called "classical liberal" and "unreconstructed Bultmannian" positions, who assert the impossibility of any such endeavor since: (1) much of the exegesis of the New Testament is an arbitrary and ingenious twisting of the biblical texts going beyond the limits of any proper hermeneutic;[26] and (2) the

[26] E.g., S. V. McCasland, "Matthew Twists the Scriptures," *JBL*, LXXX (1961), pp. 143-48, who goes so far as to assert that Matthew's exegesis aptly illustrates the words of II Pet. 3:16 regarding "ignorant and unstable" men twisting Scripture to their own destruction.

self-understanding of contemporary man and the critico-historical thought of modern study separates us from the methods of the New Testament.[27] Those responding negatively do not deny that the Old Testament is important for the study of the New Testament. They insist, however, that the Old Testament represents a religion that stands outside of and apart from the religion of the New, and that it must therefore be treated not as prolegomena to the gospel but as a witness to the gospel on the part of a religion that was essentially distinct from the gospel. The New Testament writers, not realizing this, engaged in demonstrating continuity and fulfilment. But from our more knowledgeable perspective, we now see how impossible such an endeavor was—and continues to be.

Where a positive answer to our question is given, it is usually expressed in one or the other of the following ways:

1. Most conservative interpreters hold—or at least "feel"—that on so vital a matter as the New Testament's use of the Old, the descriptive must also be the normative; and therefore they believe themselves in some manner committed to explaining the principles that underlie the exegesis of the New Testament so that these same procedures may be employed today. Few would accept the flexible axiom of Cocceius that "the words of Scripture signify all that they can be made to signify"; but taking their cue from such earlier writers as F. W. Farrar,[28] many insist that the exegetical methods of Christ and the apostles ought to control our exegetical procedures today.[29]

2. A number of Roman Catholic scholars have recognized that the New Testament frequently employs the Old Testament in a way that gives to the biblical texts a fuller meaning, and have credited the origin of this *sensus plenior*

[27] E.g., F. Baumgärtel, "The Hermeneutical Problem of the Old Testament," *Essays on Old Testament Interpretation*, ed. C. Westermann (ET 1963), pp. 134-159; cf. R. Bultmann, "Prophecy and Fulfilment," *ibid.*, pp. 50-75, and *idem, History and Eschatology* (ET 1957), pp. 35-37.

[28] F. W. Farrar, *History of Interpretation* (1886), pp. 434-36.

[29] E.g., L. Berkhof, *Principles of Biblical Interpretation* (1950), pp. 140ff., who, in discussing the interpreter's handling of the "mystical sense of Scripture," begins by saying: "The necessity of recognizing the mystical sense is quite evident from the way in which the New Testament interprets the Old."

in one way or another to the historic Jesus. Explicating a doctrine of the dual basis of revelational authority, they then go on to argue that in like manner theology today can carry on the New Testament exegetical procedures—but only as interpreters are guided by the Magisterium of the Church, the visible expression of the "Mystical Body of Christ."[30]

3. Many existential exegetes (particularly the so-called "post-Bultmannians") are prepared to argue in regard to the more distinctive modes of New Testament interpretation that it is "open to us to go beyond the New Testament types and to mention other similar correspondences,"[31] since the faith that unites Old and New Testaments is ours as well. These interpreters agree with the "classical liberals" and Rudolf Bultmann in their disavowal of any real continuity of detail between the testaments and in their insistence that "modern scientific exegesis cannot be simply derived from its use within the New Testament."[32] But they insist that because of the continuity of faith that exists between prophets, apostles and ourselves, each in his own way and employing categories of thought relevant to his own time must engage in a similar exegetical task; for, to quote H. W. Wolff, "the witnessing word waits on its encounter with each new hearer."[33]

While it is precarious to generalize, yet it seems to be the case that many Christians have found themselves unhappy with the presuppositions underlying (1) the "No" answers of the "classical liberals" and "unreconstructed Bult-

[30] E.g., E. F. Sutcliffe, "The Plenary Sense as a Principle of Interpretation," *Bib*, XXXIV (1953), pp. 333-343; R. Bierberg, "Does Sacred Scripture Have a Sensus Plenior?" *CBQ*, X (1948), pp. 182-195; R. E. Brown, *The "Sensus Plenior" of Sacred Scripture* (1955); *idem*, "*Sensus Plenior* in the Last Ten Years," *CBQ*, XXV (1963), pp. 262-285.

[31] W. Eichrodt, "Is Typological Exegesis an Appropriate Method?" *Essays on Old Testament Interpretation*, ed. C. Westermann (ET 1963), p. 244.

[32] *Ibid.*, p. 231.

[33] H. W. Wolff, "The Hermeneutics of the Old Testament," *Essays on Old Testament Interpretation*, ed. C. Westermann (ET 1963), p. 164. In addition to the articles cited above by Eichrodt and Wolff, note the seminal article in the same volume by Gerhard von Rad, "Typological Interpretation of the Old Testament."

mannians," and (2) the "Yes" responses of the Roman Catholic and "post-Bultmannian" interpreters, and have therefore held themselves—in their sympathies, if not always in their formal practice—to some form of the thesis that the descriptive is also in some manner normative for exegesis today. But in light of the nature of New Testament exegesis, especially as illumined to a great extent by first-century Jewish practice, the question must be raised: Is there not a better way to solve the problem of relationships?

It is the thesis of this book that at least three matters must be taken into consideration when asking about the relation of New Testament exegesis and a proper hermeneutic today. In the first place, it is essential that we have an adequate understanding of the New Testament exegetical procedures themselves—not only the literalist modes, but also the pesher, midrash and allegorical treatments. This is principally an historical issue, which it has been our purpose throughout the preceding pages to clarify; and it is for this reason that these pages are offered to the reader. Secondly, it is necessary that we have an appreciation for the purpose of biblical revelation. This is almost entirely a theological question, which, though influenced by historical considerations, is finally determined on a theological basis. We have not spoken directly to such an issue in what has preceded, though we must inevitably consider it here when asking theological as well as historical questions. And thirdly, in light of historical and theological considerations, we must develop a sensitivity as to what is descriptive and what is normative in the biblical revelation. This, admittedly, is more of the nature of awareness and artistry than statement or science (though a scientific treatment of both history and theology must always precede it), but it is vitally important if our hermeneutics are to be kept from being wooden and sterile.

F. J. A. Hort succinctly characterized the Christian's attitude toward the New Testament when he said:

> Our faith rests first on the Gospel itself, the revelation of God and His redemption in His Only begotten Son, and secondly on the interpretation of that primary Gospel by the Apostles and Apostolic men to whom was Divinely committed the task of applying

> the revelation of Christ to the thoughts and deeds of their own time. That standard interpretation of theirs was ordained to be for the guidance of the Church in all after ages, in combination with the living guidance of the Spirit.[34]

As students of history we can appreciate something of what was involved in their exegetical procedures, and as Christians we commit ourselves to their conclusions. But apart from a revelatory stance on our part, I suggest that we cannot reproduce their pesher exegesis. While we legitimately seek continuity with our Lord and his apostles in matters of faith and doctrine—and may inadvertently sound at times as if we are speaking direct from the courts of heaven—we must also recognize the uniqueness of Jesus as the true interpreter of the Old Testament and the distinctive place he gave to the apostles in the explication of the prophetic word.[35]

Likewise, I suggest that we should not attempt to reproduce their midrashic handling of the text, their allegorical explications, or much of their Jewish manner of argumentation. All of this is strictly part of the cultural context through which the transcultural and eternal gospel was expressed. This is fairly obvious where such methods are employed more circumstantially and in *ad hominem* fashion, but it is true even where they are not. H. N. Ridderbos has rightly observed that to claim inspiration by the Spirit for the teaching of Paul "does not remove the fact that this same Paul in more than one way still betrayed the traces of his rabbinistic education, for instance, in the manner in which he debates, makes use of rabbinic argumentation and traditional materials, and cites the Old Testament";[36] and Ridderbos goes on to assert quite correctly that such things help us understand the organic character of inspiration in such a way that it "can also mean connection

[34] F. J. A. Hort, *Epistle of St. James*, p. ix.

[35] Note the consciousness of the centrality of the apostles in early Christian tradition as expressed in such passages as John 15:27; Eph. 2:20; Rev. 21:14.

[36] H. N. Ridderbos, "An Attempt at the Theological Definition of Inerrancy, Infallibility, and Authority," *International Reformed Bulletin*, XI (1968), p. 38. I am indebted to A. J. Bandstra (see below) for this and the following quote from Ridderbos.

with certain Jewish or non-Christian elements, without at the same time these elements having been brought under the sanction of revelation and thus belonging to the normative character of Scripture."[37] And A. J. Bandstra has aptly pointed out that "neither the Bible as a whole nor the New Testament in particular was meant to be a textbook on the science of hermeneutics. It is meant to be proclamation which centers in creation, fall, and redemption. To proclaim their message the authors of the New Testament use and interpret the Old, but in so doing they do not intend to lay down hermeneneutical rules. To use the New Testament in such a fashion would be putting it to a use for which it was not intended."[38]

What then can be said to our question, "Can we reproduce the exegesis of the New Testament?" I suggest that we must answer both "No" and "Yes." Where that exegesis is based upon a revelatory stance, where it evidences itself to be merely cultural, or where it shows itself to be circumstantial or *ad hominem* in nature, "No."[39] Where, however, it treats the Old Testament in more literal fashion, following the course of what we speak of today as historico-grammatical exegesis, "Yes." Our commitment as Christians is to the reproduction of the apostolic faith and doctrine, and not necessarily to the specific apostolic exegetical practices. Christians have always distinguished between the descriptive and the normative in other areas; for example, in matters pertaining to ecclesiastical government, the apostolic office and the charismatic gifts, to name only a diverse few. I propose that in the area of exegesis as well we may appreciate the manner in which the interpretations of our Lord and the New Testament writers were derived and may reproduce their conclusions by means of historico-

[37] *Ibid.*, p. 39.

[38] A. J. Bandstra, "Interpretation in 1 Corinthians 10:1-11," *CTJ*, VI (1971), p. 20.

[39] While made facetiously, C. F. D. Moule's comment is illustratively apt: "I wish I had lived in the age of פשר. I would have shown how II Kings vi.5f. is an account of St. Paul's conversion in code: the lost axe-head was שאול; what rescued it was עץ!" ("Fulfilment-Words in the New Testament: Use and Abuse," *NTS*, XIV [1968], p. 297, n. 2).

grammatical exegesis, but we cannot assume that the explanation of their methods is necessarily the norm for our exegesis today. And that, I propose, is an important step in the development of a sound approach to interpretation today.

A SELECTED BIBLIOGRAPHY

I. THE HERMENEUTICS OF LATE JUDAISM

Bacher, W. *Die exegetische Terminologie der jüdischen Traditionsliteratur*, 2 vols. (Leipzig: Mohr, 1889, 1905).

Bickerman, E. J., "The Septuagint as a Translation," *PAAJR*, XXVIII (1959), pp. 1-39.

Black, M., "Theological Conceptions in the Dead Sea Scrolls," *Svensk Exegetisk Årsbok*, XVIII-XIX (1953-54), pp. 72-97.

Bloch, R., "Note méthodologique pour l'étude de la littérature rabbinique," *RSR*, XLIII (1955), pp. 194-227.

Bonsirven, J., "Exégèse allégorique chez les rabbins tannaites," *RSR*, XXIII (1933), pp. 522-24.

———. *Exégèse rabbinique et exégèse paulinienne* (Paris: Beauchesne, 1939).

Bowker, J. *The Targums and Rabbinic Literature* (Cambridge: University Press, 1969).

Brownlee, W. H., "Biblical Interpretation among the Sectaries of the Dead Sea Scrolls," *BA*, XIV (1951), pp. 54-76.

———. *The Text of Habakkuk in the Ancient Commentary from Qumran* (Philadelphia: Society of Biblical Literature, 1959).

Bruce, F. F., "The Dead Sea Habakkuk Scroll," *ALUOS*, I (1958-59), pp. 5-24.

———. *Biblical Exegesis in the Qumran Texts* (London: Tyndale; Grand Rapids: Eerdmans, 1960).

Cross, F. M., Jr., "The History of the Biblical Text in the Light of Discoveries in the Judean Desert," *HTR*, LVII (1964), pp. 281-299.

———, "The Contribution of the Qumran Discoveries to the Study of the Biblical Text," *IEJ*, XVI (1966), pp. 81-95.

Daube, D., "Rabbinic Methods of Interpretation and Hellenistic Rhetoric," *HUCA*, XXII (1949), pp. 239-264.

———, "Alexandrian Methods of Interpretation and the Rabbis," *Festschrift Hans Lewald* (Basel: Helbing & Lichtenbahn, 1953), pp. 27-44.

———. *The New Testament and Rabbinic Judaism* (London: Athlone, 1965).

Doeve, J. W. *Jewish Hermeneutics in the Synoptic Gospels and Acts* (Assen: Van Gorcum, 1954).

Drummond, J. *Philo Judaeus*, 2 vols. (London: Williams & Norgate, 1888).

Elliger, K. *Studien zum Habakuk-Kommentar vom Toten Meer* (Tübingen: Mohr-Siebeck, 1953).

Finkel, A., "The Pesher of Dreams and Scriptures," *RQ*, IV (1963), pp. 357-370.

Finkelstein, L., "The Transmission of Early Rabbinic Tradition," *HUCA*, XVI (1941), pp. 115-135.

Fitzmyer, J. A., "4Q Testimonia and the New Testament," *TS*, XVIII (1957), pp. 527-537.

———, "The Use of Explicit Old Testament Quotations in Qumran Literature and in the New Testament," *NTS*, VII (1961), pp. 297-333.

Gordis, R., "Quotations as a Literary Usage in Biblical, Oriental and Rabbinic Literature," *HUCA*, XXII (1949), pp. 157-220.

Horovitz, S., "Midrash," *The Jewish Encyclopedia*, ed. I. Singer, VIII (1904), pp. 548-550.

Jellicoe, S. *The Septuagint and Modern Study* (Oxford: Clarendon, 1968).

Johnson, A. R. *The One and the Many in the Israelite Conception of God* (Cardiff: University of Wales, 1942).

Kennedy, H. A. A. *Philo's Contribution to Religion* (London: Hodder & Stoughton, 1919).

Lauterbach, J. Z., "Peshaṭ," *The Jewish Encyclopedia*, IX (1905), pp. 652f.

———, "Talmud Hermeneutics," *The Jewish Encyclopedia*, XII (1906), pp. 30-33.

———, "Ancient Jewish Allegorists," *JQR*, I (1911), pp. 291-333 and 503-531.

LeDéaut, R., "Apropos a Definition of Midrash," *Interp*, XXV (1971), pp. 259-282.

Loewe, R., "The 'Plain' Meaning of Scripture in Early Jewish Exegesis," *PIJSL*, I, ed. J. G. Weiss (Jerusalem: Hebrew University, 1964), pp. 140-185.

Lowy, S., "Some Aspects of Normative and Sectarian Interpretation of the Scriptures," *ALUOS*, VI (1966-68), pp. 98-163.

McNamara, M. *The New Testament and the Palestinian Targum to the Pentateuch* (Rome: Pontifical Biblical Institute, 1966).

Mann, J. *The Bible as Read and Preached in the Old Synagogue*, 2 vols. (Cincinnati: Jewish Publication Society, 1940).

Roberts, B. J., "The Dead Sea Scrolls and the Old Testament Scriptures," *BJRL*, XXXVI (1953), pp. 75-96.

Robinson, H. W., "The Hebrew Conception of Corporate Personality," *Corporate Personality in Ancient Israel* (Philadelphia: Fortress, 1964), pp. 1-20.

Rosenthal, J. M., "Biblical Exegesis of 4QpIs," *JQR*, LX (1969), pp. 27-36.

Roth, C., "The Subject Matter of Qumran Exegesis," *VT*, X (1960), pp. 51-68.
Ryle, H. E. *Philo and the Holy Scriptures* (London: Macmillan, 1895).
Shroyer, M. J., "Alexandrian Jewish Literalists," *JBL*, LV (1936), pp. 261-284.
Siegfried, C. *Philo von Alexandria als Ausleger der Alten Testaments* (Jena: Dufft, 1875).
Silberman, L. H., "Unriddling the Riddle. A Study in the Structure and Language of the Habakkuk Pesher," *RQ*, XI (1961), pp. 323-364.
Skehan, P. W., "A Fragment of the 'Song of Moses' (Deut. 32) from Qumran," *BASOR*, 136 (1954), pp. 12-15.
_______, "The Biblical Scrolls from Qumran and the Text of the Old Testament," *BA*, XXVIII (1965), pp. 87-100.
Slomovic, E., "Toward an Understanding of the Exegesis in the Dead Sea Scrolls," *RQ*, VII (1969), pp. 3-15.
Sowers, S. G. *The Hermeneutics of Philo and Hebrews* (Richmond: John Knox, 1965).
Strack, H. L. *Introduction to the Talmud and Midrash* (Philadelphia: Jewish Publication Society of America, 1931).
Vermès, G. *Scripture and Tradition in Judaism* (Leiden: Brill, 1961).
_______, "The Qumran Interpretation of Scripture in its Historical Setting," *ALUOS*, VI (1966-68), pp. 85-97.
de Waard, J. *A Comparative Study of the Old Testament Text in the Dead Sea Scrolls and in the New Testament* (Leiden: Brill, 1965).
Williamson, R. *Philo and the Epistle to the Hebrews* (Leiden: Brill, 1970).
Wolfson, H. A. *Philo*, 2 vols. (Cambridge, Mass.: Harvard University Press, 1947).
Wright, A. G., "The Literary Genre Midrash," *CBQ*, XXVIII (1966), pp. 105-138, 417-457; also published as *The Literary Genre Midrash* (Staten Island: Alba House, 1968).
Zeitlin, S., "Hillel and the Hermeneutic Rules," *JQR*, LIV (1963), pp. 161-173.

II. THE NEW TESTAMENT'S USE OF THE OLD

Ackerman, J. S., "The Rabbinic Interpretation of Psalm 82 and the Gospel of John: John 10:34," *HTR*, XIX (1966), pp. 186-191.
Albright, W. F., "The Names 'Nazareth' and 'Nazoraean'," *JBL*, LXV (1946), pp. 397-401.
Allen, L. C., "The Old Testament in Romans I-VIII," *Vox Evangelica*, III, ed. R. P. Martin (London: Epworth, 1964), pp. 6-41.
_______, "The Old Testament Background of (ΠΡΟ)'ΟΡΙΖΕΙΝ in the New Testament," *NTS*, XVII (1970), pp. 104-8.
Anderson, H., "The Old Testament in Mark's Gospel," *The Use of the*

Old Testament in the New and Other Essays, ed. J. M. Efird (Durham: Duke University Press, 1972), pp. 280-309.

Bandstra, A. J., "Interpretation in I Corinthians 10:1-11," *CTJ*, VI (1971), pp. 5-21.

Barr, J. *Old and New in Interpretation* (London: SCM, 1966).

Barrett, C. K., "The Eschatology of the Epistle to the Hebrews," *The Background of the New Testament and its Eschatology*, ed. W. D. Davies and D. Daube (Cambridge: University Press, 1954), pp. 363-393.

Barth, M., "The Old Testament in Hebrews," *Current Issues in New Testament Interpretation*, ed. W. Klassen and G. F. Snyder (New York: Harper & Row, 1962), pp. 65-78.

Baumgärtel, F., "The Hermeneutical Problem of the Old Testament," *Essays on Old Testament Interpretation*, ed. C. Westermann, trans. J. L. Mays (London: SCM, 1963), pp. 134-159. The American edition of this work appears under the title *Essays on Old Testament Hermeneutics* (Richmond: John Knox, 1963).

Baumstark, A., "Die Zitate des Mt.-Evangeliums aus dem Zwölfprophetenbuch," *Bib*, XXXVII (1956), pp. 296-313.

Beecher, W. J. *The Prophets and the Promise* (New York: Crowell, 1905).

Best, E. *The Temptation and the Passion: The Marcan Soteriology* (Cambridge: University Press, 1965).

Bierberg, R., "Does Sacred Scripture Have a *Sensus Plenior*?" *CBQ*, X (1948), pp. 182-195.

Black, M., "The Christological Use of the Old Testament in the New Testament," *NTS*, XVIII (1971), pp. 1-14.

Böhl, E. *Die Alttestamentlichen Citate im Neuen Testament* (Wien: Braumüller, 1878).

Bonsirven, J. *Exégèse rabbinique et exégèse paulinienne* (Paris: Beauchesne, 1939).

Borgen, P., "Observations on the Midrashic Character of John 6," *ZNW* (1963), pp. 232-240.

Bratcher, R. G., ed. *Old Testament Quotations in the New Testament* (London: United Bible Societies, 1967).

Brown, R. E. *The "Sensus Plenior" of Sacred Scripture* (Baltimore: St. Mary's University, 1955).

Bruce, F. F., "Qumran and the New Testament," *Faith and Thought*, XC (1958), pp. 92-102.

———, "Promise and Fulfilment in Paul's Presentation of Jesus," *Promise and Fulfilment*, ed. F. F. Bruce (Edinburgh: T. & T. Clark, 1963), pp. 36-50.

———. *This is That. The New Testament Development of Some Old Testament Themes* (Exeter: Paternoster, 1968).

Bultmann, R., "Prophecy and Fulfilment," *Essays on Old Testament Interpretation*, ed. C. Westermann, trans. J. L. Mays (London: SCM, 1963), pp. 50-75. The American edition of this work appears under the title *Essays on Old Testament Hermeneutics* (Richmond: John Knox, 1963).

Caird, G. B., "The Exegetical Method of the Epistle to the Hebrews," *CJT*, V (1959), pp. 44-51.

_______, "The Descent of Christ in Ephesians 4, 7-11," *Studia Evangelica*, II, ed. F. L. Cross (Berlin: Akademie, 1964), pp. 535-545.

Cerfaux, L., "Les sources Scriptuaires de Mt. XI, 25-30," *Ephemerides Theologicae Lovanienses*, XXXI (1955), pp. 331-342.

Daniélou, J., "The New Testament and the Theology of History," *Studia Evangelica*, I, ed. K. Aland, *et al.* (Berlin: Akademie, 1959), pp. 25-34.

_______. *From Shadows to Reality*, trans. W. Hibberd (Westminster, Md.: Newman, 1961).

_______. *The Theology of Jewish Christianity*, trans. J. A. Baker (Chicago: Regnery, 1964).

_______. *Études d'exégèse judéo-chrétienne* (Paris: Beauchesne, 1966).

Davies, W. D. *Paul and Rabbinic Judaism* (London: S.P.C.K., 1948).

_______. *The Setting of the Sermon on the Mount* (Cambridge: University Press, 1964).

Diestel, L. *Geschichte des Alten Testaments in der christlichen Kirche* (Jena: Mauke, 1869).

Dittmar, W. *Vetus Testamentum in Novo* (Göttingen: Vandenhoeck & Ruprecht, 1903).

Dodd, C. H. *According to the Scriptures: The Sub-Structure of New Testament Theology* (London: Nisbet, 1952).

_______. *The Old Testament in the New* (London: Athlone, 1952; Philadelphia: Fortress, 1963).

Doeve, J. W. *Jewish Hermeneutics in the Synoptic Gospels and Acts* (Assen: Van Gorcum, 1954).

Edgar, S. L., "New Testament and Rabbinic Messianic Interpretation," *NTS*, V (1958), pp. 47-54.

Eichrodt, W., "Is Typological Exegesis an Appropriate Method?" *Essays on Old Testament Interpretation*, ed. C. Westermann, trans. J. L. Mays (London: SCM, 1963), pp. 224-245. The American edition of this work appears under the title *Essays on Old Testament Hermeneutics* (Richmond: John Knox, 1963).

Ellis, E. E. *Paul's Use of the Old Testament* (Edinburgh: Oliver & Boyd; Grand Rapids: Eerdmans, 1957).

_______, "Luke xi.49-51: An Oracle of a Christian Prophet?" *ExpT*, LXXIV (1963), pp. 157f.

_______. *The Gospel of Luke* (London: Nelson, 1966).

_______, "Midrash, Targum and New Testament Quotations," *Neotestamentica et Semitica*, ed. E. E. Ellis and M. Wilcox (Edinburgh: T. & T. Clark, 1969), pp. 61-69.

Farrer, A. M. *A Study in St. Mark* (London: Dacre, 1951; New York: Oxford University Press, 1952).

Fitzmyer, J. A., "4Q Testimonia and the New Testament," *TS*, XVIII (1957), pp. 527-537.

_______, "The Use of Explicit Old Testament Quotations in Qumran

Literature and in the New Testament," *NTS*, VII (1961), pp. 297-333.

Fjärstodt, B., "The Use of Isaiah 53 in the N.T.—Recent Scandinavian Research," *IJT*, XX (1971), pp. 109-116.

Flanagan, N., "Messianic Fulfillment in St. Paul," *CBQ*, XIX (1957), pp. 474-484.

France, R. T. *Jesus and the Old Testament* (London: Tyndale, 1971).

Freed, E. D. *Old Testament Quotations in the Gospel of John* (Leiden: Brill, 1965).

Gerhardsson, B. *Memory and Manuscript. Oral Tradition and Written Transmission in Rabbinic Judaism and Early Christianity*, trans. E. J. Sharpe (Lund: Gleerup, 1961).

———. *The Testing of God's Son* (Lund: Gleerup, 1966).

Gertner, M., "Midrashim in the New Testament," *Journal of Semitic Studies* (1962), pp. 267-292.

Glasson, T. F. *Moses in the Fourth Gospel* (London: SCM, 1963).

———, " 'Plurality of Divine Persons' and the Quotations in Hebrews i. 6ff.," *NTS*, XII (1966), pp. 270-72.

Goldsmith, D., "Acts 13:33-37: A Pesher on II Samuel 7," *JBL*, LXXXVII (1968), pp. 321-24.

Goppelt, L. *Typos. Die typologische Deutung des Alten Testaments im Neuen* (Gütersloh: Bertelsmann, 1939).

Grant, W. M. *The Bible of Jesus: An Inquiry into His Use of the Old Testament* (New York: Doran, 1927).

Gundry, R. H. *The Use of the Old Testament in St. Matthew's Gospel* (Leiden: Brill, 1967).

Hanson, A. T. *Jesus Christ in the Old Testament* (London: S. P. C. K., 1965).

———, "John's Citation of Psalm lxxxii Reconsidered," *NTS*, XIII (1967), pp. 363-67.

———. *Studies in Paul's Technique and Theology* (London: S. P. C. K., 1974), esp. pp. 126-278.

Hanson, R. P. C. *Allegory and Event* (London: SCM, 1959).

Harnack, A., "Das alte Testament in den paulinischen Briefen und in den paulinischen Gemeinden," *Sitzungsberichte der Preussischen Akademie der Wissenschaften zu Berlin* (1928), pp. 124-141.

Harris, J. R. *Testimonies*, 2 vols. (Cambridge: University Press, 1916, 1920).

Hay, D. M. *Glory at the Right Hand: Psalm 110 in Early Christianity* (Nashville-New York: Abingdon, 1973).

Hillyer, N., "Matthew's Use of the Old Testament," *Evangelical Quarterly*, XXXVI (1964), pp. 12-26.

Howard, G., "Hebrews and the Old Testament Quotations," *Novum Testamentum*, X (1968), pp. 208-216.

Hühn, E. *Die alttestamentlichen Citate und Reminiscenzen im Neuen Testament* (Tübingen: Mohr, 1900).

Jeremias, J., "Paulus als Hillelit," *Neotestamentica et Semitica*, ed. E.

E. Ellis and M. Wilcox (Edinburgh: T. & T. Clark, 1969), pp. 88-94.

Johnson, F. *The Quotations of the New Testament from the Old* (Philadelphia: American Baptist Publication Society, 1896).

Kent, H. A., "Matthew's Use of the Old Testament," *Bibliotheca Sacra*, CXXI (1964), pp. 34-43.

Kistemaker, S. *The Psalm Citations in the Epistle to the Hebrews* (Amsterdam: van Soest, 1961).

Ladd, G. E., "History and Theology in Biblical Exegesis," *Interp*, XX (1966), pp. 54-64.

Lampe, G. W. H., "The Reasonableness of Typology," *Essays on Typology* (London: SCM, 1957), pp. 9-38.

_______, "Hermeneutics and Typology," *London Quarterly and Holborn Review*, XXXIV (1964), pp. 17-25.

Lindars, B. *New Testament Apologetic* (London: SCM, 1961).

_______, "Second Thoughts—IV. Books of Testimonies," *ExpT*, LXXV (1964), pp. 173-75.

Lövestam, E. *Son and Saviour: A Study of Acts 13, 32-37*, trans. M. J. Petry (Lund: Gleerup, 1961).

McArthur, H. K., "On the Third Day," *NTS*, XVIII (1971), pp. 81-86.

McCasland, S. V., "Matthew Twists the Scriptures," *JBL*, LXXX (1961), pp. 143-48.

McConnell, R. S. *Law and Prophecy in Matthew's Gospel. The Authority and Use of the Old Testament in the Gospel of St. Matthew* (Basel: Reinhardt, 1969).

Manson, T. W., "The Argument from Prophecy," *JTS*, LXVI (1945), pp. 129-136.

Mare, W. H., "Paul's Mystery in Ephesians 3," *Bulletin of the Evangelical Theological Society*, VIII (1965), pp. 77-84.

Martin, R. A., "The Earliest Messianic Interpretation of Genesis 3:15," *JBL*, LXXXIV (1965), pp. 425-27.

Mauser, U. *Christ in the Wilderness: The Wilderness Theme in the Second Gospel and its Basis in the Biblical Tradition* (London: SCM, 1963).

Mayor, J. B. *The Epistle of St. James* (London: Macmillan, 1892).

Metzger, B. M., "The Formulas Introducing Quotations of Scripture in the NT and the Mishnah," *JBL*, LXX (1951), pp. 297-307.

_______, "A Suggestion Concerning the Meaning of I Cor. xv. 4b," *JTS*, VIII (1957), pp. 118-123.

Michel, O. *Paulus und seine Bibel* (Gütersloh: Bertelsmann, 1929).

Moore, G. F., "Nazarene and Nazareth," *The Beginnings of Christianity*, 5 vols., ed. F. J. F. Jackson and K. Lake, I (1920), pp. 426-432.

Morgan, R., "Fulfillment in the Fourth Gospel," *Interp*, XI (1957), pp. 155-165.

Morris, L. *The New Testament and the Jewish Lectionaries* (London: Tyndale, 1964).

Moule, C. F. D. *The Birth of the New Testament* (London: Black; New York: Harper & Row, 1966).

———, "Fulfilment-Words in the New Testament: Use and Abuse," *NTS*, XIV (1968), pp. 293-320.

Nepper-Christensen, P. *Das Matthäusevangelium, ein judenchristliches Evangelium?* (Aarhus: Universitetsforlaget, 1958).

Nicole, R., "The New Testament Use of the Old Testament," *Revelation and the Bible*, ed. C. F. H. Henry (Grand Rapids: Baker, 1958), pp. 137-151.

O'Rourke, J. J., "The Fulfillment Texts in Matthew," *CBQ*, XXIV (1962), pp. 394-403.

———, "Explicit Old Testament Citations in the Gospels," *Studia Montis Regii*, VII (1964), pp. 37-60.

Padva, P. *Les Citations de l'Ancien Testament dans l'Épître aux Hébreux* (Paris: Danzig, 1904).

Pereira, F., "The Galatian Controversy in the Light of the Targums," *IJT*, XX (1971), pp. 13-29.

Perrin, N., "Mark XIV. 62: The End Product of a Christian Pesher Tradition?" *NTS*, XII (1966), pp. 150-55.

Pillai, C. A. J., " 'Children of Abraham' in the Gospels," *IJT*, XX (1971), pp. 57-69.

van der Ploeg, J., "L'Exégèse de l'Ancien Testament dans l'Épître aux Hébreux," *RB*, LIV (1947), pp. 187-228.

Prabhu, G. M. S., "Matthew 4:14-16—A Key to the Origin of the Formula Quotations of Matthew," *IJT*, XX (1971), pp. 70-91.

Rendall, R., "The Method of the Writer to the Hebrews in Using OT Quotations," *Evangelical Quarterly*, XXVII (1955), pp. 214-220.

———, "Quotation in Scripture as an Index of Wider Reference," *Evangelical Quarterly*, XXXVI (1964), pp. 214-221.

Richardson, A. and W. Schweitzer, eds. *Biblical Authority for Today* (Philadelphia: Westminster, 1951).

Riesenfeld, H. *The Gospel Tradition and Its Beginnings. A Study in the Limits of "Formgeschichte"* (London: Mowbray, 1957).

———, "Observations on the Question of the Self-Consciousness of Jesus," *Svensk Exegetisk Årsbok*, XXV (1960), pp. 23-36.

von Rohr Sauer, A., "Problems of Messianic Interpretation," *Concordia Theological Monthly*, XXXV (1964), pp. 566-574.

Rothfuchs, W. *Die Erfüllungszitate das Matthäus-Evangeliums* (Stuttgart: Kohlhammer, 1969).

Sanders, J. A., "*NAZŌRAIOS* in Matt. 2.23," *JBL*, LXXXIV (1965), pp. 169-172.

Schweizer, E., " 'Er wird Nazoräer heissen' (zu Mc 1.24, Mt 2.23)," *Judentum, Urchristentum, Kirche*, ed. W. Eltester (Berlin: Töpelmann, 1960), pp. 90-93.

Scott, J. *Principles of New Testament Quotation* (Edinburgh: T. & T. Clark, 1875).

Selwyn, E. G. *The First Epistle of St. Peter* (London: Macmillan, 1947).

______, "The Authority of Christ in the New Testament," *NTS*, III (1957), pp. 83-92.

Smith, D. M., Jr., "The Use of the Old Testament in the New," *The Use of the Old Testament in the New and Other Essays*, ed. J. M. Efird (Durham: Duke University Press, 1972), pp. 3-65.

Smits, C. *Oud-Testamentische Citaten in het Nieuwe Testament*, 2 vols. (Hertogenbosch: Malmberg, 1955).

Sowers, S. G. *The Hermeneutics of Philo and Hebrews* (Richmond: John Knox, 1965).

Spicq, C. *L'Épître aux Hébreux*, 2 vols. (Paris: Gabalda, 1952, 1953).

______, "L'Épître aux Hébreux, Apollos, Jean-Baptiste, les Hellenistes et Qumran," *RQ*, I (1959), pp. 365-390.

Stanley, D. M., "Balaam's Ass, or a Problem in New Testament Hermeneutics," *CBQ*, XX (1958), pp. 50-56.

Stendahl, K. *The School of St. Matthew and its Use of the Old Testament* (Lund: Gleerup, 1954; Philadelphia: Fortress, 1968).

Stewart, R. A., "Creation and Matter in the Epistle to the Hebrews," *NTS*, XII (1966), pp. 284-293.

Suhl, A. *Die Funktion der alttestamentlichen Zitate und Anspielungen im Markus-evangelium* (Gütersloh: Mohn, 1965).

Sundberg, A. C., "On Testimonies," *Novum Testamentum*, III (1959), pp. 268-281.

Sutcliffe, E. F., "The Plenary Sense as a Principle of Interpretation," *Bib*, XXXIV (1953), pp. 333-343.

Swete, H. B. *The Apocalypse of St. John* (London: Macmillan, 1909).

Synge, F. C. *Hebrews and the Scriptures* (London: S.P.C.K., 1959).

Tasker, R. V. G. *The Old Testament in the New Testament* (London: SCM, 1954; Grand Rapids: Eerdmans, 1963).

______. *Our Lord's Use of the Old Testament* (Glasgow: Pickering & Inglis, 1953).

Thackeray, H. St.J. *The Relation of Paul to Contemporary Jewish Thought* (London: Macmillan, 1900).

Thomas, K. J., "The Old Testament Citations in Hebrews," *NTS*, XI (1965), pp. 303-325.

Toy, C. H. *Quotations in the New Testament* (New York: Scribner, 1884).

Turpie, D. M. *The Old Testament in the New* (London: Williams & Norgate, 1868).

Vis, A. *The Messianic Psalm Quotations in the New Testament* (Amsterdam: van Soest, 1936).

______, "Is Ps. CX een Messiaansche Psalm?" *Vox Theologica*, XV (1944), pp. 91-93.

Vollmer, H. *Die Alttestamentlichen Citate bei Paulus* (Freiburg: Mohr, 1895).

Vriezen, T. C., "Psalm 110," *Vox Theologica*, XV (1944), pp. 81-85.

Wenham, J. W. *Christ and the Bible* (London: Tyndale, 1972).

Westcott, B. F., "On the Use of the Old Testament in the Epistle," *The Epistle to the Hebrews* (London: Macmillan, 1889), pp. 471-497.

Westermann, C. *The Old Testament and Jesus Christ*, trans. O. Kaste (Minneapolis: Augsburg, 1970).

Wilcox, M., "The Old Testament in Acts 1-15," *Australian Biblical Review*, V (1956), pp. 1-41.

Williamson, R. *Philo and the Epistle to the Hebrews* (Leiden: Brill, 1970).

Wolf, C. U., "The Gospel to the Essenes," *Biblical Research*, III (1958), pp. 28-43.

Wolff, H. W. *Jesaja 53 im Urchristentum* (Berlin: Evangelische Verlag, 1942).

———, "The Hermeneutics of the Old Testament," *Essays on Old Testament Interpretation*, ed. C. Westermann, trans. J. L. Mays (London: SCM, 1963), pp. 160-199. The American edition of this work appears under the title *Essays on Old Testament Hermeneutics* (Richmond: John Knox, 1963).

Woollcombe, K. J., "Biblical Origins and Patristic Development of Typology," *Essays on Typology* (London: SCM, 1957), pp. 39-75.

Yadin, Y., "The Dead Sea Scrolls and the Epistle to the Hebrews," *Aspects of the Dead Sea Scrolls* (Scripta Hierosolymitana IV), ed. C. Rabin and Y. Yadin (Jerusalem: Hebrew University, 1958), pp. 36-55.

———, "A Note on Melchizedek and Qumran," *IEJ*, XV (1965), pp. 152-54.

INDEX OF AUTHORS

INDEX OF REFERENCES

I. OLD TESTAMENT

II. JEWISH APOCRYPHA AND PSEUDEPIGRAPHA

III. DEAD SEA SCROLLS

IV. PHILO

V. JOSEPHUS AND THUCYDIDES

VI. RABBINIC LITERATURE

VII. NEW TESTAMENT

VIII. CHURCH FATHERS